C.I.P.A. Guide to the Patents Acts

THIRD EDITION

Third Supplement

Introduction

This Supplement mainly comments on cases reported and other material which has become available since September 1, 1989, when the text of the Main Work was finalised, up to January 27, 1992, including: [1991] RPC No. 23; FSR and EIPR, OJEPO, EPOR and CIPA for December 1991; IPD for January 1992 and the SRIS collection of transcripts to C/1/92 and O/7/92. Some matter has also been included by way of addition to that contained in the Main Work.

Each entry in the Supplement has a marginal reference in bold type to the para. of the Main Work to which it relates, identified by headings and sub-headings corresponding to those in the Main Work.

This Supplement also contains prefatory Supplementary Tables to each of the Tables in the Main Work, as well as a further Table of County Court Rules; and a terminal Supplementary Index, each of which is to be read in conjunction with the corresponding Table or Index in the Main Work, each against the para. number quoted therein.

It is intended to continue to update this Supplement by the issue of further cumulated Supplements approximately annually.

The present Supplement has been compiled largely by the current General Editor of the Main Work (Dr. A. W. White). However, the Textbooks Committee of the Chartered Institute remains responsible for this Supplement, the present members of which are:

K. B. Weatherald (Chairman), M. J. W. Atchley; M. D. Berkson; R. J. Burt; R. J. Gallafent, T. Z. Gold, Helen Jones, R. C. Petersen, A. C. Serjeant and A. W. White.

This Committee thanks particularly C. Jones, T. Z. Gold, Helen Jones, R. P. Lloyd, R. K. Percy and R. C. Petersen for their special assistance in providing material for the Supplement.

The Controller to Her Majesty's Stationery Office is thanked for the permission given to reproduce photographically in the Main Work some of the Patents Forms.

Readers who perceive in the Main Work, or in this Supplement, any inaccuracy or omission are warmly requested to write to the Editor of the C.I.P.A. Guide, c/o The Chartered Institute of Patent Agents, Staple Inn Buildings, High Holborn, London WC1V 7PZ in order that the Work can comprehensively and accurately fulfil the promise of its title. The General

Editor would particularly like to hear from readers who encounter unusual points of British patent practice, so that the profession as a whole can benefit from the experiences of others.

TABLE OF AMENDMENTS TO THE PATENTS ACT 1977

The Act has been further amended by the following enactments:

Year	*Enactment*	*Sections affected*
1987	Debtors (Scotland) Act (c. 18) [Sched. 6]	93, 107
1990	Courts and Legal Services Act (c. 41) [Sched. 18, para. 20]	102, 102A
	Copyright, Designs and Patents Act 1988 (Isle of Man) (No. 2) Order (S.I. 1990 No. 2293)	General
	Patents Act 1977 (Isle of Man) (Variation) Order (S.I. 1990 No. 2295)	General, 130

TABLE OF CASES

(Supplemental to cases cited in the Main Work)
Cases are listed according to the paras. of the Main Work to which they refer, as supplemented by the contents of this Supplement wherein the corresponding paras. of the Main Work are indicated in bold type in the margin.
An asterisk against a case listed in this Table indicates that that case is also cited in the Main Work, see the Table of Cases therein at p. xv. An omission from the Table in the Main Work is indicated by †.
Abbreviations are used as indicated at p. lxxxiv of the Main Work as perhaps amplified thereto infra *in this supplement.*

TABLE OF STATUTES

(Supplemental to statutes cited in the Main Work)
The same notes apply as head the Table of Cases in this Supplement.

TABLE OF STATUTORY INSTRUMENTS

(Supplemental to statutory instruments cited in the Main Work)
The same notes apply as head the Table of Cases in this Supplement.

TABLE OF PATENT CONVENTIONS

(Supplemental to Table in the Main Work)
The same notes apply as head the Table of Cases in this Supplement.

TABLE OF RULES OF THE SUPREME COURT

(Supplemental to Rules of the Supreme Court cited in the Main Work)
The same notes apply as head the Table of Cases in this Supplement.

Ord. 6
  r.7 .... E006.7
Ord. 14A
  r.1 .... 61.23, **E014A.1**
  r.2 .... **E014A.2**
Ord. 18
  r.2 .... E018.2
Ord. 24
  r.13 .... 61.28
Ord. 26
  rr. 2, 3, 5, 6 .... 61.34
Ord. 34
* r.2 .... 61.38
  r.3 .... 61.38, **E034.3**
  r.8 .... 61.38, **E034.8**
  r.10 .... 61.38, **E034.10**
* Ord. 41
* r.12 .... 72.41
* Ord. 59
* r.3 .... E059.3
* r.5 .... E059.5
Ord. 64
† rr. 4, 5 .... 118.11
* Ord. 65
  r.5 .... E065.5
Ord. 107
  r.2 .... 96.19, **E107.2**

TABLE OF COUNTY COURT RULES

Ord. 38 .... 61.20
Ord. 48A 72.13, 96.22
  r.2 .... 96.21
  r.4 .... 96.22
  r.6 .... 96.22
  r.8 .... 61.36, 96.22, 96.25
  r.10 .... 37.16, 40.17, 72.29, 75.11

EUROPEAN PATENT OFFICE GUIDELINES

(Supplemental to Table in the Main Work)
The same notes apply as head the Table of Cases in this Supplement.

TABLE OF ABBREVIATIONS

(Supplemental to Table in the Main Work)

AC	Appeal Cases
CCR	County Court Rules
CLR	Commonwealth (of Australia) Law Reports
ECFI	European Court of First Instance
EPOR	European Patent Office Reports
PCC	Patents County Court
U.S.	United States Supreme Court Reports

Patents Act 1977 (c. 37)

PART I

NEW DOMESTIC LAW

SECTION 1 1.01

Erratum: In the Main Work the word "only" should be inserted after "granted" in line 1 of subsection (1).

BOOKS 1.02

N. Byrne, "The scope of intellectual property protection for plants and other life forms, Part 1" (IPB, 1989).

ARTICLES: COMPUTER PROGRAMS 1.03

J. Worthy, "Software patents in the UK after *Merrill Lynch*", [1989] EIPR 380;
B. Sherman, "The patentability of computer-related inventions in the United Kingdom and the European Patent Office", [1991] EIPR 85;
G.D. Kolle, "Patentability of software-related inventions in Europe", (1991) 22 IIC 660;
P.M. Cutforth, "Patents for software: Off course again?", (1991–92) 21 CIPA 4.

ARTICLES: MICRO-ORGANISMS, PLANTS AND ANIMALS 1.04

A. Christie, "Patents for plant innovation", [1989] EIPR 394;
R. S. Crespi, "Patenting innovation in animal biotechnology", [1989] 6 IPB 16;
R. Maufang, "Patentability of genetic inventions in animals", (1989) 20 IIC 823;
D. G. Bannerman, "Of mice and men", (1989–90) 19 CIPA 283;
V. Vossius, "Patent protection for animals: *Onco-mouse/HARVARD*", [1989] EIPR 250.

COMMENTARY ON SECTION 1

Matter excluded from patentability by not being regarded as "inventions" (subs. (2))

1.09 *—Exclusion of abstract and non-technical matter*

In *Furuno Electric's Application* (SRIS O/133/90, *noted* IPD 14040) a claim to a method of detecting fish shoals by the use of radar was refused as a performance of a mental act contrary to subsection (2)(*c*).

Computer programs

1.10 *—The EPO Guidelines*

The EPO attitude to the patenting of inventions relating to computer programs and their use is illustrated by: *EPO Decision T* 22/85, "*Document abstracting and retrieving/IBM*" (OJEPO 1–2/1990, 12; [1990] 2 EPOR 98), where the mere setting out of steps does not lead to patentability because no technical effect is there involved; *EPO Decision T* 52/85, "*Semantically-related expressions/IBM*" ([1989] 8 EPOR 454), where semantic relationships were not regarded as of technical character and the processing of the applicant's system involved only conventional computer techniques and programing; and likewise in *EPO Decision T* 36/86, "*Text processing/IBM*" (OJEPO 9/1990, 384; [1990] EPOR 606) in relation to a computer thesaurus, and in *EPO Decision T* 65/86, "*Text processing/IBM*" ([1990] 3 EPOR 181) in each of which the technical acts were held analogous to carrying out purely mental acts. Also, in *EPO Decision T* 158/88, "*Character form/SIEMENS*" (OJEPO 11/1991, 566), no technical effect was found merely in modifying data in a computer for the purpose of affecting its screen display. However, in *EPO Decision T* 115/85, "*Computer-related invention/IBM*" (OJEPO 1–2/1990, 30; [1990] 2 EPOR 107), the giving of visual instructions automatically according to specified conditions was patentable because a technical problem and its solution were involved, and likewise in *EPO Decision T* 6/83, "*Data processor retrieval/IBM*" (OJEPO 1–2/1990, 5; [1990] 2 EPOR 91). The EPO decisions concerning computer programs are well reviewed in the papers by G.D. Kolle and P.M. Cutforth listed in para. 1.03 *supra*).

1.11 *—Decisions of the Comptroller*

The *Merrill Lynch* decision, cited in the Main Work, was discussed in the paper by J. Worthy listed in para. 1.03, *supra*. Following rejection of the claims in that case by the Court of Appeal revised claims were allowed in a form directed to the operation of a programed computer, see Patent No. 2,180,380B.

In *Gale's Application* the Comptroller refused claims to a computer read-only memory encoded with the ability to calculate square roots, the physical embodiment of the invention being likened to a computer floppy disk. However, this decision was reversed by the Patents Court where the "ROM" was considered as an article of novel construction and not akin to a disk containing merely encoded information and therefore being more than a claim to matter disqualified from protection under section 1(2), but on further appeal ([1991] RPC 305 (CA)) the Comptroller's decision was reinstated because no difference existed between the hardware in question and a computer program and no novel *technical* effect resulted.

In *Wang's Application* ([1991] RPC 463), where the Patents Court upheld the Comptroller in refusing claims to "computer systems operable as an expert system", the claim features were seen as a collocation rather than a combination with the technical contribution to a mental act—the opinion of an expert—being provided by the program: the claim was therefore to a method of performing a mental act and hence unpatentable under section 1(2)(*c*). In *Hitachi's Application* ([1991]) RPC 415) claims to operating a computer using a compiler program were likewise rejected as being claims to a computer program as such.

The approaches of the EPO and of United Kingdom courts to the patentability of computer-related inventions are discussed at some length in the papers by B. Sherman, G.D. Kolle and P.M. Cutforth, each listed in para. 1.03 *supra*. However, their views and to some extent also the views of the EPO, have not been accepted by the Comptroller, see *e.g. Sharp K.K.'s Application* (SRIS O/75/91, *noted* IPD 14171). Here, it was held that computer-based inventions must, to be patentable, solve a technical problem which is not one of the matters excluded by section 1(2): accordingly, claims to an interactive translation machine system were rejected following decisions of the Patents Court and the Court of Appeal which the Comptroller held were binding upon him, even if these were contrary to decisions of the EPO. In two further decisions (*Sharp K.K.'s Applications*, SRIS O/113/91 and O/114/91), it was likewise held that the field of linguistics is non-technical. Also, in *Apple Computer's Application* (SRIS O/76/91, *noted* IPD 15001), it was held that claims to a conventional computer containing a novel program (here because of its hierarchical file structure) were claims to performing a mental act, not allowable irrespective of any technical advance over the prior art.

—Other protection for computers and computer programs **1.12**

The *E.C. Directive on the Legal Protection of Computer Programs* has been issued in final form (OJEC L122/42, 17.5.91; [1991] EIPR 327), replacing the Draft Directive referred to in the Main Work and to be implemented by January 1, 1993 to ensure that Member States provide for the protection of computer programs under copyright law. Its contents have been discussed by R.J. Hart ((1991–92) 21 CIPA 26).

Exclusion of presentation of information (subs. (2)(d)) **1.13**

In *Waring's Application* (SRIS O/73/90, *noted* IPD 13138) claims to a "traffic violation ticket" were held unpatentable as being merely a presentation of information, the other characteristics of the ticket being known in a stationery pad intended for other purposes.

The EPO has held that a colour television signal characterised by the technical features of the system in which it occurs is not a mere presentation of information excluded by EPCa. 52(*d*) (*EPO Decision T* 163/85, "*Colour television signal/BBC*", OJEPO 9/1990, 379; [1990] EPOR 599), but where an invention only concerns a feature of using a specified colour, or range of colours, the EPO regards it as excluded from patentability under EPCa. 52 (*EPO Decision T* 119/88, "*Coloured disk jacket/FUJI*", OJEPO 9/1990, 395; [1990] EPOR 615).

Specific exclusions from patentability despite being inventions (subs. (3))

1.15 *—Exclusion on grounds of public policy (subss. (3)(a) and (4))*

The test under subsection 3(*a*) is, probably, whether use of the invention would offend moral principles of right-thinking members of the public, such that it would be wrong for the law to protect it, following a similar principle on the registrability of designs (*Masterman's Design*, [1991] RPC 89).

1.16 *—Exclusion for plant and animal varieties (subs. (3)(b))*

This exclusion has been further discussed in the book by N. Byrne and the papers by A. Christie, R. S. Crespi, R. Moufang and D. G. Bannerman listed in paras. 1.02 and 1.04 *supra*, the paper by D. G. Bannerman containing a layman's guide to the science of genetic engineering. The Main Work refers to two EPO decisions which have now respectively been reported as "*Onco-mouse/HARVARD*" (OJEPO 11/1989, 451; [1990] 1 EPOR 4) and *EPO Decision T* 320/87, "*Hybrid plants/LUBRIZOL*," OJEPO 3/1990, 71; [1990] 3 EPOR 173). In the latter case it was stated that hybrid plants (and seed therefrom), lacking stability in some trait of the complete genetic population, cannot be classified as plant varieties within EPCa. 53(*b*). These decisions are commented upon in the paper by V. Vossius listed in para. 1.04, *supra*. Subsequently, the EPO Appeal Board, in *EPO Decision T* 19/90, "*Onco-mouse/HARVARD*" (OJEPO 12/1990, 488; [1990] EPOR 501), referred the *Onco-mouse* case back to the Examining Division for further study, while pointing out that a clear distinction exists between "animals" and an "animal variety" and that the claims need not be limited to "rodents".

1.17 *Plant breeders' rights*

An EEC Draft Regulation on Plant Variety Rights has been published ([1990] 3 CMLR 196). If these proposals were adopted, Community-wide industrial property rights for plant varieties would arise and patent protection for plant varieties would be prohibited. The prohibition against dual protection for plant varieties under plant breeders' rights and the patent system are further discussed in the book by N. Byrne listed in para. 1.02 *supra*. The view for the abolition of this prohibition has been criticised (M. Llewelyn, [1989] EIPR 303).

SECTION 2—RELEVANT RULE

2.02 **Rule 5 [1990]**—*International exhibitions*

In rule 5(4) [1990], the words "rule 85(2A) below" have been amended to "rule 85(3)".

2.03

SECTION 2—ARTICLES

A. W. White, "The novelty-destroying disclosure: Some recent decisions", [1990] EIPR 315;

J.R. Lane, "What level of disclosure is required to anticipate a patented invention by prior publication or use?", [1990] EIPR 462;

G.D. Paterson, "The patentability of further uses of a known product under the European Patent Convention", [1991] EIPR 16;

R.S. Crespi, "Novelty in patent law: diverging views in Europe", (1991) 3(1) IPB 9;

R.S. Crespi, "The 'state of the art' in patent law: Reflections on recent UK and European cases", (1991) 3(5) IPB 17.

COMMENTARY ON SECTION 2

Novelty destroyed by the state of the art (subss. (1) and (2))

—The state of the art **2.05**

A disclosure is not an anticipation unless it was clearly not affected by a bar of confidentiality (*Quantel* v. *Spaceward Microsystems*, [1990] RPC 83).

The EPO has held that whether an act of publication has occurred has to be determined on the balance of probabilities and, on this basis, a document probably placed in a library on a certain date was published on that date if anyone could then ask to see it, even if it had not then been indexed (*EPO Decision T* 381/87, "*Publication/RESEARCH ASSOCIATION*", OJEPO 5/1990, 213). Likewise, an additional example post-filed in a Japanese application has been regarded as a prior publication because this was inspectable (*EPO Decision T* 444/88, "*Foam Particles/JAPAN STYRENE PAPER*", [1991] EPOR 94). However, submission of a paper to a scientific society for publication, including the vetting of this in confidence, is not an act of publication (*EPO Decision T* 381/87, *supra*). Also to be discounted is a publication which is *ex facie* erroneous, as in the case of an abstract inconsistent with the, inevitably cross-referenced, document which it purports to summarise (*EPO Decision T* 77/87, "*Erroneous abstract/ICI*", OJEPO 7/1990, 280). However, post-priority documents can be used as evidence of the content of pre-priority disclosures (*EPO Decision T* 316/86, "*Electrical connecting apparatus/NILED*" ([1990] 3 EPOR 217).

—The general test for lack of novelty **2.06**

The Patents Court has specifically stated that the tests for lack of novelty set out by the Court of Appeal in the *General Tire* case, cited in the Main Work, apply under the 1977 Act (*Helitune* v. *Stewart Hughes*, [1991] FSR 171).

—The "post infringement" or "right to work" test **2.07**

The validity of the "right to work" test of novelty now seems to be impaired as the result of the decision of the House of Lords (*Asahi's Application*, [1991] RPC 485 (HL)) that, for a disclosure to be an anticipating one, such must also be an "enabling" one, for which see para. 2.18 *infra*. While that decision did not advert to a prior user situation, the concept of the enabling disclosure had previously been applied by the Patents Court to hold a prior use non-anticipatory because the public had not thereby been enabled to practise the invention for themselves (*Quantel* v. *Spaceward Microsystems*, [1990] RPC 83). The difficulties that are created by a prior use being held non-anticipatory if this does not amount to an enabling disclosure are discussed in the papers by A.W. White and R.S. Crespi listed in para. 2.03 *supra*.

—Mere novelty of purpose **2.10**

The EPO Enlarged Board of Appeal has accepted the proposition that, in addition to inventions of a further medical indication (as discussed in the Main

Work), novelty can be conferred on a claim by including therein a statement of novel technical purpose (*EPO Decision G* 2/88, "*Friction reducing additive/ MOBIL III*, OJEPO 4/1990, 9; [1990] 2 EPOR 73 and *EPO Decision G* 6/88, "*Second non-medical indication/BAYER*" (OJEPO 4/1990, 114; [1990] 4 EPOR 257), which specifically endorsed *EPO Decision T* 231/85 cited in the Main Work. These decisions are discussed in the papers by G. D. Paterson, A. W. White and R. S. Crespi listed in para. 2.03 *supra*, see also para. 2.13 *infra*. If they are adopted by United Kingdom courts, they will over-rule the decision in *Adhesive Dry Mounting* v. *Trapp* ((1910) 27 RPC 341) discussed in the Main Work. Then, presumably, the stated purpose should also be taken into account in assessing whether a claim, which is valid only because of a statement of purpose, is infringed, see para. 125.08. As a result of *EPO Decisions G* 2/88 and *G* 6/88 (*supra*), it may be that (at least in the EPO) objections of lack of novelty can be overcome in many cases if a different technical effect from the effects indicated by the prior art can be demonstrated, see *EPO Decision T* 20/88, "*Polymer-polyol compositions/UNION CARBIDE*" ([1990] 3 EPOR 212); *EPO Decision T* 361/88, "*Hollow filaments/DU PONT*" ([1991] EPOR 1); and also in the continuation of the first of these decisions (*EPO Decision T* 59/87, "*Friction reducing additive/ MOBIL IV*", OJEPO 11/1991, 561; [1990] 7 EPOR 514), and in *EPO Decision T* 290/86, "*Cleaning plaque/ICI*" ([1991] EPOR 157, *noted* OJEPO 8/1991). However, anticipation is not avoided by adding a test procedure as a feature of the claim where there is no evidence that prior art products would fail that test (*EPO Decision T* 627/88, "*Resin composition/ASAHI*", [1991] EPOR 81).

2.13 —*EPO decisions concerning lack of novelty*

The EPO Enlarged Board of Appeal has allowed an appeal in *EPO Decision T* 59/87, "*Friction reducing additive/MOBIL II*", cited in the Main Work, (see *EPO Decision G* 2/88, "*Friction reducing additive/MOBIL III*" (OJEPO 4/1990, 93; [1990] 2 EPOR 73), discussed in (1989–90) 19 CIPA 111 and 171 and the paper by G. D. Paterson listed in para. 2.03 *supra*. In this decision it was stated that "A claim to the use of a known compound for a particular purpose, which is based on a technical effect which is described in the patent, should be interpreted as including that technical effect as a functional technical feature, and is accordingly not open to objection under EPCa. 54(1) provided that such technical feature has not previously been made available to the public", as was then held in that case (*EPO Decision T* 59/87, "*Friction reducing additive/MOBIL IV*", OJEPO 11/1991, 561; [1990] 7 EPOR 514). Thus, at least according to the EPO, a claim may be valid if its sole feature of novelty is an expressed statement of *technical*, and not merely informative, purpose, in this case a statement that the known use of a composition had a previously unknown utility so that the invention, when considered as a whole, has not (according to the EPO) been "made available to the public". A similar decision is *EPO Decision G* 6/88, "*Second non-medical indication/BAYER*" (OJEPO 4/1990, 114; [1990] 4 EPOR 257). These decisions, if adopted into United Kingdom law, will have a profound effect on the traditional concept of the novelty criteria for patentability, see also para. 2.10 *supra*.

The availability to the public of a cited document at a sufficiently early date must be proved if not apparent and, in *EPO Decision T* 308/87, "*Yarn finish applicator/DU PONT*" ([1991] EPOR 464), a brochure was disregarded for lack of proof of its distribution date. However, if a document is capable of being inspected by the public, even if not so inspected, it is to be considered as part of the state of the art (*EPO Decision T* 444/88 "*Foam particles/JAPAN STYRENE PAPER*", [1991] EPOR 94): here the pleaded art was an example added to the file of a Japanese patent application after this had been published. A case where a prior oral disclosure was proved is *EPO Decision T* 534/88, "*Ion etching/IBM*" ([1991] EPOR 18). Also, a disclosure makes its teaching available to the public if the skilled person would seriously contemplate applying its technical teaching in a particular area; but, where the document contains a reasoned statement dissuading its reader from doing certain acts, novelty can reside as regards those acts but the claims must be limited thereto (*EPO Decision T* 26/85, "*Thickness of magnetic layers/TOSHIBA*" (OJEPO 1–2/1990, 23; [1990] 4 EPOR 267).

The technical teaching of a prior art document is to be considered in its entirety and parts of it may not be arbitrarily isolated from it to derive a technical teaching which is distinct from, or even in contradiction with the integral teaching of, the whole document (*EPO Decision T* 56/87, "*Ion chamber/SCANDITRONIX*", OJEPO 5/1990, 188; [1990] 5 EPOR 352): see also *EPO Decision T* 356/89, "*Novelty/FORD*" ([1990] 5 EPOR 370), where the drawings of the citation could not be taken in isolation. Thus, while there is a lack of novelty if the *inevitable* result of carrying out a described process is the product now being claimed as an invention (*EPO Decision T* 12/81, "*Diastereomers/BAYER*", OJEPO 8/1982, 296), this is not so if the prior document contains a contrary teaching (*EPO Decision T* 310/88, "*Photosensitive resin/TORAY INDUSTRIES*", [1991] EPOR 10). Also, a finding of "inevitable result" will only be made if the prior disclosure has been experimentally repeated exactly as stated (*EPO Decision T* 173/89, "*Gamma-sorbitol/ICI*", [1991] EPOR 62). Further, a chemical substance is new if it differs from a known substance by a reliable parameter, including a special configuration (*EPO Decision T* 296/87, "*Enantiomers/HOECHST*," OJEPO 5/1990, 195; [1990] 5 EPOR 337), though the claims may lack inventive step if this parameter is an obvious one to investigate, see para. 3.48 *infra*. Although "product-by-process" claims are not normally allowed by the EPO, there is an exception when it is the process which renders the product novel (*EPO Decision T* 130/90, "*Recombinant monoclonal antibody/UNIVERSITY OF TEXAS*", *unreported*).

A difference in properties does not itself demonstrate a difference of composition from that previously disclosed (*EPO Decision T* 25/87, "*Polyacrylate molding composition/UNION CARBIDE*", [1989] 7 EPOR 381); and, while a disclaimer may provide a claim with novelty, such cannot make an obvious teaching inventive (*EPO Decision T* 170/87, "*Hot-gas cooler/SULZER*," OJEPO 11/1989, 441; [1990] 1 EPOR 14), see para. 3.48 *infra*.

If an objection of lack of novelty is overcome, it should be expected that a the question of inventive step will then fall for consideration (*EPO Decision T* 493/88, "*Spacer grid/CEA-FRAMATOME*", [1991] EPOR 393).

—*Selection inventions* **2.14**

The Comptroller still requires the criteria of the *I. G. Farben* case, cited in the Main Work, to be met even when claims are held not to lack novelty. This is because a purported selection must not be an arbitrary one, on which see *Compagnie Centrale des Emeris's Application* ((1935) 52 RPC 167). However, after grant, the onus falls upon an applicant for revocation to demonstrate the absence of these criteria, see *Haynes International's Patent* (SRIS O/27/90, *noted* IPD 13145) noted in para. 2.07 *supra*. In *Hallen* v. *Brabantier* ([1991] RPC 195 (CA)) the patent was not supported as a selection invention because it failed to describe the particular advantage which the claimed device had been found to provide.

2.16 —*The EPO approach (to selection inventions)*

There is lack of novelty where four ranges of numbers define the claimed compositions and overlapping ranges are combined in the same way as the prior art (*EPO Decision T* 25/87, "*Polyacrylate molding composition/UNION CARBIDE*", [1989] 7 EPOR 381). There is also lack of novelty when the prior art describes a process for the production of a class of products and the skilled person can prepare all members of that class, because thereby the whole class (and not merely those similar to the specific examples of the prior patent) have been made available to the public, and thus no invention of selection arises when further members of the class are made (*EPO Decision T* 124/87, "*Copolymers/DU PONT*", cited in the Main Work and now also reported OJEPO 12/1989, 491). However, the Comptroller has formulated the novelty test for a selection invention in rather different terms, see paras. 2.07 and 2.14 *supra*.

The EPO has, however, found novelty when the subject matter claimed could only be found by combining various pieces of information contained in the cited document in a certain manner (*EPO Decision T* 137/90, "*Amino-triazine/SHELL*", [1991] EPOR 381); and also in the case of a catalogue where it was doubted whether it was proper to regard this as a single document, rather than as a selection of documents (*EPO Decision T* 305/87, "*Shear/GREHAL*", OJEPO 8/1991, 429; [1991] EPOR 389).

2.17 —*Special considerations in cases of prior use*

The EPO has authoritatively stated that a hidden or secret use is not a ground of objection to the validity of a European patent because such use has not "been made available to the public" (*EPO Decision G* 2/88, "*Friction reducing additive/MOBIL III*", OJEPO 4/1990, 93; [1990] 2 EPOR 73 and *EPO Decision G* 6/88, "*Second non-medical indication/BAYER*", OJEPO 4/1990, 114; [1990] 4 EPOR 257.

However, it has made findings of prior use based on the balance of probability (*EPO Decision T* 627/88, "*Resin composition/ASAHI*", [1991] EPOR 81), and where there was no reason to doubt the authenticity of the evidence or the witness presenting them (*EPO Decision T* 124/88, "*Electric motor/PEUGEOT*", [1991] EPOR 255), but not where it was far from clear that the public had sufficient access to the alleged prior used apparatus to ascertain its nature (*EPO Decision T* 245/88, "*Atmospheric vaporizer/UNION CARBIDE*", [1991] EPOR 373).

When judging an alleged prior user, it is necessary to consider what was actually used, and also what was "made available to the public," and the evidence needs very careful scrutiny when the allegation is against a commercially successful invention (*Quantel* v. *Spaceward Microsystems*, [1990] RPC 83). Here it was held that a demonstration, at which no-one was allowed near the machine and no engineering description was given, did not amount to a prior user because there had not been an "enabling disclosure", but as to which see *infra*. Other examples of failure to prove prior uses, with evidence of personal recollection of events occurring over 10 years previously not being accepted, are: *Van der Lely* v. *Ruston's Engineering (No. 2)* (SRIS C/2/90, *noted* IPD 13075); and *John Deks* v. *Aztec Washer* (SRIS C/25/90, *noted* IPD 13094), with an allegedly contemporaneous written record also being rejected in the *Van der Lely* case.

An example of failure to prove a prior use is *Van der Lely* v. *Ruston's Engineering (No. 2)* (SRIS C/2/90) where the recollections of a witness, then 13 years old, of events 26 years previously, and an alleged contemporaneous written record of those events, were each not accepted.

To prove a prior use in EPO opposition proceedings, the material provided must: verify the point or period of time for the alleged use; identify the object of indicating unobviousness, but has been prepared to do so where the adoption of the invention appears to have been uninfluenced by other factors, *e.g.* where the invention was adopted in hospitals (*EPO Decision T* 69/89, "*Disinfection/SURGIKOS*", [1990] EPOR 632).

Identification of problem to be solved by the invention **3.37**

If a technical problem is solved by the invention, the EPO apparently regards it as patentable, see *EPO Decision T* 6/83, "*Data processor retrieval/IBM*" (OJEPO 1–2/1990, 5; [1990] 2 EPOR 91). However, where detailed instructions for solving a particular problem are not to be found in the specification, the claim will probably lack an inventive step: otherwise, if inventive, the description will be insufficient, see *EPO Decision T* 292/87, "*Ticket-issuing machines/CONTROL SYSTEMS*" ([1989] 6 EPOR 333).

Restatement and reformulation of the problem **3.38**

It is possible that the problem formulated in relation to the inventive step over the cited art can be regarded as overshadowed by the need for a radical simplification of the apparatus *EPO Decision T* 428/88, "*Automatic dispenser/ELECTROLUX*" ([1990] 5 EPOR 385).

Obvious and unobvious problems and solutions **3.39**

The perception of a problem can not contribute to the assessment of inventive step if that problem is not of a technical nature (*EPO Decision T* 579/88, "*Automatic programmer/ESSWEIN*", [1991] EPOR 120).

Assessment of the solution

—The "obvious to try" test in the EPO **3.40**

The main authority for the "would, not could" test is seen by the EPO as *EPO Decision T* 2/88, "*Simethicone tablet/RIDER*" (OJEPO 6/1984, 265, cited in para. 3.39 of the Main Work), see *EPO Decision T* 726/89, "*Cylinder block/NISSAN*" ([1991] EPOR 107) where a document was discounted as applicable only by *ex post facto* analysis. However, a skilled man must not be precluded from optimising parameters in a known device (*EPO Decision T* 490/90, "*Avalanche diode/FUJITSU*", [1991] EPOR 423).

—Probability of attainment of solution **3.41**

It is not sufficient that a person faced with the problem would be led only partly to its solution (*EPO Decision T* 335/88, "*Injection moulding machine/NISSEI*", [1990] 7 EPOR 552).

Structural obviousness **3.43**

Although a chemical process may lack an inventive step, products made according to that process may nevertheless be unobvious (*EPO Decision T* 189/88, "*Polyethylene terephthalate fibres/ASAHI*", [1990] 7 EPOR 543).

3.44 *—Patentability of chemical intermediates*

The patentability of intermediates is to be measured by the same yardstick as other chemical compounds and this requires a non-obvious (*i.e.* unexpected) enhancement of the art. This can be because the compound has been made in connection with an inventive preparation, or an inventive further processing, or as part of an inventive complete process (*EPO Decision T* 648/88, "*(R,R,R,)-alpha-tocopherol/BASF*", OJEPO 6/1991, 292; [1991] EPOR 305).

3.45 *EPO attitude to selection inventions*

There is no novelty in the selection of a sub-group of chemical compounds if such can be inferred as a particular area of a previously disclosed general formula and, for patentability, the compounds of the selected group must provide a different technical teaching (*EPO Decision T* 12/90, "*Amino acid derivatives/ BAYER*", [1991] EPOR 312), see also *EPO Decision T* 11/89, "*Naphthyridinone derivatives/GODECKE*" ([1991] EPOR 336) where extreme overlap between the selected groups of compounds was found. Also, the use of a known material, on the basis of a known property of it, to obtain a known effect in a new combination is not normally considered inventive, but special cases are recognised where selection of the material brings an unexpected advantage, or overcomes a known prejudice, or unforeseen difficulties are encountered such as a need to alter another component of the combination, see *EPO Decision T* 130/89, "*Profile member/KÖMMERLING*" (OJEPO 10/1991, 514) where the claims were disallowed because, although two disparate problems were solved, neither solution involved inventive ingenuity.

If the problem is only to find a further solution to those already known, because no unexpected effect has been demonstrated, small changes (such as reversal of the known arrangement) are unlikely to be held inventive, see *EPO Decision T* 170/87, "*Hot gas cooler/SULZER*" ([1990] 1 EPOR 14).

Demonstration of advantages in support of inventive step

3.46 *—Advantages must be unpredictable*

Comparative tests are not required by the EPO if it was not prima facie obvious to make the claimed compositions (*EPO Decision T* 390/88, "*Photographic film/ KONISHIROKU*", [1990] EPOR 417). Also, the advantage can be a surprising effect of a generally known process coupled with some further development of that process (*EPO Decision T* 361/88, "*Hollow filaments/DU PONT*", [1991] EPOR 1).

3.47 *—Advantages must be demonstrated*

The improved effect must convincingly be shown to have its origin in the distinguishing feature of the invention, so that it may be necessary to modify the elements of comparison so that they differ only by the specific distinguishing characteristic (*EPO Decision T* 197/86, "*Photographic complexes/KODAK*", OJEPO 9/1989, 371; [1989] 7 EPOR 395).

3.48 *Unpatentability of the "one-way street" solution*

While a disclaimer may provide a claim with novelty, such cannot make an obvious teaching inventive (*EPO Decision T* 170/87, "*Hot-gas cooler/SULZER*", OJEPO 11/1989, 441; [1990] 1 EPOR 14).

Although an isomer of a known chemical substance may possess novelty (for which see para. 2.13 *supra*), its isolation will probably lack inventive step as it is often mere routine to test each isomer for some activity found in the first prepared mixture of isomers, but a different position obtains where the activity of that mixture had not previously been reported (*EPO Decision T* 296/87, "*Enantiomers/HOECHST*", OJEPO 5/1990, 195; [1990] 5 EPOR 337). Also, the replacement of polyclonal antibodies by a monoclonal antibody in an immuno-purification process has been held to be the next logical step to take and hence lacks an inventive step (*EPO Decision T* 499/88, "*Immunoglobulins/UNILEVER*" (*noted* (1990) 2(6) IPBB 7).

While the Main Work refers to unpatentability if the claimed invention is obvious for *any* purpose, the EPO has, more recently, developed the concept of a dual purpose invention which has to be considered as a whole thereby allowing a bonus effect to be taken into account in recognising the existence of an inventive step (*EPO Decision T* 236/88, "*Preparation of acetic anhydride*" [1990] 3 EPOR 227).

PRACTICE UNDER SECTION 3

Pleading of commercial success **3.51**

While discovery of documents relating to the issue of commercial success must be given, extending to those documents which could in any way assist the case either offensively or defensively, the court will not make an oppressive order in this regard, see *Mölnlycke* v. *Procter & Gamble (No. 3)* ([1990] RPC 498) discussed in para. 61.28 *infra*. Also, RSC Ord. 104, rule 6(5) does not seem to apply to proceedings before a patents county court, see CCR Ord. 48A, rule 4(4) reprinted in para. H48A.04.

SECTION 4 **4.01**

Erratum: In the reprinting of subsection (1) in the Main Work, the word "industrial" should be "industry".

COMMENTARY ON SECTION 4

Unpatentability of medical and veterinary treatment (subss. (2) and (3))

—Decisions in the EPO **4.07**

In *EPO Decision T* 584/88, "*Anti-snoring means/REICHART*" ([1989] 8 EPOR 449) a claim was allowed in the form: "Use of X to combat *troublesome* snoring," this type of snoring not being regarded as medical treatment: claims in the "Swiss form" were also allowed as regards "the therapeutic treatment of snoring which might be harmful to health", see para. 2.29, *supra*. However, claims to use of a known composition as an oral hygiene agent have been refused as being inevitably a therapeutic treatment of the human body (*EPO Decision T* 290/86, "*Cleaning plaque/ICI*", [1991] EPOR 157, *noted* OJEPO 8/1991), following the *Oral Health* decision cited in para. 4.06 of the Main Work and distinguishing *EPO Decision T* 144/83, "*Appetite suppressant/DU PONT*" (cited in the Main Work) on the basis that therein the cosmetic treatment was differentiated from the use of the medicament for therapeutic purposes.

SECTION 5—RELEVANT RULE

5.02 **Rule 6 [1990]**—*Declaration of priority for the purpose of section 5*

In rule 6(5), "17.1(a)" has been changed to "17.1(a) or (b)". In rule 6(6), after "English" (first occurrence) ", subject to rule 85(3)(c) and (d)" has been added, and the proviso to that sub-rule has been replaced by a new sub-rule reading:

> (7) In the case of an international application for a patent (UK), the application of paragraph (6) above shall be subject to the provisions of rule 85(3)(c) and (d).

COMMENTARY ON SECTION 5

5.06 *According an earlier priority date (subs. (2))*

The interpretation accorded by the Patents Court to section 130(3) in the *Asahi* case was not followed by the higher courts in that case, see *Asahi's Application* ([1990] FSR 546 (CA) and [1991] RPC 585 (HL)), and in that case the House of Lords held that, to accord priority, the earlier application must contain an "enabling" disclosure, *i.e.* it must itself satisfy the requirement of sufficiency under section 14(3).

In *A. C. Edwards* v. *Acme Signs* ([1990] RPC 621 and SRIS C/80/91 (CA) following the *Asahi* case), the meaning of section 130(3) was explained as requiring a claim in a priority document to be treated as part of its disclosure, to be read in conformity with it.

5.07 *The necessity for a valid declaration of priority*

In the last line of page 79 of the Main Work, "document" should read "declaration."

From July 1, 1992, the PCT Regulations will be amended to permit (by PCTr. 90*bis*.3(a)) withdrawal of a priority declaration at any time during the international phase. This should require some amendment of rule 2(*d*) because it will then be possible to withdraw a priority declaration for an international application at any time during the international phase, that is possibly after publication of the international application. It should be noted that the definition of "declared priority date" is of no relevance to the *validity* of a priority declaration for establishing the priority date of an invention under section 5(2)(*a*) in relation to the state of the art (under s.2(2)), nor for establishing under section 5(2)(*b*) the prior art effect (under s.2(3)) of the international application against an invention of later priority.

5.09 *Decisions under the present section 5*

The Comptroller's decision in *Asahi Kasei's Application*, cited in the Main Work, has been reversed by the House of Lords (*Asahi's Application*, [1991] RPC 485), see para. 2.18 *supra*, it being held that for priority purposes an earlier application must contain an "enabling" disclosure, *i.e.* one which meets the requirements of sufficiency under section 14(3), see also para. 2.06 *supra*.

Relevant EPO Decisions 5.11

The EPO interprets EPCa. 87 as only according a priority date to an earlier application if this was "for the same invention", *i.e.* that the subject-matter of the later application must be clearly identifiable in the documents of the earlier application when these are taken as a whole, though identical wording is not required. Accordingly, if any essential element for which the European patent is sought is missing, then there is no right to priority, it not being possible to fill gaps with after-acquired knowledge (*EPO Decision T* 81/87, "*Preprorennin/COLLABORATIVE*", OJEPO 6/1990, 250; [1990] 5 EPOR 361). However, a general teaching in the priority document can provide sufficient support for a feature more specifically delimited in the later application (*EPO Decision T* 73/88, "*Snackfood/HOWARD*", [1990] 2 EPOR 112 and *EPO Decision T* 212/88, "*Theta-1/BP*", [1990] 7 EPOR 518).

Where the Applicants had filed a British application more than 12 months before filing a European application describing the same apparatus as that of the earlier British application, priority was held to be lost with the result that that earlier application became effective prior art invalidating a claim to a different, but obvious, method of operating that apparatus (*EPO Decision T* 229/88, "*Target apparatus/DETRAS*", [1991] EPOR 407). Also, the fact that the claim in the priority document was broad enough to cover a particular specified feature in the later claim does not necessarily mean that that feature has been sufficiently disclosed in the priority document for priority to be accorded therefrom (*EPO Decision T* 490/90, "*Avalanche diode/FUJITSU*", [1991] EPOR 423).

The sufficiency requirement of a priority application 5.12

In *EPO Decision T* 81/87, "*Preprorennin/COLLABORATIVE*" (OJEPO 6/1990, 250; [1990] 5 EPOR 361) the EPO reiterated its view that a priority document has to contain a sufficient (and therefore "enabling") disclosure before priority can be accorded from it. In *Asahi's Application* ([1991] RPC 485), the House of Lords followed this view and that of *EPO Decision T* 206/83 (considered in the Main Work). Accordingly, the decisions of the Comptroller and Patents Court (each noted in the Main Work) and also that of the Court of Appeal ([1990] FSR 546) were reversed.

Resolution of conflicts based on implicit disclosure 5.15

The decision in *Asahi's Application*, cited in the Main Work, was reversed by the House of Lords ([1991] RPC 485), see paras. 5.06 and 5.09 *supra*. Accordingly, the tests for lack novelty and priority are essentially the same, each requiring the prior document to contain an "enabling" disclosure.

First convention filing and re-filing (subs. (3)) 5.16

Genentech's [Human Growth Hormone] Patent, cited in the Main Work, has now been reported ([1989] RPC 613).

PRACTICE UNDER SECTION 5

Supply of translation of certified copy of priority application (r. 6(6)) 5.21

In its application to international applications (UK), rule 6(6) must now be read in conjunction with rule 6(7) (see para. 5.02 *supra*). These provisions now enable translations of a priority document for such an application to be filed up to 22 months from the declared priority date or 32 months therefrom if Chapter II of PCT has been invoked.

COMMENTARY ON SECTION 6

6.04 *Relevant EPO decisions*

Although EPCaa. 87–89 (with EPCr. 38) form a complete code of law in relation to priority claims, these are to be considered as based on the same principles as the priority provisions of the Paris Convention (*EPO Decision T* 301/87, "*Alpha-interferons/BIOGEN*," OJEPO 8/1990, 335; [1990] 3 EPOR 190). As a result of this decision the interpretation of the EPC now seems aligned with section 6 because it held that the contents of a prior application, published elsewhere, are not to be deemed to be part of the state of the art against matter contained in an application claiming priority from that application: however, additional matter contained in such a publication will enter the state of the art and therefore can impugn the validity of a later-dated invention, see comment by R. S. Crespi ((1990) 2(2) IPB 24). The difficulties in drafting claims where there are multiple priorities and intervening publications have been discussed by J. C. H. Ellis ((1989–90) 19 CIPA 187).

COMMENTARY ON SECTION 7

7.05 *Entitlement to grant of a patent (subs. (2))*

In *Kokta's Patents* (SRIS O/88/91) a general policy document issued by a University stating that patent rights in University inventions would pass to the appropriate professor was held sufficient to pass to the professor rights to inventions made by a co-inventor with him who at the time was a University employee.

7.08 *Entitlement to grant (subs. (4))*

CPCaa. 27 and 68–71, referred to in the Main Work, have been re-numbered as CPCaa. 23 and 66–69 [1989] respectively, see para. 86–03 *infra*.

7.09 *Revocation after grant to non-entitled person*

CPCaa. 57 and 27, referred to in the Main Work, have been re-numbered as CPCaa. 56 and 23 [1989] respectively, see para. 86.03 *infra*.

SECTION 8—RELEVANT RULES

8.02 **Rule 7 [1990]**—*References under section 8(1)(a) or 12(1)(a)*

In paragraph (2)(b), "application" has been added after "patent". In paragraph (2)(c), "(not being a party to the reference)" has been added after "person"; and at the end of paragraph (2) there has been added:

"; and

The Comptroller has declined to deal with entitlement questions when these relate to the contractual relationship between the parties (*J. Downs (Jersey)'s Application*, SRIS O/66/90, *noted* IPD 13146), though here the relationship was an alleged oral contract probably arising under Scots law. For other cases where referral to the court has been considered or ordered, see para. 37.10 in the Main Work and *infra*.

Nature of the invention to be considered under section 8 **8.09**

The Comptroller has confirmed that questions of patentability cannot be raised pre-grant in entitlement proceedings under section 8 (*Coin Controls' Application*, SRIS O/95/89, *noted* IPD 13034 and *Kokta's Applications*, SRIS O/16/90).

Relief under section 8

—General **8.10**

The Comptroller has no power to declare an application void *ab initio* in order that a later-filed application can validly stand in its place, but a replacement application can be filed claiming priority from the earlier application, see *Amateur Athletic Association's Application* ([1989] RPC 717). The Comptroller also appears to have no power to require an applicant to maintain the application pending determination of entitlement proceedings: a replacement application can be ordered if the entitlement application succeeds (*Vet Health's Patent*, SRIS O/49/90, *noted* IPD 13165).

—Filing of new application **8.11**

In *Amateur Athletic Association's Applications* (cited in the Main Work and now reported, [1989] RPC 217) it was indicated that, by analogy with reviving an apparently abandoned application by extension of time under former rule 110(3A), it might be possible to allow an application to proceed in the name of the referrer notwithstanding that it had previously been treated as withdrawn. *Coin Controls' Application* (SRIS O/95/89), also cited in the Main Work, has been *noted* at IPD 13034. However, this type of relief is not possible where the priority application was filed other than as one under the Act (when s. 8(3) or 37(4) may apply) or as a European or international application (when s. 12(6) may apply), see *Dodge's European Application* (SRIS O/20/90, *noted* IPD 13136).

A replacement application was also allowed in *Earl Engineering's Application* (SRIS O/18/91) where the original applicant had abandoned his application and did not contest the entitlement proceedings.

PRACTICE UNDER SECTION 8

8.12 *Raising of questions under subsection (1)*

The periods for lodging opposition and for each stage of successive submissions of evidence have each been reduced to two months from the date of dispatch (see paras. 8.02 and 8.03 *supra*), but extension is still possible under rule 110(1). A referrer will not be permitted to allege a new case at the evidence in reply stage of the proceedings, for example that the invention had in fact been made some years earlier by another, when by due diligence that point could have been raised earlier (*Manthorpe's Application*, SRIS O/1/91): however, the possibility was there seen of a new reference being made to raise the intended new allegation.

Security for costs is now only required from a referrer who neither resides nor works within the EEC, and proceedings on related applications can be consolidated with the filing of a single PF 2/77 and one set of evidence, see *Kokta's Applications* (SRIS O/16/90).

8.13 *Orders made under section 8 or 12*

The Comptroller is not required to decide a case adversely to the referrer if he withdraws his reference (*Lupa's Application*, SRIS O/59/90, *noted* IPD 13167).

When the Comptroller decides to refer a dispute to the court under section 8(7), a notice to this effect occurs in the O.J., see O.J. July 4, 1990.

SECTION 10—RELEVANT RULE

10.02 Rule 12 [1990]—*Request by joint applicant under section 10 or 12(4)*

In paragraph 2, the words "three months of the receipt" have been changed to "the period of two months beginning on the date when such copies are sent to him".

COMMENTARY ON SECTION 10

10.03 *General*

Because of the exception contained in section 12(4), in the case of European patent applications, and international applications in the international phase, the Comptroller only has power under section 10 to determine disputes as to ownership and not as to the manner in which such application may be prosecuted, contrary to the statement in the Main Work. Of course the Patents Court could be asked to make orders binding upon the parties to a section 10 dispute, but it would probably not do so unless it had jurisdiction over the person(s) involved. Once an international application has entered the UK phase (for which see paras. 89.13 and 89A.08 in the Main Work), then (by virtue of ss.89(1) and 89A(3)) section 10 fully operates upon it in the same way as it does on an application filed under the Act.

10.04 *Application of section 10 in practice*

In *Cange Controls' Application* (SRIS O/34/91, *noted* IPD 14149) C and E were joint applicants. E became uncontactable after instructing different agents. C obtained an order that the application proceed solely in its name, but with an undertaking that, upon request from E, C should grant E a free, personal, non-assignable licence under the patent, which C was not required to keep in force. In *Melco Products' Application* (SRIS O/49/91) a verbal agreement was found for collaboration in the filing, but with no concluded agreement on future exploitation. Because it was not considered appropriate for the application to proceed in only one of the joint applicants' names, nor for exploitation to be governed by section 36, the matter was adjourned to give the parties a chance to agree an exploitation agreement.

PRACTICE UNDER SECTION 10 **10.05**

The period for lodging opposition (under r. 12(2)) is now two months from the date of dispatch of the copy request and statement, see para. 10.02 *supra*.

SECTION 11—RELEVANT RULE

Rule 13 [1990]—*Referral to the Comptroller under section 11(5)* **11.02**

In paragraph 2, the words "three months of the receipt" have been changed to "the period of two months beginning on the date when the copies are sent to him".

COMMENTARY ON SECTION 11

General **11.03**

Rules 58 and 59 [1982] have become, respectively, rules 57 and 58 [1990].

Result of making order under subsection (2) **11.05**

The periods of two months and four months under rule 9, referred to in the Main Work, now run from the date when the notification is sent to the new proprietor.

PRACTICE UNDER SECTION 11 **11.06**

The period for lodging opposition (under r. 13(2)) is now two months from the date of dispatch of the copy request and statement, see para. 11.02 *supra*.

COMMENTARY ON SECTION 12

General **12.03**

CPCa. 70, referred to in the Main Work, has been re-numbered as CPCa. 68 [1989], see para. 86.03 *infra*.

Application of section 12 in practice **12.04**

In *Cannings' U.S. Application* (SRIS O/127/90, *noted* IPD 14041 and SRIS O/51/91, *noted* IPD 14164) a former employee-inventor had refused to execute an assignment of a United States' application in favour of his employer, but had not contested the section 12 proceedings. On the uncontested facts, the employer was held to be entitled to the benefit of the application and the inventor was ordered to execute an assignment. However, while the Comptroller noted that he had no express power to authorise another to execute the assignment if the inventor failed to obey this order (as can be done under section 8(5)), the Comptroller held that he had such a power by analogy with that section. Subsequently, he only exercised this power after efforts to have the inventor sign had failed and after an assurance that an assignment executed by another under his authorisation would at least be recorded in the United States Patent and Trademark Office.

12.05 *New applications under subsection (6)*

In *Dodge's European Application* (SRIS O/20/90, *noted* IPD 13136) the Comptroller allowed a new European application to be filed even though five years had elapsed since the filing of the non-entitled application. Although there is no provision for protection for those who might have started to work the invention in reliance on the initial application having been abandoned, the Comptroller left it to the Courts to devise relief in any such circumstances. However, a problem arose in that the non-entitled application had claimed priority and the priority application would have been a novelty-destroying disclosure but for the original form of section 78(5) by which the abandonment of the non-entitled application caused this to be removed from the prior art. It was recognised that the position would have been different if the amendment to section 78(6) had been brought into force: obviously a future case on similar facts will face the same problem, apparently without solution where the Comptroller cannot permit the filing of a new back-dated application solely for priority purposes, as was done in *Amateur Athletic Association's Application* ([1989] RPC 217) discussed in para. 8.11 of the Main Work.

12.06 PRACTICE UNDER SECTION 12

The Comptroller can make no order under section 8 or 37 relating to foreign applications or patents. Such requires a separate reference under section 12 and the Comptroller will not permit amendment of an existing reference (under s. 8 or 37) if that would delay the conclusion of that reference (*Vet Health's Patent*, SRIS O/49/90, *noted* IPD 13165).

SECTION 13—RELEVANT RULES

13.02 Rule 14 [1990]—*Mention of inventor under section 13*

In the preamble to paragraph 2, the word "an" has been changed to "any such", and the words "under section 13(2)" have been deleted. In paragraph (3), the words "three months of its receipt" have been changed to "the period of two months beginning on the date when the copies are sent to him".

13.03 Rule 15 [1990]—*Procedure where applicant is not the inventor or sole inventor*

In paragraph (1), reference to rule "85(3)(*a*)" has been changed to rule "85(7)(a)".

Paragraph (4) has been amended to read:

> (4) Where the application is an international application for a patent (UK), the requirements of paragraphs (1) and (2) above shall be treated as having been complied with if the provisions of rules 4.1(a)(v) and 4.6 of the Regulations made under the Patent Co-operation Treaty have been complied with, whether or not there was any requirement that they be complied with.

COMMENTARY ON SECTION 13

Inventor designation in international and European applications (UK) **13.07**

Rule 85(3)(*a*), cited in the Main Work, has become rule 85(7)(a) [1990], see para. 89A.02 *infra*.

Amendment of inventorship entities **13.10**

Hago Products' Patent (SRIS O/40/91, *noted* IPD 14140) is an example of deletion of a named inventor. The case concerned a divisional application for which the deleted inventor had been named as sole inventor. Although the case was uncontested, deletion was only ordered after the Comptroller had satisfied himself that deletion of that person from the parent application was appropriate.

PRACTICE UNDER SECTION 13

Amendment of named inventor(s) **13.13**

The period for lodging opposition (under r. 14(3)) is now two months from the date of dispatch of the copy request and statement, see para. 13.02 *supra*.

If in an application for change of inventorship the named inventors are notified of the proceedings and do not oppose, the Comptroller will, apparently, allow the application and order issue of an erratum slip (*Ferguson Ltd.'s Patent*, SRIS O/85/91).

SECTION 14

Note. The repeal of subsections (4) and (8), and their replacement by section 125A, took effect from January 7, 1991 (S.I. 1990 No. 2168). **14.01**

SECTION 14—RELEVANT RULES

Rule 18 [1990]—*Drawings* **14.03**

At the end of sub-paragraph (2)(i), "and" has been added; and, in sub-paragraph (2)(j), "rule 20(10) below" has become "rule 20(9)".

Rule 19 [1990]—*The abstract* **14.04**

In paragraph (4), the words "Patents Form No. 1/77" have been changed to "the abstract".

14.05 Rule 20 [1990]—*Size and presentation of documents*

In paragraph (1) the words "other than drawings" have been replaced by "(including drawings)," and in paragraph (3) the words ", including drawings," have been deleted. In paragraph (4), "All such documents and drawings" has been changed to "All documents referred to in paragraph (1) above". Previous paragraphs (10)–(16) have been renumbered as (9)–(15) respectively; and, in present paragraphs (12) and (15), the words ", including drawings," have been deleted in each instance.

14.06 Rule 22 [1990]—*Claims in different categories*

At the end of sub-paragraph (a), "or" has been added.

COMMENTARY ON SECTION 14

The request (subs. (2)(a))

14.10 —*General*

For amendment of PF 1/77, see para. 123.19 *infra*.

The specification (subs. (2)(b))

14.13 —*General*

In *Alps Electric's Application* (SRIS O/12/90, *noted* IPD 13083) the Comptroller refused to follow *EPO Decision J* 04/85, "*Correction of drawings/ETAT Français*, cited in the Main Work, because neither of sections 15 and 117 is mentioned in section 130(7).

EPO Decision T 260/85, "*Coaxial connector/AMP*", also cited in the Main Work, has also been published ([1989] 7 EPOR 403).

Sufficiency of description (subs. (3))

14.15 —*General*

Rule 20(14), cited in the Main Work, has become rule 20(13).

Despite the change of wording between section 32(1)(*h*) [1949] and section 14(3) [1977], the Patents Court does not regard this as a matter of substance (*Helitune* v. *Stewart Hughes*, [1991] FSR 171). Here the addressee would have appreciated that the specification contained an error; this he would notionally, and automatically, have corrected to render the specification sufficient.

14.16 —*Date at which sufficiency of the specification is required*

There is a view in the EPO that a specification must be sufficient to support a claimed invention as of its claimed priority date, see *EPO Decision T* 301/87,

"*Alpha-interferons/BIOGEN*" (OJEPO 8/1990, 335; [1990] 3 EPOR 190), see also para. 5.12 in the Main Work and *supra.*

The Patents Court has specifically left open whether it is the filing or the publication date which controls the sufficiency of a specification (*Mentor* v. *Hollister*, [1991] FSR 557).

—Addressee as a person skilled in the art **14.17**

A specification is not insufficient if the skilled addressee can carry out its concepts without difficulty and without using ingenuity (*Helitune* v. *Stewart Hughes*, [1991] FSR 171), or through using his skill to perform the invention while seeking success (*Mentor* v. *Hollister*, [1991] FSR 557). Thus, the skilled person can make use of his common general knowledge (*EPO Decision T* 51/87, "*Starting compounds/MERCK*", OJEPO 3/1991, 177), but he cannot be presumed to have special knowledge (*Yen Wei Hsiung's Patent*, SRIS C/5/91, *noted* IPD 14079).

The EPO has held that a chemical specification need not contain an illustrative example if performance of the invention would require routine experimental investigations only (*EPO Decision T* 407/87, "*Semiconductor device/TOSHIBA*," [1989] 8 EPOR 470).

—Comparison with requirement of sufficiency under the 1949 Act **14.18**

Section 14(3) only requires *some* method of performing the invention to be described: there is "no requirement to disclose every possible way in which it may be performed", see *Quantel* v. *Spaceward Microsystems* ([1990] RPC 83) where an inutility-type of objection failed for this reason.

EPO decisions on insufficiency **14.18A**

The Main Work discusses EPO decisions on insufficiency in para. 14.25, but that paragraph should only deal with consideration of clarity. Consequently, this new paragraph has been created to discuss EPO decisions arising from insufficiency of the description rather than from a defect in the claims. That para. of the Main Work indicates the EPO view that a specification is sufficient if it describes *one* method of practising the invention. This view that claims to a class of substances with the same biological activity do not require instructions for the preparation of each member of the class has been endorsed in *EPO Decision T* 301/87, "*Alpha-interferons/BIOGEN*" (OJEPO 8/1990, 335; [1990] 3 EPOR 190). Also, a mere statement in opposition proceedings that one of the patent examples has been repeated "exactly as described" but without obtaining the stated result is inadequate to establish insufficiency in those proceedings (*EPO Decision T* 182/89, "*Extent of opposition/SUMITOMO*", OJEPO 7/1991, 391).

Within the EPO, sufficiency can be demonstrated by adding to the content of the specification the common general knowledge of the person skilled in the relevant art. While this knowledge is normally demonstrated by reference to textbooks and basic handbooks (*EPO Decision T* 206/83, "*Pyridine Herbicides/ICI*", OJEPO 1/1987, 5; [1986] EPOR 232), in an appropriate case it can consist of a recently published patent application (*EPO Decision T* 51/87, "*Starting compounds/MERCK*", OJEPO 3/1991 177; [1991] EPOR 329).

In *EPO Decision T* 787/89, "*Diamond identification/BRITISH PETROLEUM*" ([1991] EPOR 178) the EPO refused an application because the applicant did not respond to the invitation to provide a pre-published document indicating how a particular claimed feature could in practice be attained.

The claims (subs. (5))

14.21 —*General*

EPO Decision T 23/86, "*Computer controlled switch/NAIMER*" has been further reported (OJEPO 7/1987, 316).

While absence of clarity of claims is not available post-grant as a ground of invalidity (as indicated in the Main Work), the EPO will consider the point if amendments are proposed in EPO opposition proceedings (*EPO Decision T* 434/87, "*Toothbrush fibres/FABRE*", [1990] 2 EPOR 141), provided that the objection arises out of these amendments (*EPO Decision T* 301/87, "*Alpha-interferons/BIOGEN*", OJEPO 8/1990, 335; [1990] 3 EPOR 190).

14.22 —*EPC requirements as to claims*

For the EPO, a product-by-process claim is only allowable if the product is novel *per se* (*EPO Decision T* 434/87, "*Toothbrush fibres/FABRE,*" [1990] 2 EPOR 141), for example because it is the process which renders the product novel as in *EPO Decision T* 130/90, "*Reconbinant monoclonal antibody/UNIVERSITY OF TEXAS*" (*unreported*) where a distinction was also drawn between the words "produced by" and "obtainable by".

14.23 —*Types of claims*

The EPO Enlarged Board of Appeal has decided that novelty can be imparted to a claim by the inclusion therein of a statement of novel purpose, see *EPO Decision G* 2/88, "*Friction reducing additive/MOBIL III*" (OJEPO 4/1990, 93; [1990] 2 EPOR 73), discussed in paras. 2.10 and 2.13, *supra*, and at (1989–90) 19 CIPA 111 and 171. If adopted into United Kingdom law, this decision also, presumably, alters the interpretation of a claim which refers to a stated technical purpose so that this becomes limited to the use of the claimed article or method to effect that particular purpose.

14.24 —*Claims to be clear and concise (subs. (5)(b))*

The EPO accepts that an invention may be functionally defined by an unambiguous mathematical formula if a skilled person can determine therefrom whether the claim is infringed (*EPO Decision T* 126/89, "*Fluid filter cleaning system*", [1990] 4 EPOR 292).

The EPO has held the phrase "artificial diamond or zircon" to lack clarity because it indicates that zircon is not an artificial diamond (*EPO Decision T* 787/89, "*Diamond identification/BRITISH PETROLEUM*" ([1991] EPOR 178); and has also refused to allow a claim containing an internal disclaimer to materials claimed in an earlier application (*EPO Decision T* 11/89, "*Naphthyridinone derivatives/GODECKE*", [1991] EPOR 336). The EPO has also refused to allow the word "approximately" to appear in a claim as inherently vague, but did allow the word to remain in the specification on the Applicant's representation that the word merely implied a possible lack of perfection (*EPO Decision T* 194/89, "*Brushless DC motor/IBM*", [1991] EPOR 411); and has stated that the word "comprising" is inherently ambiguous as meaning either "includes" or "comprehends", but accepted "consisting essentially of" as meaning that unspecified components could be present if the characteristics of the claimed composition were thereby not materially affected (*EPO Decision T* 472/88, *"Thermoplastic resin/GENERAL ELECTRIC"*, [1991] EPOR 486).

The fact that a claim to a process does not explicitly specify certain steps does not mean that these are implicitly excluded if that would mean that some of the protected embodiments could not then be reproduced (*EPO Decision T* 07/88, *"Flange formation process (2)/DUPONT"*, [1990] 2 EPOR 149).

—Claims to be supported by the description (subs. (5)(c)) **14.25**

In *Schering Biotech's Application* (SRIS C/4/90, *noted* IPD 13031) the Patents Court upheld an objection from the Comptroller (SRIS O/77/88) that, while claims to the preparation of a plasmid containing a specified cDNA insert were allowable, extension of these claims to cover use also of a nucleotide capable of hybridisation with such insert should not be permitted as not being supported by the description, particularly because it was admitted that such hybridised product would not necessarily produce the same result as a plasmid with the specified insert. It was stated that "the word support requires the description to be the base which can fairly entitle the patentee to a monopoly of the width claimed", and a mere mention in the specification of the features of the claims is not sufficient support for them. Leave to appeal further was granted.

Unity of invention (subs. (6)) **14.27**

The "single general concept" required by the EPO for unity of invention to be present must have an "inventive character": otherwise unity of invention will be denied (*EPO Decision W* 6/90, *"Single general concept/DRAENERT"*, OJEPO 8/1991, 438; [1991] EPOR 516).

Non-unity of remaining claims may arise during prosecution as a result of rejection of a broader claim. In the EPO at least, filing of a divisional application would normally be appropriate in such a case provided that the subject-matter for that divisional application had not been abandoned during the prosecution (*EPO Decision T* 178/84, *"Lack of unity/IBM"*, [1989] 6 EPOR 364, *noted* OJEPO 5/1989, 157 and *EPO Decision W* 08/87, *"Protest/ELECTRO CATHETER"*, [1989] 7 EPOR 390, *abridged* OJEPO 4/1989, 123).

—The abstract (subs. (7) and r. 19) **14.29**

Rule 19(4) now requires that any figure of drawings which the applicant suggests should accompany the abstract be indicated on the abstract itself, see para. 14.04 *supra*.

Documents and language **14.30**

Rule 20(1) now requires *all* wording (including that contained in drawings) to be in the English language.

Practice under Section 14

Physical requirements

—Form of documents **14.35**

Sub-rules 20(10)–(16) have been renumbered as sub-rules 20(9)–(15) respectively.

The listing in specifications of sequences of nucleotides or amino acids to indicate a DNA or protein structure is now, effectively, the subject of stringent presentation requirements, for which see new para. 125A.22 *infra*.

The EPO has held that, somewhat contrary to *EPO Decision J* 5/87, cited in the Main Work, that individual statements of desired protection will only rank as "claims" if presented as such (*EPO Decision J* 15/88, "*Claims fees/NEORX*", OJEPO 11/1990, 445) and *EPO Decision J* 28/89, *noted* (1990) 2(8) IPBB 7).

14.38 *Cross-references between applications*

To ensure that no new matter is added when a cross-reference to a copending application is initially made by citing an agent's case reference, the examiner no longer *replaces*, but supplements, that reference with the publication number of the cross-referenced application (O.J. May 2, 1990). The agent's case reference should be uniquely identifiable as such and, therefore, this should preferably appear on the Patent Office file copy of the specification of that other application.

14.39 *Withdrawal*

The EPO has allowed a withdrawal made erroneously by an agent as a correction under EPCr. 88, though only because publication of the withdrawal in the OJEPO had not then been made (*EPO Decision J* 10/87, "*Retraction of withdrawal/INLAND STEEL*", [1989] 7 EPOR 437, *abridged* OJEPO 8/1989, 323).

When an application is to be unequivocally withdrawn with a view to permitting a re-filed application to claim priority under article 4(C)4 of the Paris Convention, it is useful to send the letter of withdrawal to the Patent Office in duplicate asking that the copy be stamped as received and returned to the applicant/agent. This stamped duplicate will then readily be available as evidence when advantage is taken of this article 4(C)4.

15.01

SECTION 15

Note. The amendment to section 15, noted in the Main Work, came into effect on January 7, 1991 (S.I. 1990 No. 2168).

SECTION 15—RELEVANT RULES

15.02 **Rule 23 [1990]**—*Late filed drawings*

In rule 23, the words "Patent Office" have been changed to "comptroller".

15.03 **Rule 24 [1990]**—*New applications under section 15(4)*

Paragraphs (1) and (2) of this rule have been totally replaced as follows:

24.—(1) Subject to paragraph (2) below, a new application for a patent, which includes a request that it shall be treated as having as its date of filing the date of filing of an earlier application, may be filed in accordance with section 15(4) not later than the latest of—

(a) the beginning of the sixth month before the end of the period ascertained under rule 34 in relation to the earlier application as altered, if that be the case, under rule 100 or rule 110 ("the rule 34 period");
(b) where the earlier application is amended as provided by section 18(3) so as to comply with section 14(5)(d), the expiry of the period of two months beginning on the day that the amendment is filed; and
(c) where the first report of the examiner under section 18 is made under subsection (3), the expiry of the period specified for reply to that report:

Provided that, where the first report of the examiner under section 18 is made under subsection (4) and the comptroller notifies the applicant that the earlier application complies with the requirements of the Act and these Rules, notwithstanding the foregoing provisions of this paragraph but subject to paragraph (2) below, a new application may be filed not later than the expiry of the period of two months beginning on the day that the notification is sent.

(2) Where any of the following dates falls before the date ascertained under paragraph (1) above, a new application may only be filed before that date instead of the date so ascertained—

(a) the date when the earlier application is refused, is withdrawn, is treated as having been withdrawn or is taken to be withdrawn;
(b) the expiry of the rule 34 period ascertained in relation to the earlier application; and
(c) the date when a patent is granted on the earlier application.

Previous paragraph (2) has been renumbered as paragraph (3) and at its end there have been added the words:

> "and shall indicate the matter for which protection is claimed in the other application."

Rule 25 [1990]—*Periods prescribed under sections 15(5)(a) and (b) and 17(1) for filing claims, abstract and request for preliminary examination and search* **15.04**

The title to this rule has been changed to that indicated above; and, in the preamble to paragraph (2), reference is now made instead to "rules 81(3), 82(3) and 85(7)(a)"; and the word "below" has been deleted.

15.05 Rule 26 [1990]—*Extensions for new applications*

This rule has been extensively amended and is therefore reprinted below:

26.—(1) Where a new application is filed under section 8(3), 12(6), 15(4) or 37(4) after the period of sixteen months prescribed in either rule 6 or rule 15, then, subject to the following provisions of this rule,

(a) the requirements of those rules shall be complied with at the time of filing the new application; and
(b) the requirements of paragraph 1(2)(a)(ii) and (3) of Schedule 2, in a case to which they apply, shall be complied with not later than the later of the time ascertained under the said paragraph 1(3) and the time of filing the new application.

(2) Where a new application is filed under any of those sections—

(a) within the period prescribed in paragraph (6) of rule 6 as modified, in the case of an international application, by rule 85(3), the requirement of that paragraph shall have effect as provided therein; or
(b) after that period, the requirements of that paragraph shall be complied with at the time of filing.

subject, in either case, to paragraph (3) below.

(3) Where a new application is filed under section 15(4) after—

(a) the period of sixteen months prescribed in rule 6(2) or rule 15(1); or
(b) the period prescribed in rule 6(6) as modified, in the case of an international application, by rule 85(3),

but within an extension of that period under rule 110(3) or (4) in respect of the earlier application, the requirements of rule 6(2) and (3), rule 6(6) or rule 15, as the case may be, shall be complied with before the end of the extended period.

COMMENTARY ON SECTION 15

15.09 *Missing drawings (subss. (2), (3) and (3A))*

No distinction is to be drawn between a missing sheet of drawings and a drawing omitted from a filed sheet (*Alps Electric's Application*, SRIS O/12/90, *noted* IPD 13083). However, now that new subsection (3A) has been brought into effect, it should be possible to correct a mis-filing of drawings provided that the original intent of the applicant can be shown, for example by referring to the drawings in a priority document as was done in *EPO Decision J* 04/85, "*Correction of drawings/ETAT FRANÇAIS*" (OJEPO 7/1986, 205; [1986] 6 EPOR 331), over-ruling *EPO Decision J* 01/82 cited in the Main Work.

Times for filing claims, abstract and for paying search fee (subss. (5)) **15.10**

The previously misleading title to rule 25 has now been corrected, see para. 15.04 *supra*.

Divisional applications (subs. (4))

—Time for filing **15.13**

New rule 24 [1990] renders obsolete much of para. 15.13 in the Main Work. The new rule significantly broadens the period within which the filing of a divisional application may be filed. Subject to rule 24(2) (which prohibits the filing of a divisional application after the earlier application has been refused, withdrawn, deemed to be withdrawn, or granted, or for which the rule 34 period has expired), a divisional application may now be filed up to the latest of the following dates:

(a) six months before the end of "the rule 34 period" (that is the period permitted by that rule for placing the application in compliance with the Act and Rules, including any extension thereof under rule 100 or 110);
(b) two months after amendment to meet a non-unity objection under section 14(5)(d); and
(c) the expiry of the period specified for response to the first substantive examination report under section 18(3).

However, where the first examination report is made under section 18(4) (*i.e.* that the application is already in compliance with the Act and Rules), the time period for filing divisional applications is limited to two months from the date of such report (r. 24(1) proviso). Where a divisional application is filed in such circumstances, an accompanying letter should be filed marked "URGENT" in order that the parent application should not proceed to grant before the divisional application is accorded a filing date, see O.J. October 9, 1991.

Thus, in most circumstances, an applicant should be able to file a divisional application up to six months before the end of the rule 34 period, provided that before then the fate of the earlier application has not been determined, for example by issue of a letter under section 18(4) which operates as the administrative date of grant (on which see the Main Work): unless late issuance of a non-unity objection or the first examination report (which is most likely to occur in the case of an application which is already a divisional application, or a replacement application filed under one of sections 8(3), 12(6) or 37(4) permits recourse to rule 24(1)(b) or (c). However, what is not clear is whether the (usually longer) period under rule 24(1)(a) will apply to over-ride rule 24(1)(b) in a case where the application has earlier been restricted to overcome an objection of non-unity: otherwise rule 24(1)(b) will only apply where a non-unity objection is made at a late stage of the substantive examination.

—Content of divisional applications **15.14**

Rule 24(2), cited in the Main Work, is now rule 24(3). This now requires the parent and/or divisional application, where necessary to describe the matter for which protection is sought, to "indicate the matter for which protection is claimed in the other application". It is thought that there will be sufficient "indication" for this purpose if the reference number of the other application is related to the appropriate part of the text in the description and to state that the matter concerned is claimed in the other application.

As the amendment of section 76 has now come into force, the effect of the *Hydroacoustics* decision, cited in the main work, has now been much reduced, as is indicated in paras. 15.29 and 76.07 in the Main Work.

Time limits for filing other documents on divisional applications

15.19 *—Filing of inventorship statement on PF 7/77*

Rule 26(3) has been reworded so that PF 7/77 will (if 16 months has elapsed since the declared priority date) be required to be filed within any period extended under rule 110(3) or (4), the latter being formerly rule 110(3A), but otherwise by the date of filing the new application.

15.20 *—Filing of priority document*

Rule 26 has been reworded and rule 110(3A) has become rule 110(4).

15.21 *—Verified translation of the priority document*

Rule 26(3) has been reworded and rule 110(3A) has been renumbered as rule 110(4), but the periods for filing verified translations of the priority documents remain unchanged.

PRACTICE UNDER SECTION 15

15.29 *—Content of divisional application*

Rule 24(2), cited in the Main Work, is now rule 24(3) and is discussed in para. 15.14 *supra*.

Divisional applications

15.30 *—Time for filing divisional application*

In view of the rewording of rule 24 (for which see para. 15.03 *supra*), the second paragraph of para. 15.30 in the Main Work should now be read in conjunction with para. 15.13 *supra*. As there indicated, apparently (but not certainly), the extended period for filing a divisional application up to six months before the end of the rule 34 period can now overcome the difficulty which arises when an objection of non-unity is successfully contested.

The established practice of the Comptroller is only to permit late filing of a divisional application "in instances where the applicant can show that the circumstances are exceptional, and that he has been properly diligent," see *Asahi's Application* (SRIS O/98/89, *noted* IPD 12113) where the case failed for both of these reasons.

The Main Work refers to the division of an application that already has divisional status. This permits a series of "cascading divisionals" and, while this practice is inhibited under the Part I of the Act because of the overall time limit for acceptance being calculated from the declared priority date, the absence of a fixed acceptance period under the EPC does (at least in theory) enable a determined applicant to keep a divisional application pending throughout the maximum term which a patent granted thereon would have.

—Register entries for divisional applications **15.32A**

Since the register of patents (maintained under s. 32) became computerised (late in 1989) entries have been made therein against the entry of a parent application of the filing of any divisional applications thereon.

COMMENTARY ON SECTION 16

General **16.04**

Although a request for early publication, either of the "A" or "B" specifications, can be made and will be acted upon to place the application in the queue for publication, it is not possible to expediate the actual preparations for publication thereafter ((1990–91) 20 CIPA 415).

Extent of publication under section 16 **16.05**

Starting from April 1992, the front sheet of the application as published has included the list of documents contained in the search report ((1991–92) 21 CIPA 157). This has brought the position into accord with that stated (erroneously at the time) in the Main Work.

SECTION 17 **17.01**

Note. The amendments to section 17, noted in the Main Work, came into effect on January 7, 1991 (S.I. 1990 No. 2168).

SECTION 17—RELEVANT RULES

Rule 28 [1990]—*Preliminary examination and search under section 17* **17.02**

This rule is identical with paragraphs (1) and (2) of former rule 29 as printed in the Main Work, to which a further paragraph has been added which reads:

"(3) The Comptroller may, if he thinks fit, send to the applicant a copy of any document (or any part thereof) referred to in the examiner's report under section 17(5)".

Rule 29 [1990]—*Procedure where earlier application made* **17.02A**

Rule 29 is identical with former rule 29(3) as printed in para. 17.02 of the Main Work, except that after "examination" the words "under rule 28" have been added.

17.03 **Rule 31 [1990]**—*Formal Requirements*

In paragraph (1), the words "of that rule" have been omitted; and the words "paragraph (12) or paragraph (13) of (15) of that rule)" have been changed to "paragraph (11) and in paragraphs (12) and (14))".

17.04 **Rule 32 [1990]**—*Searches under section 17(6) and (8)*

The rule title has been slightly changed to that given above; and new paragraphs (3) and (4) added, reading:

(3) The fee for a supplementary search under section 17(8) shall be accompanied by Patents Form No. 9/77.

(4) The Comptroller may, if he thinks fit, send to the applicant a copy of any document (or any part thereof) referred to in the examiner's report under section 17 pursuant to subsection (6) or (8) thereof.

COMMENTARY ON SECTION 17

Preliminary examinations (subss. (1)–(3))

17.06 —*Scope and definitions*

Rule 29(3) [1982] has become rule 29 [1990].

17.07 —*Meeting of formal requirements (r. 31)*

Rule 29(2) [1982] has become rule 28(2) [1990].

EPO Decisions J 08/87 and *J* 09/87, "*Submitting culture deposit information/IDAHO*" (OJEPO 1/1989, 9; [1989] 3 EPOR 170), cited in the Main Work, have been overruled by the EPO Examining Division in "*Deposit number/ROCKEFELLER*" (OJEPO 4/1990, 156; [1990] 4 EPOR 303): thus failure to supply a culture deposit number before the end of the stipulated period now appears to be an irremediable defect.

In the Main Work the reference in the final line to para. 17.16 should have been to para. 17.07.

17.08 *Declaration of priority*

Rule 29(2) [1982] has become rule 28(2) [1990].

17.09 *The search (subs. (4)–(7))*

New rule 28(3) (reprinted in para. 17.02 *supra*) makes provision for the Comptroller to supply copies of documents (or parts thereof) cited in the search report. New rule 33(4) (reprinted in para. 18.02 *infra*) makes like provision for new citations during substantive examination. It is understood that the supply of copies of cited prior art is a long-term aim and a fee may be required for an optional service. The supply of such copies is now permitted without breach of copyright under sections 45 and 178 [1988].

Search against further inventions and supplementary search (r. 32) **17.10**

The fee for a supplementary search, either under subsection (6) or the new subsection (8), is paid by filing a PF 9/77 together with the prescribed fee (r. 32(3)). The Comptroller now has power to supply copies of documents (or any parts thereof) which are referred to in that supplementary search report (r. 32(4)).

Practice under Section 17

Time limits

—General **17.13**

Rule 29(3) is now rule 29(1).

Preliminary examination **17.17**

Rule 29(3) is now rule 29(1).

Supplementary searches **17.19**

Subsection (8) was brought into effect from January 7, 1991 (see para. 17.01 *supra*), requiring a fee for a supplementary search unless the Comptroller should direct otherwise. Such fee is to be paid by filing PF 9/77, see rule 29(2) [1990] (reprinted in para. 17.02A *supra*).

Amendment after the search **17.20**

If amended claims are filed after receipt of the search report and it is desired that these be published in the A-print under section 16, the amendments should be filed in a communication marked "URGENT" (O.J. July 10, 1991).

SECTION 18 **18.01**

Note. The amendment to section 18, noted in the Main Work, came into effect on January 7, 1991 (S.I. 1990 No. 2168).

Section 18—Relevant Rules

Rule 33 [1990]—*Request for substantive examination under section 18* **18.02**

In paragraph (2) the reference to rule "85(3)(*c*)" has been changed to rule "85(7)(b)". In paragraph (3) as printed in the Main Work, "section 22(2)" should be "section 22(1)". There is a new paragraph (4) reading:

(4) When he gives the applicant the opportunity under section 18(3) to make observations on the examiner's report under subsection (2) of that section, the comptroller may, if he thinks fit, send to the

applicant a copy of any document (or part thereof) referred to in the report.

Former paragraph (4) is now renumbered (5).

18.03 Rule 34 [1990]—*Period for putting application in order*

This rule has been extensively amended and is therefore reprinted below:

34.—(1) Subject to the provisions of paragraph (2) below and of rule 83(3), for the purposes of sections 18(4) and 20(1), the period within which an application for a patent shall comply with the Act and these Rules,—

(a) subject to the following provisions of this paragraph, shall be the period of four years and six months calculated from its declared priority date or, where there is no declared priority date, from the date of filing of the application; and
(b) in the case of an application under section 8(3), 12(6) or 37(4), shall be—
  (i) the period of four years and six months calculated from the declared priority date for the earlier application or, where there is no such declared priority date, the date of filing of the earlier application; or
  (ii) the period of eighteen months calculated from the actual date of filing of the application,

whichever expires the later.

(2) In a case where—

(a) before or after these Rules come into force, a third party makes observations under section 21 on an application;
(b) the examiner, for the first time in a report under section 18(3), relies upon the substance of those observations to report that the patentability requirements of the Act are not met; and
(c) following that report, and within the last three months of the period ascertained under paragraph (1) above (including any alteration thereof under rule 100 or rule 110 or an alteration thereof previously made under this paragraph) but after these Rules come into force, the comptroller gives the applicant the opportunity under section 18(3) to make observations on the report and to amend the application,

the period within which an application for a patent shall comply with the Act and these Rules shall expire at the end of the period of three months beginning on the date when the comptroller sends notification to the applicant of that opportunity.

COMMENTARY ON SECTION 18

Substantive examination (subss. (2) and (3)) **18.07**

New rule 33(3) (reprinted in para. 18.02 *supra*) now permits the Comptroller to provide copies of prior art newly cited during substantive examination, for which see also para. 17.09 *supra*.

Grant of the patent (subs. (4)) **18.09**

Rule 24, cited in the Main Work, has been significantly reworded, see paras. 15.03 and 15.13, *supra*. Thus, now, once the administrative letter of grant has issued under section 18(4), the filing of a divisional application is precluded, unless that letter was a "first report" from the substantive examination when two months from the date of that report are allowed under the proviso to rule 24(1).

Time for complying with Act and Rules **18.10**

The new wording of rule 34 (for which see para. 18.03, *supra*) maintains the period of four years six months (from the filing date or declared priority date, if any) as the normal period within which an application must be placed in compliance with the Act and Rules if a patent is to be granted thereon. However, rule 34 also provides two exceptions to the general rule. Firstly, in the case of a replacement application (under ss.8(3), 12(6) or 37(4)), a minimum period of 18 months from the actual date of filing such application is allowed (r. 34(1)(b)), but note that this extension is *not* applicable to a divisional application (under s.15(4)). Secondly, where third party observations are (or have been) made under section 21 and lead to a new objection of unpatentability thereover and the applicant is (after January 7, 1991) given an opportunity to respond to such objection during the last three months of the normal rule 34 period (including any alteration thereof under r. 100 or 110), then three months from the notification of that opportunity to respond are allowed for meeting the compliance obligation (r. 34(2)). The possibilities for extension of the rule 34 period discussed in the Main Work remain unchanged.

PRACTICE UNDER SECTION 18

Request for substantive examination **18.12**

A request for accelerated substantive examination will only be accepted if the Comptroller is satisfied that the applicant is suffering substantial hardship; and, while accelerated examination can be commenced immediately after publication, no favourable communication under section 18(4) will be sent until at least three months after publication (O.J. July 3, 1991). Also, once examination has been concluded, the administrative procedure for publication of the B-print has to take its normal course, see para. 16.04 *supra*.

Plurality of inventions **18.13**

Rule 24, cited in the Main Work, has been significantly reworded, see paras. 15.03 and 15.13 *supra*, but the advice given in the Main Work seems still to be applicable.

Substantive examination

18.14 *—Filing of response*

Toyama's Application, cited in the Main Work, has been reported ([1990] RPC 555); and *General Electrics' Application*, also cited in the Main Work, has been noted (IPD 12103).

SECTION 19—RELEVANT RULES

19.02 Rule 35 [1990]—*Amendment of request for grant*

Rule 35 now reads:

"Subject to rule 45(3), an application for amendment of the request for the grant of a patent shall be made on Patents Form 11/77 and shall be accompanied by a document clearly identifying the proposed amendment."

19.03 Rule 36 [1990]—*Amendment of application before grant*

Paragraphs (1) and (2) of former rule 36 have been replaced by new paragraphs (1)–(3) which read:

36.—(1) Unless the comptroller so requires, the applicant may not amend the description, claims and drawings contained in his application before the comptroller sends to the applicant the examiner's report under section 17(5).

(2) An applicant may of his own volition amend his application in accordance with the following provisions of this rule but not otherwise.

(3) After the comptroller has sent to the applicant the examiner's report under section 17(5) and before he sends to the applicant the first report of the examiner under section 18, the applicant may of his own volition amend the description, claims and drawings contained in his application.

Former paragraph (3) is renumbered as (4). New rule 36(5) repeats former rule 36(4), but with the addition at the end of the words:

> "accompanied by a document clearly identifying the proposed amendment".

Former rule 36(5) has been deleted: its content has been assimilated into new rule 36(1).

COMMENTARY ON SECTION 19

19.05 *Amendments to the specification*

Rule 36 has been recast in form (see para. 19.03 *supra*), but not in substance. The prohibition against voluntary amendment prior to issue of the preliminary examination report under section 17(5) is now in rule 36(1) and rule 36(2) states that voluntary amendment thereafter is only permitted in the circumstances set out in rule 36(3)–(5). These are: between receipt of the preliminary examination report and the first examiner's report under section 18 (r. 36(3)); *one* voluntary amendment made during the period set for response to the *first* substantive examination process (in addition to amendments required to meet the examiner's objections), or within two months if that report is made under section 18(4) (r. 36(4)); and otherwise only with the Comptroller's consent (r. 36(5)). Where amendment is sought under rule 36(5), but apparently not otherwise, application must be made on PF 11/77 and be accompanied by a document "clearly indicating the proposed amendment". The previous requirement to indicate the proposed amendment in red ink is removed, unless the Comptroller so requires, see the comments in para. 19.12 *infra* which apply generally when PF 11/77 is required.

—Change of applicant **19.08**

The statement in the Main Work that no evidence is required if PF 11/77 is filed for amendment of the applicant entity prior to the filing of PF 7/77 is understood to be no longer true, the practice having changed so that supporting evidence by way of a statutory declaration is now required.

PRACTICE UNDER SECTION 19

Amendment of the description, claims or drawings **19.11**

When amendments are filed under present rule 36(4), following a favourable first examination report under section 18(4), the accompanying letter should be prominently marked "URGENT" in order to alert the Patent Office to the need to deal with the requested amendments prior to the administrative act of grant; and similarly upon filing amendments when less than six months remains of the period under rule 34 for placing the application in order for acceptance, especially where the application is: a divisional application filed under section 15(4); a converted European application (UK) filed under section 81; or an international application (UK) entering the national phase under section 89, see O.J. October 9, 1991.

Amendment of the request (PF 1/77) **19.12**

Because rule 35 has been made subject to rule 45(3) (for which see para. 18.02 *supra* and para. 32.05 *infra*), correction of an address can now be made without fee or formality but must be made in writing, see para. 32.24 *infra*. Also, PF 11/77 no longer requires a copy of the request (PF 1/77) to be supplied on which the amendments are shown in red ink, provided that the proposed amendments are otherwise clearly identified. However, the Comptroller can call for the submission of a red ink amendment if he considers this the best way of showing the changes.

SECTION 21—RELEVANT RULE

Rule 37 [1990]—*Observations on patentability under section 21* **21.02**

Rule 37 has been completely revised and now reads:

37.—(1) Subject to paragraph (2) below, the comptroller shall send to the applicant a copy of—

(a) any document containing observations which he receives under section 21 in connection with the application; and
(b) any document referred to in any such observations being a document which he receives from the person making them.

(2) Nothing in paragraph (1) above shall impose any duty on the comptroller in relation to any document—

(a) a copy of which it appears to the comptroller is readily available for retention by the applicant; or
(b) which in his opinion is not suitable for photocopying, whether on account of size or for any other reason.

(3) If the period ascertained under rule 34 (as altered, if that be the case, under rule 100 or rule 110) has not expired and the comptroller has not sent to the applicant notice in accordance with section 18(4) that the application complies with the requirements of the Act and these Rules, the observations shall be referred to the examiner conducting a substantive examination of the application under section 18; and the examiner shall consider and comment upon them as he thinks fit in his report under that section.

COMMENTARY ON SECTION 21

21.05 *Time for making observations*

The new form of rule 37 (reprinted in para. 21.02 *supra*) now removes any obligation of the Comptroller to consider third party observations submitted after the applicant has been informed (under s.18(4)) that the application may proceed to grant or if the rule 34 period for compliance with the Act and Rules (including any extension thereof under r. 100 or 110) has expired. However, otherwise the observations have to be referred to an examiner who may "consider and comment upon them as he thinks fit" in a (further) report made to the applicant under section 18.

However, the hardship of a late report of unpatentability following third party observations made near to the end of the rule 34 period for placing an application in compliance with the Act and Rules (referred to in the Main Work) has now been somewhat alleviated by new rule 34(2) (reprinted in para. 18.03 *supra*). This permits a minimum three month period from the date of such report for meeting the compliance requirements, see para. 18.10 *supra*.

21.06 PRACTICE UNDER SECTION 21

The new form of rule 37 (reprinted in para. 21.02, *supra*) now requires the Comptroller to include with a report made to an applicant of third party observations the documents which constitutes those observations, unless the Comptroller considers any such document will already be available to the applicant or if the document is not, for some reason, suitable for photocopying. It would appear from the wording of rule 37 that the original documents received as the observations are to be forwarded: presumably the Comptroller will keep copies thereof. However, new rule 93(5)(a) (reprinted in para. 118.05 and commented upon in para. 118.16 *infra*) should be noted: this gives the Comptroller power to exclude any document from public inspection which contains disparaging, offensive, immoral or anti-social matter. It is not clear whether, in such circumstances, a report may be made by an examiner but without him placing the offending document on the public file of the application.

PRACTICE UNDER SECTION 22

Procedure on imposition, and effect, of secrecy order **22.09**

Correspondence concerning applications subject to a secrecy order, and any other matters involving sections 22 or 23, should be addressed or delivered by hand to "The Patent Office, Room GR70, Concept House, Newport, Gwent" (telephone for enquiries: 0633 813558). Applications and documents to which section 22 applies, or may apply, may also be delivered by hand to Hazlitt House, 45 Southampton Buildings, Chancery Lane, London WC2A 1AR between 10.00 am and 4.00 pm. Persons delivering such documents should indicate to the receptionist that a Room GR70 filing is required. Fees for applications subject to a secrecy order should be paid separately from those on normal applications.

Export of Goods (Control) Order **22.14**

The substantive Export of Goods (Control) Order is one which is frequently amended and re-issued. Enquiry of the current position should therefore be made as indicated in the Main Work.

COMMENTARY ON SECTION 23

General purpose of section **23.04**

On the meaning of "resident" under European Community law, see *Rigsadvokaten* v. *Ryborg* (*The Times*, May 2, 1991).

Obtaining leave to file application abroad **23.08**

Clearance to file a foreign application under section 23(1) should now be sought from one of the addresses indicated in para. 22.09 *supra.*

Filing application abroad while secrecy order is in place **23.09**

If it is desired to seek to file an application for a European patent for an invention covered by a secrecy order, contact should be made with Room GR70 at the Patent Office, as indicated in para. 22.09 *supra.*

When a European application is not allowed to proceed and application is made to convert the application into national applications in the designated countries, a list of the proposed foreign associates should be supplied with PF 41/77. It should be noted that documents relating to the conversion process must be forwarded from the United Kingdom Patent Office to reach the Patent Office concerned in Europe by 20 months from priority of the application concerned. In general, agents are advised to send early instructions to associates through the address supplied by the Ministry of Defence to enable associates to monitor the receipt of documents.

SECTION 24—RELEVANT RULE

24.02 **Rule 38 [1990]**—*Certificates of grant*

The words "to these Rules" have been deleted from this rule.

COMMENTARY ON SECTION 24

24.05 *Notification of grant (subs. (1))*

While substantive examination can, perhaps, be accelerated when the applicant is suffering hardship, it is understood that the process for granting the patent after completion of the examination is not now administratively possible.

24.07 *Publication of patent specification (subs. (3))*

Unlike the position now with granted European patents (for which see para. 77.09 *infra*), the "B-print" does not indicate whether any divisional applications were filed which could mature into individual patents.

PRACTICE UNDER SECTION 24

24.12 *Specification of granted patent*

Rule 20(16), cited in the Main Work, has become rule 20(15).

SECTION 25—RELEVANT RULES

25.02 **Rule 39 [1990]**—*Renewal of patents*

The rule title has been slightly changed to that set out above.

Paragraph (1) has been amended to read:

> "If, except in the case of a European patent (UK), it is desired to keep a patent in force for a further year after the expiration of the fourth or any succeeding year from the date of filing an application for that patent as determined in accordance with section 15, Patents Form 12/77, in respect of the next succeeding year, accompanied by the prescribed renewal fee for that year, shall be filed in the three months ending with the fourth or, as the case may be, succeeding anniversary of the date of filing:

Provided that, where a patent is granted in the three months ending with the fourth or any succeeding anniversary as so determined or at any time thereafter, Patents Form 12/77, accompanied by the prescribed renewal fee, in respect of the fifth or succeeding year may be filed not more than three months before the expiration of the fourth or relevant succeeding year but before the expiration of three months from the date on which the patent is granted."

In paragraph (2), the words "before the expiration of that year" have been changed to "ending with the fourth or, as the case may be, succeeding anniversary of the date of filing as so determined; and the proviso to paragraph (2) has been reworded to read:

"Provided that, where any renewal fee is due on, or within the period of three months after, the date of publication in the European Patent Bulletin of the mention of the grant of the patent, being a date on or after that on which these Rules come into force, that renewal fee may be paid within those three months; but, where the date of such publication is before that on which these Rules come into force, the proviso to rule 39(2) of the Patents Rules 1982(a) shall continue to apply."

In paragraph (3) the words "(if the patent has been granted)" have been added before the word "issue". Paragraph (5) has been reworded to read:

(5) The comptroller shall send a notice under paragraph (4) above to—

(a) the address in the United Kingdom specified by the proprietor on payment of the last renewal fee; or
(b) where another address in the United Kingdom has been notified to him for that purpose by the proprietor since the last renewal fee, that address,

and, in any other case, the address for service entered in the register."

Paragraph (6) has been reworded to read:

"(6) A request for extending the period for payment of a renewal fee shall be made on Patents Form 12/77 and shall be accompanied by the prescribed renewal fee and the prescribed additional fee for late payment."

Rule 42 [1990]—*Notification of lapsed patent* **25.03**

The word "above" has been deleted.

COMMENTARY ON SECTION 25

25.06 *Grant and term of patent (subss. (1) and (2))*

The E.C. Council of Ministers has approved a draft E.C. Regulation which would have the effect of restoring a patent for a pharmaceutical invention subject to regulatory approval by way of a "supplementary protection certificate" ("SPC") to take effect from the date of expiry of the first patent protecting the approved product, conferring the same rights as the expired patent, and to last for a period corresponding to the delay between patent filing and the first EC marketing authorisation for the product, less five years, *i.e.* for an effective term of 15 years, but with a maximum term of five years. However, the E.C. Member States have an option to choose their own date, provided that this is within three years either way of January 1, 1985, from which patents dated thereafter become eligible for the grant of an SPC. The original SPC proposal however, aroused doubts as to its compatibility with the EPC and, to overcome this, a conference in December 1991 agreed (subject to subsequent signature and ratification by individual Member States) to amend EPCa. 63 in order to provide the Member States with an optional power to grant patent term extensions in defined situations, particularly where a patented product can only be marketed after an administrative authorisation procedure.

25.07 *Renewal fees (subs. (3))*

Rule 39 (reprinted at para. 25.02, and not as stated in the Main Work) has been amended to clarify its wording and simplify its operation. Note, in particular, that the proviso to rule 39(2) (concerning publication of grant of a European patent (UK) about the time when a renewal fee is due) has been amended to increase the specified period to three months (though without retroactive effect), thereby bringing this provision into line with the proviso in rule 39(1) for patents granted under the Act within the period of three months before the renewal fee falls due: thus, in such circumstances, both types of patents can now be renewed within three months from their date of grant.

25.09 *Reminders (subs. (5))*

Under new rule 39(5) (reprinted in para. 25.02 *supra*), the rule 39 reminder letter will now be sent by the Patent Office to the address specified on the PF 12/77 filed with the last previous renewal fee, unless since then a different address (in the United Kingdom) has been notified for the purpose, and otherwise (*e.g.* for the first renewal fee) to the recorded address for service. The commentary in the Main Work is therefore superseded on this point. Also, rule 30 (*Address for service*) has not been amended and therefore must still be one in the United Kingdom, see para. 32.16 *infra*. Where no such address has been recorded and no other address is available under rule 39(5), it is understood that the Patent Office will send the rule 39 reminder to the proprietor's address, even though this may be abroad.

25.10 *Existing patents*

The word "working" in Schedule 1, paragraph 4(2)(*b*) is not limited to acts of "manufacture" but (by analogy with ss. 30(4) and 60(6), where the word is also used) includes acts of sale and export: however, where corresponding foreign patents continue to exist, royalties may be payable for use thereof; but, although the effect of the 1977 Act was to extend the terms of corresponding patents in Hong Kong and Singapore, these extensions were subject to the same conditions so that sales in these countries (as well as those in the United Kingdom) had become royalty-free under a licence granted before June 1, 1978 once the patents had reached the end of the 16th year of their life (*National Research Development Corp.* v. *Wellcome Foundation*, [1991] FSR 663).

PRACTICE UNDER SECTION 25

Payment of renewal fees 25.12

The revised form of PF 12/77 (reprinted in para. 141.12, *infra*) now requires there to be stated thereon: the date on which the renewal fee is due; the number of the year for which it is paid; the amount of the fee being paid; and requires the name and address of the person paying the fee to be stated. The form also contains a statement that any reminder that has to be sent (under r. 39(5)) of non-payment of the next renewal fee due will be sent to the address for service entered on the register *unless* some other address, in the United Kingdom (or the Isle of Man), is entered in the box which is provided for this purpose. However, there is no requirement that the address given for the person paying the fee need be in the United Kingdom.

As anticipated in the Main Work, PF 13/77 has been discontinued so that, when an additional fee is paid upon late renewal, the combined extension and renewal fees are now paid together on PF 12/77, see rule 39(6) (reprinted in para. 25.02 *supra*).

Legal obligations of agents in respect of statutory notices 25.15

Although an agent may purport to have his address removed from the register as the address for service, it appears that, until some other address for service is notified to the Patent Office, the former address is not removed from the register and, consequently, reminder letters under rules 39 and 42 continue to be sent to that address.

SECTION 27—RELEVANT RULE

Rule 40 [1990]—*Amendment of specification after grant* 27.02

In paragraph (2), the words "three months" have been changed to "two months". In paragraph (4), the words "three months of the receipt of such copies" have been changed to "the period of two months beginning on the date when such copies are sent to him". Paragraph (6) has been replaced by:

(6) An application under this rule shall be accompanied by—

(a) a copy of the specification as published on which the proposed amendment is clearly identified;
(b) if the specification as published is not in English, a document containing a translation into English of the part of the specification

proposed to be amended and a translation into English of the part as proposed to be amended being verified to the satisfaction of the comptroller as corresponding to the original text; and

(c) in the case of an application for amendment of a European patent (UK), a copy of the specification for that patent as published,

and, if the specification as published is not in English, the applicant shall, if the comptroller so requests, supply a translation thereof into English verified to his satisfaction as corresponding to the original text.

In paragraph (7), the final word "above" has been deleted.

COMMENTARY ON SECTION 27

Discretion

27.05 *—Duty of full disclosure*

Smith Kline & French's (Bavin's) Patent (No. 2), cited in the Main Work, has been reported as *Smith Kline & French* v. *Evans Medical* ([1989] FSR 561).

It has again been stressed that a patentee seeking amendment "has a duty, whether discovery is sought or not, to make full disclosure of all relevant matters" (*Yen Wei Hsiung's Patent*, SRIS C/5/91, *noted* IPD 14079). Here amendment was refused because there had been no disclosure whether there were corresponding patents in other countries and, if so, whether other patent offices had raised an objection of the prior art cited in the present proceedings; and because no evidence had been put forward to show whether there had been any culpable delay between the date of grant and the commencement of these proceedings.

Although full disclosure must be given, and this may involve the waiving of privilege in certain documents, the Court has been prepared to protect a patentee against use of those documents in other proceedings by agreeing to hear the evidence *in camera* and imposing an injunction against use of the documents other than in the amendment proceedings in issue (*Bonzel* v. *Intervention (No. 2)*, [1991] RPC 231).

27.06 *—Undue delay*

Smith Kline & French's (Bavin's) Patent (No. 2), cited in the Main Work, has been reported as *Smith Kline & French* v. *Evans Medical* ([1989] FSR 561). This decision has been held conveniently to summarise the relevant principles for the exercise of discretion (*Hugh Steeper's Patent*, SRIS O/33/90), but (as there pointed out), even if full details of the prior art were known to the patentee, it does not necessarily follow that as a consequence he knew that the patent was invalid: amendment should only be refused when the patentee obtains and maintains claims which he knew, or in the circumstances ought to have known, were invalid. Thus, where there has been a failure of communication between applicant and patent agent so that the relevance of the prior art was not appreciated by the applicant, discretion to permit amendment can be exercised (*Rockwool International's Patent*, SRIS O/63/90, *noted* IPD 13164).

In *Glaverbel's Patent* (SRIS O/19/90) the Comptroller reviewed the cases concerning delay and held that denial of amendment is only appropriate where the delay in dealing with amendment is in some way to be classified as culpable conduct, this not being so here in contrast to that in the *Smith Kline & French* case. This view was reiterated in *Corning Glass Works' Patent* (SRIS O/88/90, *noted* IPD 13213) where it was indicated that mere delay does not bar amendment, this requiring delay after the patentee had appreciated the need to amend or resulting prejudice to some other person.

In *N.L. Petroleum's Patent* (SRIS O/112/90, *noted* IPD 14043) a delay of two years plus was sufficient for amendment to be denied.

Opposition to application to amend a patent (subs. (5)) **27.12**

The period for opposition has been reduced to two months from the date of advertisement in the O.J. of the proposed amendment, see para. 27.18 *infra*. There is now specific power for the Comptroller to stay the amendment proceedings on a European patent (UK) when there is a pending opposition against that patent in the EPO, if one of the parties should so request (new r. 40(6) reprinted in para. 27.23 *supra*), see para. 27.15 *infra*.

Grounds of opposition **27.13**

Minister of Agriculture's Patent, cited in the Main Work, has been reported ([1990] RPC 61). Also, *EPO Decision T* 301/87, "*Alpha-interferons/BIOGEN*", cited in the Main Work, has been reported (OJEPO 8/1990, 335; [1990] 3 EPOR 190) and discussed (1988–89) 18 CIPA 396 and [1990] IPBB 6.

PRACTICE UNDER SECTION 27

Procedure for applying to amend a patent **27.14**

New rule 39(7) (reprinted in para. 27.02 *supra*) dispenses with the former requirement of providing a copy of the patent showing in red ink the amendments sought. However, a document must be supplied which clearly identifies the proposed amendment in the specification as published. For amendment of a European patent (UK), see para. 27.15 in the Main Work and *infra*.

Minister of Agriculture's Patent, cited in the Main Work, has been reported ([1990] RPC 61). Here it was held that the Comptroller has power to allow amendment of an opposition statement in order that this should fully set out the facts relied upon.

Amendment of European patent (UK) **27.15**

Revised rule 40(6) specifies that, where a European patent (UK) is sought to be amended, there must be supplied a copy of the specification as published; and, where the specification is not in English, there must be supplied a translation of the part of the specification to be amended *and* a translation of that part as proposed to be amended, as well (if the Comptroller so requests) a translation of the entire specification. If that patent is under opposition in the EPO, the Comptroller has inherent discretion to stay the amendment proceedings before him, but it is understood that the proceedings are likely to continue if the proprietor indicates good reason why a stay may be prejudicial to him.

Statement of reasons for amendment **27.16**

In *PSC Frayssinet's Patent* (SRIS O/117/91) the Patentee was criticised for not referring on PF 14/77 to a pertinent patent cited in an EPO search report, PF

14/77 referring only to a German *Gebrauchsmuster* also cited in that report. However, the amendment was allowed as the opponent had raised the point only at the hearing and that patent was held not to affect patentability in the absence of evidence from skilled persons. The fact that the Patentee had supplied only the published abstract of the *Gebrauchmuster*, and not the full text, was held in the circumstances not to be sufficient to prevent the requested amendment.

27.18 *Procedure on opposition*

The period within which opposition may be lodged has been reduced to *two* months from the date of advertisement in the O.J. and this period remains inextensible under rule 110(2). To contest the opposition, the proprietor must file a counter-statement within the reduced period of two months from the date of dispatch to him of the opposition statement, but this period is extensible under rule 110(1).

For amendment of a European patent not in the English language see para. 27.15 in the Main Work and *supra.*

28.01

SECTION 28

Note. The amendments to section 28 noted in the Main Work came into effect on January 7, 1991 (S.I. 1990 No. 2168).

SECTION 28—RELEVANT RULE

28.02 **Rule 41 [1990]**—*Restoration of lapsed patents under section 28*

Paragraph (1) has been amended to read:

"(1) An application under section 28 for the restoration of a patent, including an application for restoration of a patent which lapsed not more than twelve months before these Rules came into force (being in any case a patent which has lapsed by reason of a failure to pay any renewal fee),—

(a) may be made at any time within the period of nineteen months beginning on the day on which it ceased to have effect; and
(b) shall be made on Patents Form 16/77 supported by evidence of the statements made in it:

and the comptroller shall publish in the Journal notice of the making of the application."

In paragraph (4), after "require him" there has been inserted the words:

", within two months after the notification is sent to him,"; "the unpaid" has been changed to "any unpaid";

and a proviso has been added reading:

"Provided that, in a case where a notification under this paragraph is sent to the applicant before these Rules come into force, this paragraph shall have effect as if the words "within two months after the notification is sent to him" were omitted."

Notes. 1. New rule 41(1) defines the "prescribed period" (for s. 28(1)) as 19 months calculated from the date on which the patent ceased to have effect.

2. The date when the "Rules came into force" was January 7, 1991, see para. 139.02 *infra.*

3. New rule 41(1) is subject to the proviso to Schedule 5, para. 6(4) [1988] reprinted in the *Note* to para. 28.01 in the Main Work, namely that the 19 month restoration period only applies to patents which lapsed on or after January 7, 1990.

SECTION 28—ARTICLES **28.03**

P. A. Chandler and J. A. Holland, "Systems of patent renewal: Controlling employees' frolics", [1989] EIPR 460.

COMMENTARY ON SECTION 28

Amendments to section 28 **28.05**

The amendments to section 28 took effect from January 7, 1991, see para. 28.01 *supra*. The "prescribed period" has been defined as 19 months from the date on which the patent ceased to have effect, *i.e.* from the end of the normal period for payment of a renewal fee (s. 25(3)). However, the new rule cannot be used for restoration of a patent which had lapsed more than 12 months prior to the above date (r. 41(1) and Sched. 5, para. 5 [1988] proviso).

Application for restoration (subs. (1)) **28.06**

The prescribed period is now 19 months, rather than 12 months as previously, see para. 28.05 *supra*. This period remains inextensible (r. 110(2)).

The prescribed period for requesting restoration cannot be evaded by seeking to convert PF 12/77 (filed in ignorance that the patent had lapsed) into an application for restoration (*Commissariat à l'Energie's Patent*, SRIS O/143/90, *noted* IPD 14027 and on appeal *Electricité de France's Patents*, SRIS C/73/91), following *Dynamics Research's Patent* ([1980] RPC 179).

Grounds for restoration (subs. (1))

—Lack of reasonable care **28.09**

The article by P. A. Chandler and J. A. Holland listed *re.* para. 28.03 *supra* reviews many of the decisions discussed in the Main Work, particularly in the context of the control of employees' actions, and also comes to the conclusion that the repeal of subsection (3)(*b*) may, in practice, make little difference to the outcome of particular cases.

British Broadcasting's Patent (SRIS O/49/89), cited in the Main Work, has been noted at [1989] 10 IPBB 10. An appeal against the Comptroller's refusal of restoration was successful in *Sony Corp.'s Patent* ([1990] RPC 152), following *Textron's Patent* ([1989] RPC 441 (HL), cited in the Main Work): in *Sony*, the Patentee had satisfactory fail-safe procedures but these did not apply to an isolated patent acquired by assignment. A junior employee omitted to notice this and then the official reminder was lost in the post because a foreign agent had moved his office.

Restoration was refused in *Norfield Corp.'s Patent* (SRIS O/50/90, *noted* IPD 13144) because of a failure to respond to agent's reminders or adequately instruct staff to deal with these; and, in *Linkrose's Patent* (SRIS O/117/90, *noted* IPD 14025), it was held that severe mental strain and accompanying physical run-down of the proprietor were not in themselves a sufficient basis for restoration to be allowed. Restoration was also refused in *BWS Management's Patent* (SRIS O/113/90, *noted* IPD 14026) where the responsible person, although over-worked, had found time to sell the patent; in *Fisher Westmoreland's Patent* (SRIS O/151/90) where an agreement, which would have changed responsibility for patent maintenance, had not been signed and should therefore have not been treated by the proprietor as having effect; in *Hechmati's Patent* (SRIS O/36/91, *noted* IPD 14116), where the proprietor had entrusted matters to a relative who was unaware of the need to pay a renewal fee; in *University of Chicago's Patent* (SRIS O/44/91, *noted* IPD 14162), where renewal responsibility had been delegated without proper check on the delegatee's renewal system and where the addressee for service had not been provided with a dependable address for the forwarding of renewal reminders; and in *Soldek Systems' Patent* (SRIS O/57/91, *noted* IPD 14195), where the proprietor failed to make alternative arrangements for renewal reminders to be received when it became apparent that he would be unable to play his part in the system which he had set up. A standing instruction to a patent agent to renew the patent may be ineffective if the agent reasonably refuses to implement that instruction, *e.g.* because he is owed money by the patentee (*Revmarine's Patent*, SRIS O/91/91). Restoration will also be refused when a proprietor, on the basis of uncertain facts, whether actual or presumed, decides to allow the patent to lapse, and then changes his mind when these facts subsequently prove to be incomplete or inaccurate (*Walters' Patent*, SRIS O/105/91).

The EPO has accepted that failure to pay fees due to financial circumstances outside the proprietor's control does not preclude reinstatement under EPCa. 122, and that this is possible provided that the proprietor took all steps open to him to find the necessary finance (*EPO Decision J 22/88*, "*Re-establishment of rights/RADAKOVIC*", [1990] EPOR 495).

PRACTICE UNDER SECTION 28

28.12 *Filing application for restoration*

An application for restoration must now be advertised in the O.J. (s.28(2A) and r. 41(1)). Once the "prescribed period" has expired no patent then exists upon which action can be taken, see *Electricité de France's Patents* (SRIS C/73/91) where unsuccessful attempts were made to amend the renewal form filed within this period into one seeking restoration.

28.13 *Determination of the restoration application*

The one month period allowed under rule 41(2), for requesting a hearing when the Comptroller considers that a case for restoration has not been made out, is now inextensible under rule 110(2) [1990], see para. 123.10 *infra*.

Allowance or refusal of restoration **28.14**

Upon allowance of restoration (after January 7, 1991), the filing of PF 12/77 and PF 17/77 must now be made within two months of the date when the Comptroller's notice of allowance of restoration is sent to the patentee (r. 41(4)). This period is extensible by one month under rule 110(3) [1990], see para. 123.10 *infra*.

SECTION 28A **28A.01**

Note. The new section 28A set out in the Main Work came into effect on January 7, 1991 (S.I. 1990 No. 2168).

COMMENTARY ON SECTION 28A

Origin of the section **28A.02**

On reflection the statement in the Main Work on the effect of section 28A on matters occurring before its commencement on January 7, 1991 may not be correct. There is no transitional provision and section 28A(1) refers to the "effect of an order for the restoration of a patent". These words would seem apposite to cover *any* restoration order whensoever made. The new section may, therefore, even apply to orders made before that date, and certainly to orders made thereafter on restorations filed prior thereto. However, there is the possibility of a saving of accrued rights, for which see para. 127.09 in the Main Work.

SECTION 29—RELEVANT RULE

Rule 42 [1990]—*Surrender of patents* **29.02**

In paragraph (2) "three months" has been changed to "two months". In paragraph (4), the words "three months of the receipt of such copies" have been changed to "the period of two months beginning on the date when such copies are sent to him".

COMMENTARY ON SECTION 29

Opposition to surrender (subs. (2)) **29.05**

The period within which opposition may be lodged has been reduced to *two* months from the date of the advertisement in the O.J. (r. 43(1), reprinted in para. 29.02 *supra*), and remains inextensible (r. 110(2)).

Acceptance of offer to surrender (subs. (3)) **29.06**

It appears that an offer to surrender the patent will not terminate entitlement proceedings under section 37 (*Weston Hydraulics' Patent*, SRIS O/153/90, *noted* IPD 14117), though here the patent was revoked for anticipation.

PRACTICE UNDER SECTION 29

29.08 *Opposing surrender*

The period for lodging opposition is now only two months from the date of advertisement (r. 43(1)); and, if the patentee wishes to contest such an opposition he must now file a counter-statement within *two* months calculated from the date when the statement was sent to him (r. 43(4)).

30.02

SECTION 30—BOOKS

A. Shipwright, "UK Taxation and Intellectual Property" (ESC Publishing, 1990).

SECTION 30—ARTICLES

M. Anderson, "The application of real property laws to intellectual property transactions", *Patent World*, October 1990, 24.

COMMENTARY ON SECTION 30

30.07 *Execution of documents (subs. (6))*

New section 36A of the Companies Act 1985 (c. 6) (inserted by s.130 of the Companies Act 1989, c. 40) now renders it unnecessary for a company to have a seal and (whether or not it does have a seal) a document signed by a director and the secretary of a company (or by two directors thereof), which is expressed in some way to be executed by the company, has the same effect as if that document had been executed under its seal; and such document has the effect of a deed if, *ex facie*, it is indicated as intended to have that effect.

Likewise, a personal seal is no longer required for an individual. A document is executed as a deed if it is signed personally in the presence of a witness who attests the signature and the document indicates that it is to have effect as a deed (Law of Property (Miscellaneous Provisions) Act 1989 (c. 34), s.1).

It has been confirmed that even an exclusive licence need not be in writing because a licence is not a right "in a patent", but a right "under a patent" (*Insituform* v. *Inliner*, SRIS C/77/91).

PRACTICE UNDER SECTION 30

30.09 *Liability of assignor*

The effect of section 76 of the Law of Property Act 1925 (13 Geo. 5, c. 20), mentioned in the Main Work, is more fully discussed in the article by M. Anderson listed in para. 30.03 *supra*.

30.10 *Transfer of rights by companies*

The sections of the Companies Act 1985 (c. 6) referred to in the Main Work have been prospectively amended by sections 92–107 of the Companies Act 1989

(c. 40). When these amendments are brought into force charges on "intellectual property" will be required to be registered under new section 396(1)(*c*) of the 1985 Act, this term being defined by new section 396(2)(*d*) thereof (for which see s. 93 of the 1989 Act). The provisions for late or incomplete delivery of particulars of the charge to the registrar of companies are now to be a little less severe (see new ss. 399–407 of the 1985 Act prospectively substituted by ss. 95–99 of the 1989 Act).

Stamp duty **30.12**

From a date when the "Taurus" computerised system of share transfers comes into operation (expected in late 1992), stamp duty will no longer be payable on a conveyance of intellectual property rights (arising from an agreement entered into after that date), provided that no transfer of land (or interest in or licence over land) is included in the same conveyance: consequently, from that date the certification clause set out in the Main Work need no longer be included in any such conveyance (Finance Act 1991, c. 31, ss. 110–114).

Value added tax **30.13**

The effect of VAT law on intellectual property is considered in the book by A. Shipwright listed in para. 30.02 *supra*.

Income and corporation tax **30.14**

The book by A. Shipwright, listed in para. 30.02 *supra*, also deals with the impact of taxation law on intellectual property.

COMMENTARY ON SECTION 31

Nature of patents and patent rights under Scots law (subss. (2)–(5)) **31.04**

The registration of company charges under Scots law is now to be dealt with in the same provisions which govern their registration under English law, for which see para. 30.10 *supra*.

Assignations and grants of security under Scots law (subss. (6) and (7))

—Manner of execution **31.06**

A probative deed under Scots law may now be executed on behalf of a company by it being signed on behalf of the company by two directors of the company, or by one director and the company secretary, or by two persons authorised to sign the document on behalf of the company, no sealing or witnessing now being needed (Companies Act 1985 (c. 6, s. 36B), introduced by the Companies Act 1989 (c. 40, s. 130), as further affected by the Law Reform (Miscellaneous Provisions) (Scotland) Act 1990 (c. 40, s. 72)). However, unlike the position under English law (as noted in para. 30.07 *supra*), there is no presumption under Scots law that a person signing as a director or the company secretary has such a position, or that a purported authorised signatory was in fact so authorised: thus proof of capacity should be requested upon delivery of the executed instrument.

SECTION 32—RELEVANT RULES

32.03 **Rule 30 [1990]**—*Address for service*

In rule 30, after "proceedings or patent" there has been added "(as appropriate".

Note. This rule has *not* otherwise been amended as predicted in the Main Work, see para. 32.16 *infra.*

32.04 **Rule 44 [1990]**—*Entries in the register*

At the end of sub-paragraph (2)(f), "and" has been added. Sub-paragraph (3)(b) has been amended to read:

> "(b) the date on which the application is withdrawn, taken to be withdrawn, treated as having been withdrawn, refused or treated as having been refused;".

32.05 **Rule 45 [1990]**—*Alteration of name or address*

Paragraph (1) has been amended to read:

(1) A request by any person, upon the alteration of his name, for that alteration to be entered in the register or on any application or other document filed at the Patent Office shall be made on Patents Form 20/77.

Paragraph (3) has been replaced by:

(3) A request by any person for the alteration or correction of his address or address for service entered in the register or on any application or other document filed at the Patent Office shall, if not made on a form filed under any provision of these Rules, be made in writing and shall identify any relevant application or patent.

(4) If the comptroller is satisfied that a request to alter a name or to alter or correct an address or address for service may be allowed, he shall cause the register, application or other document to be altered accordingly.

32.06 **Rule 46**—*Registrations under section 33*

Paragraph (2) has been reworded to read:

(2) Unless the comptroller otherwise directs, an application under paragraph (1) above shall be accompanied by—

(a) a certified copy of any document which establishes the transaction, instrument or event; or

(b) a certified copy of such extracts from such document as suffice to establish the transaction, instrument or event.

Rule 47 [1990]—*Request for correction of error* 32.07

Paragraph (1) has been amended to read:

(1) Without prejudice to rule 45(3), a request for the correction of an error in the register or in any document filed at the Patent Office in connection with registration shall be made on Patents Form 22/77; and the correction shall be clearly identified on a document annexed to the form or, if not, on the form itself.

Rule 51 [1990]—*Entries relating to sections 8(1), 12(1) and 37(1)* 32.09

The word "above" has been deleted after "rule 44(1)."

Rule 52 [1990]—*Certificates and copies supplied by comptroller* 32.10

In paragraph (3), the two references to "rule 93(5)" are now to "rule 93(4)"; the words "for information" have been deleted and the final two lines now read:

> "or extracts from any document or file of a description referred to in rule 93(5)."

Rule 53 [1990]—*Order or direction by court* 32.11

The final four lines of this rule now read:

> "the person in whose favour the order is made or the direction is given—
> (i) shall file Patents Form 25/77 accompanied by an office copy of the order or direction; and
> (ii) if the comptroller so requires and before a time is fixed by him, shall file a specification as amended (prepared in accordance with rules 16, 18 and 20),
> and thereupon the specification shall be amended or the register rectified or altered, as the case may require.

COMMENTARY ON SECTION 32

Address for service (r. 30) 32.16

Rule 30 has not been amended as predicted in the Main Work. Section 281(5) [1988] requires the Comptroller not to refuse recognition of an agent who resides outside the EEC (or the Isle of Man) but, to act as an agent in proceedings under the Act, such agent is still required to give an address for service which is within the United Kingdom (or the Isle of Man). An address for service can now be altered or corrected merely by notifying the Comptroller of the same in writing (r. 45(3), reprinted in para. 32.05 *supra*).

While it has been held that a recorded address for service in respect of a trade mark can be used for the service of court proceedings, such as an appeal against an unsuccessful opposition (*Johnson & Johnson's Application*, [1991] RPC 1), the reasoning there applied does not necessarily apply in relation to proceedings under the Patents Act because this appears to contain no rule-making power similar to that in section 40(1)(*a*) of the Trade Marks Act 1938 (1 & 2 Geo. 6, c. 22).

32.17 *Entries made automatically (r. 44)*

Now that the register has been computerised, there are entered against the entry for a published parent application details of any divisional application filed under section 15(4), see para. 15.32A *supra.*

32.20 *Legal proceedings*

Rule 53 now provides that, where a court order permits amendment of the patent, the Comptroller can require the submission to him (within a time specified by him) of an amended specification prepared in accordance with rules 16, 18 and 20, see para. 32.11 *supra.*

PRACTICE UNDER SECTION 32

32.23 *Alteration of address for service*

PF 20/77 is no longer required for recording an alteration or correction of an address for service. Written notification of such to the Comptroller now suffices (r. 45(3), reprinted in para. 32.05 *supra*).

32.24 *Alteration of name or address of proprietor*

Under the new form of rule 45 (reprinted in para. 32.05 *supra*), PF 20/77 is now only required for notification of an alteration of name in the register: an alteration of address can now be made simply in writing (r. 45(3)), see O.J. February 13, 1991.

Registration of transactions, instruments and events

32.26 *—Inter-company transfers*

Contrary to the statement in the Main Work, the Patent Office does not now regard a merger of two companies under United States law as being a mere change of name. The merger is treated as an "event" and a certificate from the Secretary of the State of the merged company is required as evidencing this, together with PF 21/77 rather than PF 20/77 for a change of name.

32.29 *—Filing request for registration*

No fee is now payable on PF 21/77, see para. 144.01 *infra*, and consequently there is now no "additional fee" as referred to in the Main Work.

Correction of errors in register and documents 32.32

PF 22/77 is no longer required for the correction of an address or address for service as new rule 47 is made subject to rule 45(3), for which see paras. 32.23 and 32.24, *supra*. For other corrections the nature of the correction sought must be clearly identified, either on PF 22.77 or on a document annexed thereto. However, the correction need no longer be presented in coloured ink, unless the Comptroller should so require to clarify the correction sought.

Requests for correction of the register are now advertised in the O.J., see *e.g.* O.J. August 28, 1991.

Inspection of register and documents 32.33

Following a Patent Office audit of its records, a list of patents which had erroneously been recorded in the register as having lapsed was published (O.J. December 4, 1991): these were all "existing patents". While this audit is thought to have been complete, the Patent Office has requested, through the Chartered Institute, that it be notified if any inconsistencies or irregularities in register entries should be discovered ((1991–92) 21 CIPA 157).

Rule 52 now restricts the copying from the patent file of documents not available to inspection under rule 93(4) and (5), see para. 32.10, *supra*, and para. 118.12, *infra*.

The card index of assignees, mentioned in the Main Work, is maintained on a yearly basis and is available for inspection in the Public Search Room at the Patent Office on filing PF 23/77. This provides a useful supplement to the name indices of applicants of published applications to cover those cases where assignment has, after publication of the application, resulted in a change in proprietorship.

Certificate from Comptroller 32.36

No photocopy charges are now levied in respect of documents attached to Comptroller's certificates requested by filing PF 24/77, the fee payable on this form having been increased to compensate for this (O.J. July 24, 1991). If an application has not yet been published under section 16, PF 24/77 will only be accepted if filed by the applicant or his *previously authorised* agent, see para. 118.20 *infra*.

Certification of priority documents 32.37

Certified copies of priority documents are now created within the nine formalities units within the Patent Office (determined according to the final digit of the application number). Enquiries concerning expedited or delayed certification should be addressed to the appropriate unit, followed up if necessary by a general enquiry to 0633 814611 ((1990–91) 20 CIPA 414). Certified copies of applications not yet open to public inspection are, however, only supplied to the applicant personally or to his agent of record.

When an application is abandoned, withdrawn, taken to be withdrawn or refused before publication under section 16, the Patent Office file is destroyed at the end of the fifth year from its date of filing (O.J. April 25, 1990): certified copies, as may still be required for foreign applications, will then not be available and should therefore have been obtained in advance of destruction. However, the date of destruction can be obtained from the Patent Office who are also prepared to re-certify a copy of a previously certified document obtained from some other Patent Office, see (1990–91) 20 CIPA 415.

COMMENTARY ON SECTION 36

36.03 *Prima facie entitlement of co-owners to equal undivided shares in patent*

The article by M. Anderson listed in para. 30.03 *supra* discusses the concept of co-ownership of intellectual property with particular reference to the Law of Property Act 1925 (15 Geo. 5, c. 20, s. 34).

37.01

SECTION 37

Note. The amendments to section 37 noted in the Main Work came into effect on January 7, 1991 (S.I. 1990 No. 2168).

SECTION 37—RELEVANT RULES

37.02 **Rule 54 [1990]**—*Reference of question under section 37*

Rule 54 now has a slightly different title and has been amended to read:

54.—(1) A reference under section 37(1) shall be made on Patents Form 2/77 and shall be accompanied by a copy thereof and a statement in duplicate setting out fully the nature of the question, the facts upon which the person making the reference relies and the order which he is seeking.

(2) The comptroller shall send a copy of the reference and statement to every person who is not a party to the reference being—

(a) a person who is shown on the register as having any right in or under the patent; or
(b) a person who is alleged in the reference to be entitled to a right in or under the patent.

(3) If any person who is sent a copy of the reference and statement under paragraph (2) above wishes to oppose the making of the order sought ("the opponent"), he shall, within the period of two months beginning on the date when such copies are sent to him, file in duplicate a counter-statement setting out fully the grounds of his opposition and the comptroller shall send a copy of the counter-statement to the person making the reference and to those recipients of the copy of the reference and statement who are not party to the counter-statement.

(4) The person making the reference or any such recipient, may, within the period of two months beginning on the date when the copy of the counter-statement is sent to him, file evidence in support of his case and shall send a copy of the evidence,—

(a) in any case, to the opponent; and
(b) in the case of evidence filed by such a recipient, to the person making the reference.

(5) Within the period of two months after the copy of such evidence is sent to him or, if no such evidence is filed, within two months of the expiration of the time within which it might have been filed, the opponent may file evidence in support of his case and shall send a copy of that evidence to the person making the reference and to those recipients; and within the period of two months after the copy of the opponent's evidence is sent to him, that person or any of those recipients may file further evidence confined to matters strictly in reply and shall send a copy of it to the persons mentioned in sub-paragraphs (a) and (b) of paragraph (4) above.

(6) No further evidence shall be filed by any party except by leave or direction of the comptroller.

(7) The comptroller may give such directions as he may think fit with regard to the subsequent procedure.

Rule 55 [1982]—*Reference by joint proprietors under section 37(1)* **37.03**

Note. The subject-matter of former rule 55 [1982] is now to be found within rule 54 [1990], see para. 37.02 *supra*.

Rule 55 [1990]—*Applications under section 37(3)* **37.04**

This rule is merely rule 56 [1982], renumbered, except that, in paragraph (1), the words "in duplicate" have been added after "statement".

Rule 56 [1990]—*Time limit for new application* **37.05**

This rule is merely rule 57 [1982], renumbered.

SECTION 37—ARTICLES **37.07**

T. Z. Gold, "Entitlement disputes: A case review", [1990] EIPR 382.

COMMENTARY ON SECTION 37

General **37.08**

In line 1 of the third paragraph in the Main Work, "37.09" should read "37.10".

The paper by T. Z. Gold, listed in para. 37.07 *supra*, reviews decisions given by the Comptroller on entitlement and inventorship disputes.

Scope of section 37 **37.09**

Amateur Athletic Association's Application (SRIS O/53/89), cited in the Main Work, has been reported ([1989] RPC 717); and *Coin Controls' Application*, also so cited, has been *noted* at IPD 13034.

The Comptroller does not have the power to revoke a patent in entitlement proceedings as such. However, such proceedings can be coupled with an application for revocation under section 72 or a referrer can seek a declaration of entitlement and then seek revocation under section 72(1)(*b*) based on that declaration (*Kokta's Patents*, SRIS O/88/91). The Comptroller also has no power to decide entitlement questions concerning foreign patents under section 37. This can only be done by separate application under section 12, see *Vet Health's Patent*, SRIS O/49/90, *noted* IPD 13165 and para. 8.10 *supra*.

37.10 *Powers of the court to determine entitlement disputes*

Entitlement disputes arising in England or Wales may now be brought before the patents county court, see para. 96.17 *infra*. The procedure will be that normally prevailing in this court, for which see para. 96.22 and Appendix H *infra*.

In *La Baigue's Patent* (SRIS O/124/89) the Comptroller refused to refer an entitlement question to the court under section 37(8) even though infringement proceedings were there pending: the proceedings before the Comptroller would be conducted more cheaply and, if resolved one way, would terminate the infringement proceedings. Subsequently, the parties asked the Comptroller to dismiss these proceedings without making any finding: this was done, but the Comptroller pointed out that, until any such finding, the register would reflect the *status quo* (SRIS O/9/90, *noted* IPD 13042). Reference to the court was also refused in *Vet Health's Patent* (SRIS O/49/90) because, although infringement proceedings were there pending, these did not involve the person claiming entitlement so that revocation under section 72(1)(*b*) would not be possible in those proceedings, see paras. 72.17 and 74.05 in the Main Work.

The Civil Jurisdiction and Judgments Act 1982 (c. 27) is now in force also for Denmark and Greece. This has resulted in the replacement of Schedule 1 of that Act by the Civil Jurisdiction and Judgments Act 1982 (Amendment) Order 1989 (S.I. 1989 No. 1346). The Act will also have application to Portugal and Spain when the Civil Jurisdiction and Judgments Act 1982 (Amendment) Order 1991 (S.I. 1990 No. 2591) is brought into force, and is also prospectively applied to Contracting States to the Lugano Convention (*i.e.* members of the EFTA group of countries) by the Civil Jurisdiction and Judgments Act 1991 (c. 12).

37.12 *Relief granted under section 37*

The reference in the Main Work to para. 8.08 should have been to para. 8.07, and the reference to *Norris's Patent* should have been to [1988] RPC 159. In subsequent proceedings in this case (*Norris's Patent,* SRIS O/130/91) it was held that the invention had been made in the applicant's own time and that rights therein had never belonged to his then employer; and, moreover, that a subsequent "arrangement" between him and a company set up to exploit the invention had never been sufficiently definite to be an agreement to transfer ownership of the patent.

The paper by T. Z. Gold, listed in para. 37.07 *supra*, reviews many of the Comptroller's decisions given in entitlement and inventorship disputes and discusses the kinds of relief which these decisions have provided. The Comptroller is also prepared to grant relief when the parties consent, as in *Bowling & Scott's Patent* (SRIS O/35/90) where it was agreed the patent should be transferred to the referrer. In *Kokta's Patents* (SRIS O/88/91) the referrer was found to be a co-inventor on one of the referred patents, but his rights as co-owner had been subjugated to the patentee via the referrer's employer.

In *Leighton* v. *Vickerys Holdings* (SRIS C/59/91, *noted* IPD 14158) the Plaintiff (an employee) threatened to sue for damages the agent who had filed an application on behalf of the Defendant (his employer) if the agent took any step on it other than on the Plaintiff's instructions. The agent interpleaded in the entitlement proceedings brought before the court and successfully claimed his costs to be borne equally by the Plaintiff and Defendant pending determination of the main proceedings.

Time bar for orders under section 37 (subss. (5) and (9)) **37.13**

CPCaa. 27 and 57, referred to in the Main Work, have been re-numbered as CPCaa. 23 and 56 [1989], see para. 86.03 *infra*.

In *Norris's Patent* (SRIS O/130/91) the original order for the referrer to become a joint proprietor had been discharged on appeal pending further determination of possible employer ownership. However, when this had been done, it was then held too late to make a further order to this effect because of the time bar under subsection (5). Thus, it is important that a referrer obtains an order within the two year time limit of this subsection.

PRACTICE UNDER SECTION 37

Proceedings under section 37 before the Comptroller **37.14**

Rules 54 and 55 [1982] have been combined into rule 54 [1990]. This rule indicates with some particularity to whom copies of documents filed in the proceedings must be sent. The various time periods are now reduced to *two* months and these now, where appropriate, begin with the date when the counter-statement or evidence from the other party is sent to the person to whom the time period applies. Rule 56 [1982] has been renumbered as rule 55 [1990].

The Comptroller has refused to make an interim order that the patent (under which a reference under section 37 has been made) should be kept in force pending his decision: it was pointed out that the referrer could be given an opportunity to file a replacement application under subsection (4) if he is eventually successful (*Vet Health's Patent*, SRIS O/49/90). Here it was also pointed out that no relief in respect of any foreign patent or application is possible under section 37, though there may be a possibility of parallel proceedings under section 12 in respect of any foreign applications not yet granted.

In *Fritsch's Patent* (SRIS O/115/91) the Comptroller ordered a stay of proceedings under sections 37 and 72(1)(*b*), under Article 22 of the Brussels Convention (for which see para. 61.25 of the Main Work), because proceedings already pending before the Irish Court were sufficiently related to the matters referred to the Comptroller, and discretion to grant a stay should be exercised because the Irish Court was the *forum conveniens* for resolution of the dispute. However, the issues before the two tribunals were not identical and thus no automatic stay under Article 21 of that Convention was required.

Filing of replacement application under subsection (4) **37.15**

Rule 57 [1982] has been renumbered as rule 56 [1990].

Procedure before the court in entitlement proceedings **37.16**

When the Comptroller declines to deal with entitlement proceedings originally brought before him under any of sections 8(7), 12(2) or 37(8), the referrer now has a choice of bringing the matter before a patents county court, rather than before some other court also having jurisdiction, see para. 72.13 *supra*: CCR Ord. 48A, rule 10(2) (reprinted in para. H48A.10 *infra*) then applies.

SECTION 38—RELEVANT RULES

38.02 Rule 57 [1990]—*Request under section 38(3)*

This rule is merely rule 58 [1982], renumbered.

38.03 Rule 58 [1990]—*Reference to comptroller under section 38(5)*

This rule is rule 59 [1982], renumbered but, in line 5 of paragraph (1) in the Main Work, "fact" should read "facts". In paragraph (2) the words "three months of their receipt" have been changed to "the period of two months beginning on the date when such copies are sent to him".

38.05 PRACTICE UNDER SECTION 38

Rules 58 and 59 [1982] have been renumbered as rules 57 and 58 [1990].

39.01 SECTION 39

Notes. 1. The amendment to section 39 noted in the Main Work came into effect on January 7, 1991 (S.I. 1990 No. 2168).

2. In line 4 of the reprinting of subsection (1) at the bottom of page 302 of the Main Work, "employer" should read "employee".

39.03 ARTICLES

Susan Cox, "Creative employees and the law", (1991) 3(1) IPB 2.

COMMENTARY ON SECTION 39

39.05 *General scope of section 39*

The provisions of sections 39–43 have been summarised, from the point of view of industrial relations, in the paper by Susan Cox listed in para. 39.03 *supra*.

39.06 *Meaning of "invention" in section 39–43*

The reference in the Main Work to *Viziball's Application* should be to [1988] RPC 213.

39.08 *The status of the inventor as employee*

In *Stablocel's Application* (SRIS O/3/91, *noted* IPD 14101) the referrer in entitlement proceedings failed to prove that he had made the invention during a short period when he was unemployed following redundancy from, and liquidation of, his former employer and his re-engagement by the successor thereto.

Ownership of employee inventions by an employer

—The basic rule **39.09**

The paper by T. Z. Gold, listed in para. 37.07 *supra*, reviews decisons given by the Comptroller on entitlement and inventorship disputes.

The Comptroller has been prepared to hold (in an uncontested case) that all rights in an invention belong to the employer when the inventor had apparently been employed on duties relating to the invention (*Travenol Laboratories' Application*, SRIS O/45/90, *noted* IPD 13141). In an interlocutory application in a copyright case, it was held not to be unarguable that "moonlighting" falls within the phrase "in the course of employment" (*Missing Link Software* v. *Magee*, [1989] FSR 361). The test of "economic reality" in relation to the concept of employment, referred to in the Main Work, has been approved by the Privy Council (*Lee Ting Sang* v. *Chung Chi-Keung*, [1990] ICR 409), but that case involved compensation for employee injury where the Plaintiff wished to be considered as an employee, whereas the opposite may be true in a case under section 39.

—The employee's normal duties **39.10**

In *Secretary of State for Defence's Application* (SRIS O/135/89, *noted* IPD 13063) the Comptroller saw no distinction between "official" and "normal" duties; and, where research workers had investigated whether a particular topic should become an approved research product, this was regarded as part of their normal duties.

—Duties specifically assigned to employee **39.11**

In *Secretary of State for Defence's Application* (see para. 39.10 *supra*) specifically assigned duties were stated to be duties which are not the standard or everyday duties on which a person is normally employed.

Decisions under the former law **39.15**

In *Harris's Patent* ([1985] RPC 19), it was suggested that pre-1978 case law was not relevant to cases under section 39(1)(*a*) but was useful, though not binding, in cases under section 39(1)(*b*).

Settlement of disputes by employers **39.17**

It is now considered that the third sentence of the commentary in the Main Work would be more accurate if it read: Failure to treat an employee reasonably may be taken as an indication of a breakdown of the mutual trust and confidence between an employer and an employee: the subsistence of such mutual trust and confidence is an implied term of every contract of employment. That implied term is considered in the case law of this branch of contract law to be a fundamental one, a breach of which may entitle an employee (with a qualifying . . .".

SECTION 40—RELEVANT RULE

40.02 Rule 59 [1990]—*Application under section 40 for compensation*

This is rule 60 [1982], renumbered and amended. In paragraph (3), the words "three months of receiving them" have been changed to "the period of two months beginning on the date when such copies are sent to him"; and the word "relief" has been changed to "award". In paragraph (4), the words "three months of the receipt of the copy of the counter-statement" have been changed to "the period of two months beginning on the date when the copy of the counter-statement is sent to him". Paragraph (5) has been reworded to read:

> "(5) Within the period of two months beginning on the date when the copy of the employee's evidence is sent to him or, if the employee does not file any evidence, within two months of the expiration of the time within which the employee's evidence might have been filed, the employer may file evidence in support of his case and shall send a copy of the evidence to the employee; and within the period of two months beginning on the date when the copy of the employer's evidence is sent to him, the employee may file evidence confined to matters strictly in reply and shall send a copy of that evidence to the employer."

COMMENTARY ON SECTION 40

40.05 *When a compensation award may not be "just"*

Where the nature of an invention is such that it was the expected and reasonable result of the inventor's duties and responsibilities for which he was paid, the benefits should be exceptional for it to be just that the inventor be further compensated (*Memco-Med's Patent,* SRIS O/106/91, *noted* IPD 15003).

40.07 *Time for making application for compensation*

Rule 60 [1982] has become rule 59 [1990].

In *British Steel's Patent* (SRIS O/80/91, *noted* IPD 14163) the application was made only a few months after the patent grant. In those circumstances the case for compensation at that stage would have had to have been "an exceptional one".

40.08 *Forum for seeking an award of compensation*

Proceedings under sections 40(1), (2) or 41(8) arising in England or Wales may now be brought before the patents county court, see para. 96.17 *infra*. The procedure will be that normally prevailing in this court, for which see para. 96.22 and Appendix H *infra*.

Patent belonging to the employer (subs. (1))

—*Meaning of "patent of outstanding benefit"* 40.10

Subsection (1) requires that a successful application can only be made where "the patent *is* of outstanding benefit to the employer". This means that the patent must *now* be of benefit, which is to be measured in money or money's worth (s.43(7)), see para. 43.08 *supra* and *British Steel's Patent* (SRIS O/80/91, *noted* IPD 14163) where the claim was dismissed. Here the words "outstanding benefit" were referred to as connoting a superlative; and the term "employer's undertaking" was taken, somewhat reluctantly by the Comptroller and on the case as pleaded, as the entire business of the proprietor. The invention had found use in only one of the *British Steel* locations and, though this had led to significant economic savings in absolute terms, the savings represented only a very small proportion of the total turnover and profit of the employer: it was held not germane that the employer could have made greater efforts to exploit the invention. It was held sufficient that the benefit should come partly from the patent and it will normally be for the proprietor to demonstrate, if he so wishes, that savings, profits etc. gained from use of the invention have *in no way* resulted from the existence of the patent. Thus (as in the *Elliott Brothers'* case, cited in the Main Work), the onus is on the employer to show that a patent for a product which is in commercial use has not been beneficial, at least to some degree.

However, if the total benefits are not substantial, there is no onus on the patentee to prove that these did not result from the patent (*Memco-Med's Patent,* SRIS O/106/91, *noted* IPD 15003). Here, anyway, the benefits were modest and were held to result more from an established line of business than from the patent, particularly as sales contracts had been made even before the patent application was filed and, though pre-grant sales can be regarded as a benefit, such should be looked at carefully to see that they did result from the patent.

Procedure, hearing, costs and appeals 40.14

Care should be taken that all foreign patents from which benefit is alleged to have resulted are included on PF 26/77 (*British Steel's Patent,* SRIS O/80/91, *noted* IPD 14163): otherwise late amendment may be refused. Likewise applications for discovery should be made in good time (*Memco-Med's Patent,* SRIS O/106/91, *noted* IPD 15003).

From the decision in *British Steel's Patent* (*supra*), it would appear that the several headings of benefit (under s. 41(4)) are a useful check-list of matters to which evidence should be directed. The Comptroller also there indicated that the amount of any compensation should be settled at the substantive hearing, and not left to a subsequent enquiry, with the procedure being similar to that in settling the terms of a licence of right under section 46(3).

In *Trett's Application (supra)*, costs of £700 were awarded against the unsuccessful Applicant.

PRACTICE UNDER SECTION 40

Application to the Comptroller 40.16

Rule 60 [1982] has become rule 59 [1990] and rule 93(5)(*d*) [1982] has become rule 93(4)(*d*) [1990]. Each of the subsequent periods of three months specified for the pleadings and evidence stages in new rule 60(3) and (4) have been reduced to two months, now calculated, where appropriate, from the date of dispatch by, rather than the date of receipt of documents from, the Patent Office or the other party as the case may be, see para. 40.02 *supra*.

It is understood that the *Ibstock* case (SRIS O/64/88), incorrectly cited in the Main Work, was settled before a substantive hearing. For the importance of specific citation of foreign patents, see para. 40.14 *supra*.

40.17 *Application to the court*

While application under sections 40(1), (2) or 41(8) may now be made to the patents county court, it is odd that CCR, Ord. 48A, rule 10 (reprinted in para. H48A.10 *infra*) does not explicitly provide a procedure for this unless the Comptroller has declined to deal with a matter originally brought before him. CCR Ord. 48A, rule 10(2) then stipulates the procedure if a party decides to refer the question or application to the patents county court instead of some other court having jurisdiction.

SECTION 41—RELEVANT RULE

41.02 **Rule 60 [1990]**—*Application under rule 41(8) to vary, etc., awards of compensation*

Rule 60 [1990] is rule 61 [1982], renumbered, except that: in paragraph (1), the words "in duplicate" have been added after "statement"; and, in paragraph (2), "rule 60(3) to (7)" has been changed to "rule 59(3) to (7)", and "sub-rules" has been changed to "paragraphs".

COMMENTARY ON SECTION 41

41.06 *Fair awards (subss. (1), (4) and (5))*

The concept of a "fair" award, having regard to the contributions made by other employees to the development of the invention was discussed, but not decided, in *British Steel's Patent* (SRIS O/80/91, *noted* IPD 14163).

41.10 *Procedure*

In the Main Work at page 325 line 5, the references should be to "rr. 18(2) and (3)" and to "E104.18".

41.11 PRACTICE UNDER SECTION 41

Rules 60 and 61 [1982] have become, respectively, rules 59 and 60 [1990].

COMMENTARY ON SECTION 42

42.03 *Unenforceability of contracts with employees (subs. (2))*

M. G. Harman has suggested ((1989–90) 19 CIPA 267) two reasons for having a generally worded clause in a service contract transferring "all the employee's inventions to his employer, but subject to section 39(1)", noting particularly its utility when employees are transferred to work abroad to whom sections 39–43 may then no longer apply (s.43(2)), but as to which see T. Z. Gold ((1989–90) 19 CIPA 342).

Of course, there can be no "diminuation of rights" if it were held that a standard contract of employment under the Common Law contains an implied term that an employee must disclose *all* his inventions to his employer in order that the employer may know whether to claims rights thereunder as an invention falling within section 39(1)(*a*).

Duty of confidentiality (subs. (3)) **42.04**

Erratum: The citation in the Main Work of the *Faccenda Chicken* case should be to [1986] FSR 291.

SECTION 43 **43.01**

Note. The amendment to section 43 noted in the Main Work came into effect on January 7, 1991 (S.I. 1990 No. 2168).

COMMENTARY ON SECTION 43

Meaning of "benefit" (subs. (7)) **43.08**

In assessing whether a case for compensation has been made out, the "benefit" which has accrued to the employer must be a real, not hypothetical, one: thus, the Comptroller will, in such assessment, neither consider future prospects nor any gain in general trade reputation (*i.e.* goodwill), see para. 40.10 *supra* and *British Steel's Patent* (SRIS O/80/91, *noted* IPD 14163): however, section 41(1) requires future benefits to be considered in the assessment of the quantum of compensation.

COMMENTARY ON SECTION 44

Covenant to use best endeavours **44.09**

Where a patent was assigned with a provision for the assignee to use "all reasonable endeavours" to exploit the invention, and with provision for re-assignment upon premature termination of the contract, a further assignment of the patent by the original assignee was held to be a fundamental breach of the contract resulting in its termination by repudiation and activating the requirement for re-assignment: an enquiry into damages resulting from the breach was ordered, but partly stayed until it was seen whether the plaintiff could recover patent ownership in proceedings against others (*Stephen Collins* v. *Oakside*, SRIS C/47/90).

—Settlement of litigation **44.12**

Bayer and Süllhöfer's Agreement, cited in the Main Work, has been reported ([1990] FSR 300 (ECJ)).

—The Restrictive Trade Practices Act 1976 **44.13**

A useful summary of the effect of this Act upon patent licences, and the precautions to be taken in respect thereof, is the article by Susan Singleton (1990) NLJ 1618 (November 16, 1990)).

44.16 *Contracts for the sale of goods*

In the absence of notice, the sale of a patented article imposes no restriction on its future use or re-sale (*Smith Kline & French* v. *Salim [Malaysia]*, [1989] FSR 407).

COMMENTARY ON SECTION 45

45.03 *Alternatives to use of section 45*

Ottung v. *Klee* (*Case* 320/87, ECJ), cited in the Main Work, has been reported ([1989] ECR 1172; [1991] FSR 657; [1990] 4 CMLR 915).

46.01 **SECTION 46**

Note. In the reproduction of section 46(3)(*c*) at p. 345 line 2, "licence" should read "licensee".

SECTION 46—RELEVANT RULES

46.02 **Rule 61 [1990]**—*Application under section 46(1) for entry in the register*

Rule 61 [1990] is rule 62 [1982], renumbered.

46.03 **Rule 62 [1990]**—*Application under section 46(3) to settle licences of right*

Rule 62 [1990] is rule 63 [1982], renumbered and amended to read:

62.—(1) An application under section 46(3)(a) or (b) (made on or after the date on which these Rules come into force) shall be made on Patents Form 29/77 which shall be filed in duplicate together with—

(a) in the case of an application by the proprietor of the patent, two copies of a draft of the licence he proposes and of a statement of the facts he relies on; and
(b) in the case of an application by any other person, two copies of a draft of the licence he seeks.

(2) The comptroller shall,—

(a) in the case of an application by the proprietor, send a copy of Patents Form 29/77 and a copy of the documents filed under subparagraph (a) of paragraph (1) above to the person to whom the proprietor proposes to grant the licence; and
(b) in the case of an application by any other person, send a copy of Patents Form 29/77 and a copy of the documents filed under subparagraph (b) of that paragraph to the proprietor.

(3) Within the period of two months beginning on the date when the documents are sent to him under paragraph (2) above,—

(a) in the case of an application by the proprietor, the person referred to in paragraph (2)(a) above may file a counter-statement setting out fully the grounds of his objection; and
(b) in the case of an application by any other person, the proprietor may file a statement setting out fully the grounds of his objection;

and, if he does so, at the same time shall send a copy of the statement or counter-statement, as the case may be, to the other party.

(4) Within the period of two months beginning on the date when a statement under paragraph (3)(b) above is sent to him, the person therein referred to may file a counter-statement; and, if he does so, he shall at the same time send a copy of the counter-statement to the proprietor.

(5) No further statement or counter-statement shall be served by either party without the leave or direction of the comptroller.

(6) The comptroller may give such directions as he may think fit with regard to the subsequent procedure.

(7) Notwithstanding its repeal by rule 123(3), rule 63 of the Patents Rules 1982 shall continue to apply to an application made under it before these Rules come into force.

COMMENTARY ON SECTION 46

Application to make "licence of right" entry in the register (subss. (1) and (2)) **46.06**

Rule 62 [1982] has become rule 61 [1990].

—The basic procedure **46.07**

Rule 63 [1982] has become rule 62 [1990].

In *Kaken Pharmaceutical's Patent*, cited in the Main Work and now reported ([1990] RPC 72), the Comptroller strictly decided that the current exclusive licensee had neither demonstrated a right nor a need to be joined as a party to the proceedings under section 46(3). If there was loss by the existing licensee, relief therefor (under Schedule 1, para. 4(4)) could only be granted by the Patents Court. In proceedings under section 46(3) the Comptroller can only adjudicate between patentee and applicant. However, the eventual licence can be granted as a sub-licence from the existing exclusive licensee, see para. 46.14 *infra*. Where the applicant was a foreign unincorporated partnership, namely a German Kommanditgesellschaft, the corporate partners thereof were required to be named as joint licensees because of the possible difficulty of recovering debts from such an entity under English law (*Cabot Safety's Patent*, SRIS O/146/90, *noted* IPD 14082 (*sub nom. E.A.R. Corp.'s Patent*) and SRIS C/55/91, *noted* IPD 14138).

—Comptroller only settles terms in dispute **46.08**

Appeals in the *Smith Kline & French* cases, cited in the Main Work, were dismissed and have been reported (*Smith Kline & French's (Cimetidine) Patents*,

[1990] RPC 203 (CA). The reference for *Pharmon* v. *Hoechst*, cited in the Main Work, should have been to [1985] 3 CMLR 775.

46.09 —*Other limitations on power of Comptroller*

The Comptroller has held that he has no power to vary the terms of a licence which he has previously settled (*Carl Walther's Patent*, SRIS O/50/91, *noted* IPD 14143).

46.10 —*The basic principles for settlement of terms of licence of right*

Appeals in the *Smith Kline & French* cases, cited in the Main Work, were dismissed and have been reported (*Smith Kline & French's (Cimetidine) Patents*, [1990] RPC 203 (CA). In *Cabot Safety's Patent* (SRIS C/55/91, *noted* IPD 14138) it was confirmed by the Patents Court that validity of the patent is not a relevant issue when considering the commercial value of a patent: a prospective licensee acts on the assumption that the patent is valid.

Settling terms of licence of right (subs. (3)(a) and (b))

46.13 —*Multiple applications under the same patent*

A further case where a royalty was settled by the Comptroller at the same rate as decided in a previous application under the same patent is *Allen & Hanburys' Patent [3M Health Care's Application]* (SRIS O/118/89, *noted* IPD 13080).

46.14 —*The basic criterion*

Appeals in the *Smith Kline & French* cases, cited in the Main Work, were dismissed and have been reported (*Smith Kline & French's (Cimetidine) Patents*, [1990] RPC 203 (CA)), specific reference was made to the provisions of sections 48(3)(*a*), 50(1)(*a*), (*b*) and (*c*) as each being of assistance in defining the criteria for assessment of appropriate licence terms.

A licensee should pay a commercial rate of royalty, and not that paid by an existing licensee who had undertaken the cost of development and of securing regulatory approval (*Research Corp.'s (Carboplatin) Patent*, [1990] RPC 663): here the licence was granted in a form of a sub-licence from that licensee so that the royalty paid for the licence of right would be equitably shared between the Patentee and the existing licensee.

Assessment of royalty terms

46.15 —*The different approaches*

The "comparables" approach is the guide which is the most reliable for the settlement of the royalty rate (*Smith Kline & French's (Cimetidine) Patents*, [1990] RPC 203 (CA)), but the section 41 [1949] calculations will normally be of assistance, as one of the matters to be taken into account.

46.16 —*The section 41 [1949] calculations*

In *Smith Kline & French's (Cimetidine) Patents* ([1990] RPC 203 (CA)) the allowance of full promotional costs, and the profit uplift, allowed by the Patents

Court (as discussed in the Main Work) was upheld for that case, but the Court of Appeal stated that each case had to be considered on its individual merits. This approach was followed in *Research Corp.'s (Carboplatin) Patent*, ([1990] RPC 663) where the research contribution of the existing exclusive licensee was taken into account and where the figure calculated under the section 41 [1949] approach (assessed at 43.4 per cent. of the commercial sales price of the patented drug) was adopted as the settled royalty rate, see also para. 46.18 *infra*. However, in *American Cyanamid's Patent* ([1990] RPC 309 and [1991] RPC 409 (CA)) the drug was not of an entirely new type, but it had required exceptional promotional effort by the Patentee. Nevertheless, a (small) reduction was made for brand name promotion. In the appeal on that case it was pointed out that the section 41 [1949] calculations could be no more than a pointer to, rather than an indication of, the appropriate royalty rate because, under section 46, the royalty rate had to be settled so as to provide the patentee with "reasonable remuneration from the invention" whereas, under section 46 [1949], a patentee received a "reasonable advantage from his patent".

—By considering "comparables" **46.17**

The "comparables" approach is the most reliable one, see para. 46.15 *supra*, and the Comptroller regards a 5 *per cent.* level as the "benchmark figure" for a mechanical device, see *Carl Walther's Patent* (SRIS O/22/91, *noted* IPD 14104), *W. R. Grace & Co.'s Patent* (SRIS O/28/91, *noted* IPD 14173) and *Penn's Patent* (SRIS O/33/91). In *American Cyanamid's Patent* ([1990] RPC 309 and [1991] RPC 409 (CA)) this approach was applied in respect of royalties at 27–28 per cent. of the patentees' selling prices likewise settled under section 46(3) for similar drugs, themselves also the subject of voluntary licences though these were supply contracts which justified a slightly lower royalty than would otherwise be agreed for a voluntary licence. The section 41 [1949] calculations gave a wholly different figure of 51.7 per cent. on the same basis. This was because the drug had not been launched in the United States and the Patentee had incurred most of its world-wide promotional expenditure in the United Kingdom, but this factor was held only to justify a small uplift of the "comparables" royalty to the 32 per cent. level, a view explicitly upheld on the appeal.

Kaken Pharmaceutical's Patent has been published ([1990] RPC 72), but was cited in the Main Work in error as the Comptroller only reserved, and did not decide, the point whether an existing exclusive licence should be produced by the Patentee.

In *Cabot Safety's Patent* (SRIS O/146/90, *noted* IPD 14082, *sub nom. E.A.R. Corp.'s Patent*, and SRIS C/55/91, *noted* IPD 14138) the royalty for a hearing aid was settled as equivalent to 18 *per cent.*, by comparison with royalties settled for devices of a medical nature. This rate was upheld on appeal, but a licence granted under a corresponding U.S. patent was held not strictly comparable because it arose in the settlement of litigation and was the subject of a lump sum payment. Also, a willing licensee would be prepared to pay a high rate of royalty if he could obtain a reasonable return on capital, after assuming that the licensee would undercut the Patentee's United Kingdom selling price by 10 *per cent.*

—By considering the profits available **46.18**

The "profit sharing" approach should only be used as a "last resort" (*Smith Kline & French's (Cimetidine) Patents*, cited in the Main Work and now reported [1990] RPC 203 (CA), and *American Cyanamid's Patent*, [1990] RPC 309). Indeed in the *Smith Kline* case, it was suggested that the approach was contrary to section 50(1)(*b*).

However, in *Research Corp.'s (Carboplatin) Patent* ([1990] RPC 663), the applicant was allowed its usual profit return on the basis that it would undercut the current selling price by 5 per cent., but the royalty was settled at the slightly lower rate indicated by the section 41 [1949] calculations, see para. 46.16 *supra*. On appeal in this case, the court stated that the effect of a fixed unit price royalty is to fix a floor beneath which the licensee cannot cut prices. If the settled reasonable royalty requires this floor to be set at a level at which the licensee cannot compete, "that is just too bad for him". Then, if price cutting is so likely, so that the royalty-fixing exercise is to determine where that floor should be, the "profits available" approach ceases to be useful.

46.19 *—Basis on which royalty is to be paid*

In dismissing appeals in *Smith Kline & French's (Cimetidine) Patent* ([1990] RPC 203) the Court of Appeal stated that "the principle that the rate of royalty is set at a fixed price per unit quantity sold across the whole market is one of great importance and should be used except in very exceptional circumstances": accordingly, the same rate should also apply to hospital sales of patented drugs. On a subsequent application on the same patents, the Patentee contended for a higher fixed unit royalty based on an increase in the Patentee's sales price which was alleged to have occurred after the previous rate had been calculated. This argument would have succeeded, but for a variance between the oral and written testimony given by the Patentee's witness concerning the alleged price increase (*Smith Kline & French's Patents [Harris and Becpharm's Applications]*, SRIS O/64/91, *noted* IPD 15002).

In *Research Corp.'s (Carboplatin) Patent* ([1990] RPC 663) the fixing of royalty (on a pharmaceutical product) on a fixed unit price was approved, it being pointed out that its effect is to impose a floor beneath which the licensee cannot cut prices. As the licensee is not required to be allowed a profit, it is irrelevant whether the licensee can afford to compete at the settled royalty level.

Where the patent concerns only one feature of a device, that fact may be taken into account in fixing a royalty based on the total value of the full device (*W. R. Grace & Co.'s Patent*, SRIS O/28/91, *noted* IPD 14173).

46.20 *—Miscellaneous points on royalty terms*

Appeal in *Smith Kline & French's Patents [Generics' and Harris's Applications]*, cited in the Main Work, were later rejected (*Smith Kline & French's (Cimetidine) Patents*, [1990] RPC 203 (CA)). On a further application under the same patents (*Smith Kline & French's Patent [Harris and Becpharm's Applications]*, SRIS O/64/91, *noted* IPD 15002), the Comptroller declined to include a clause for securing the royalty payments, distinguishing the facts from those in *Shiley's Patent*, cited in the Main Work. He also declined to include a policing clause with regard to possible infringement of corresponding foreign patents.

In *Research Corp.'s (Carboplatin) Patent* ([1990] RPC 663), the licence was granted as a sub-licence to an existing licence in order that that licensee could share some of the royalty paid under the licence of right, see para. 46.14 *supra*.

Delay, even culpable delay, in settling the royalty rate is no good ground for reducing the applicable royalty rate (*Cabot Safety's Patent* (SRIS O/146/90, *noted* IPD 14082, *sub nom. E.A.R. Corp.'s Patent*, and SRIS C/55/91, *noted* IPD 14138).

Security for unpaid royalties was also ordered in *Penn's Patent* (SRIS O/44/91, *noted* IPD 14194) but in a form not unduly onerous to the licensee. Here the Comptroller declined to settle the issue of damages for admitted infringement, the Act not entitling an applicant to commence working the patent before the licence of right is granted to him.

—Other terms of settled licences

—Prohibitions on importation **46.21**

The *Smith, Kline and French* decision, cited in the Main Work, was upheld on appeal (*Smith Kline & French's (Cimetidine) Patents*, [1990] RPC 203 (CA)), both as regards the ban on importation (from outside the EEC) of formulated compositions, with no ban on import of raw material, and the further decision to include imports from Spain and Portugal within that ban, though this further ban was seriously doubted as a matter of EEC law. However, both questions were referred to the ECJ, the Patents Court decision standing meanwhile. Subsequently, the Comptroller refused to allow importation from Spain on the same basis (*Research Corp.'s (Carboplatin) Patent*, [1990] RPC 663). In *American Cyanamid's Patent* ([1990] RPC 309) the Patents Court refused to draw a distinction between a drug, not patented *per se*, and a broadly claimed composition containing it because supplying the drug would be an act of indirect infringement under section 60(2): importation from outside the EEC was therefore prohibited of both the raw drug and of compositions containing it. In a further application on the *Smith Kline* patents, the licence provided for liberty to apply to remove the import bar in the licence if the ECJ judgment would justify this (*Smith Kline & French's Patent [Harris and Becpharm's Applications]*, SRIS O/64/91, *noted* IPD 15002).

On appeal in the *Research Corp.* case, in upholding the importation ban from outside the EEC, the court stated that section 48(3)(*b*)(i) requires a United Kingdom demand to be met on reasonable terms and that this meant at the prevailing price, it being irrelevant that an increased demand might result if there were price cutting by a licensed competitor.

—Export prohibitions **46.22**

The export ban imposed in *Smith Kline & French's Patents*, cited in the Main Work, was upheld on appeal (*Smith Kline & French's (Cimetidine) Patents*, [1990] RPC 203 (CA)). In *American Cyanamid's Patent* ([1990] RPC 309) an export prohibition was included in the licence, but only in respect of countries where parallel patents existed.

—Marketing controls on licensee **46.23**

In *Cabot Safety's Patent* (SRIS C/55/91, *noted* IPD 14138) no good reason was seen for the licence to contain a clause requiring the licensee to mark the product by reference to the licence of right, though the Main Work notes that a clause of this type had been approved in an earlier case.

—Sub-contracting, sub-licensing and assignment of the licence **46.25**

A provision for licence termination upon a change in control of the licensee was also imposed in *Barton-King Systems' Patent* (SRIS O/141/90, *noted* IPD 14042), where sub-contracting and sub-licensing were also not permitted. However, where an initial licence of right had excluded sub-licensing, an additional licence was ordered to permit authorised manufacture by named parties for supply to the main licensee (*Smith Kline & French's Patent [Harris and Becpharm's Applications]*, SRIS O/64/91).

46.26 *—Termination of licence by patentee*

In *Smith Kline & French* v. *Harris* (SRIS C/32/91, *noted* IPD 14160; (1991) 3(3) IPBB 7) the licence of right had contained a provision for termination if the licensee became an affiliate of another "operating in the field covered by the licence". Summary judgment that the licence could be terminated for breach of this provision was rejected because, on a literal interpretation of the quoted words, the provision was void as being in restraint of trade; and, on a narrow construction, there was no breach because the acquirer of the licensee did not supply the patented drug. However, if the licence should (after full trial) be held to have terminated, a further licence was later settled to which the acquirer would be a party (*Smith Kline & French's Patent [Harris and Becpharm's Applications]*, SRIS O/64/91).

46.27 *—Other non-royalty licence terms*

In *Allen & Hanburys' Patent [3M Health Care's Application]* (SRIS O/118/89, *noted* IPD 13080) the Patentee was refused a general indemnity against claims for lack of safety of the patented product, and the applicant was refused a *force majeure* clause as to royalty payments.

PRACTICE UNDER SECTION 46

46.29 *Making of entry in the register*

Rule 62 [1982] has become rule 61 [1990].

46.30 *Application for settlement of licence terms*

New rule 62 [1990] (reprinted in para. 46.03, *supra*) has significantly changed the procedure in order to expedite the process of settling the terms of a licence of right. Unless it is the patentee who seeks the settlement, no statement of facts relied on is now required when PF 29/77 is filed, but this form must now be accompanied by two copies of a draft of the licence proposed by the applicant (r. 62(1)). For applications filed after January 7, 1991, the Comptroller is required to send these documents to the proposed licensee or proprietor as the case may be within 21 days of receipt of PF 29/77 (r. 62(2)). That person now has two months from the date of dispatch of these documents within which to file a counter-statement (r. 62(3)). No further statement or counter-statement may then be filed without the leave or direction of the Comptroller (r. 62(4)). Thereafter, the procedure follows such directions as the Comptroller may think fit (r. 62(5)), but these are likely to provide for successive periods for filing evidence by the applicant, respondent and, by way of reply thereto, by the applicant, followed by a hearing, the date for which may be fixed at the time the Comptroller gives directions on the evidence timetable.

It is not customary for any award of costs to be made in proceedings before the Comptroller under section 46(3) (*Penn's Patent*, SRIS O/33/91), but this is not an invariable rule (*Smith Kline & French's Patent [Harris and Becpharm's Applications]*, SRIS O/90/91).

46.31 *—Sufficiency of statement of case under rule 63*

Rule 63 [1982] has become rule 62 [1990].

The citation of *Hoffmann La Roche's Patent* in the Main Work should have had the reference "SRIS O/52/88".

The new form of rule 62 (for which see paras. 46.03 and 46.30 *supra*), has been designed to obviate the many arguments concerning the sufficiency of the statement of facts. Now, no statement of facts is required, other than a draft of the licence in contemplation by the applicant, unless the application is (unusually) made by the proprietor.

Nevertheless, where now applicable, the principles for sufficiency of the statement of case under former rule 63 were summarised in *E.A.R. Corp.'s Patent* (SRIS O/140/89) as: (1) to take the place of negotiations between a willing licensor and willing licensee; (2) to set out the facts (within the applicant's knowledge) which the Comptroller will reasonably need to settle the terms; (3) to identify the facts and alleged facts in dispute; and (4) to set out the material terms of the licence, including terms which the licensor can be expected to request and which the applicant would then wish to have rejected. However, it was recognised that more relevant data are likely to be with the patentee than the applicant.

While an applicant cannot be required to disclose the intended source of the patented product if he genuinely does not know this, he will be required to amplify his statement of case, consistent with the evidence, as to intended source of supply, particularly where the patentee gives evidence that the product is not available in the stated country of supply (*Eli Lilly's Patent*, SRIS O/47/90, *noted* IPD 13142). The source of intended supply also need not be disclosed if this information would not influence the royalty rate, *e.g.* if this falls to be fixed by comparison with other licences (*Sandoz' Patent*, SRIS O/89/89, *noted* IPD 13062).

—Confidential disclosure during proceedings under subsection (3)(a) **46.33**

In *Merrell Dow's Patent* (SRIS C/53/90, *noted* IPD 13192) orders were made for discovery from the Patentee of all agreements entered into with United Kingdom companies for the supply of the patented product, and for similar agreements in other countries where the Patentee enjoyed patent protection (other than compulsory licences granted in certain countries), because these could be of assistance in evaluating a comparable royalty rate built into the supply price, see also paras. 61.28 and 72.44 *infra*. Commercial information provided in confidence during the settlement proceedings remains confidential thereafter (*Allen & Hanburys' Patent [3M Health Care's Application]*, SRIS O/118/89).

SECTION 47—RELEVANT RULES

Rule 63 [1990]—*Application by proprietor under section 47(1) for the cancellation of entry* **47.02**

Rule 63 [1990] is rule 64 [1982], renumbered.

Rule 64 [1990]—*Application under section 47(3)* **47.03**

This rule is rule 65 [1982], renumbered, except that, in paragraph (1), "three months" has been changed to "two months".

47.04 Rule 65 [1990]—*Procedure on receipt of application made under section 47*

This rule is rule 66 [1982], renumbered and amended. In paragraph (1), the words "three months" have been changed to "two months". In paragraph (2), the opening words are now "Such notice". In paragraph (3), the words "three months of the receipt of such copies" have been changed to "the period of two months beginning on the date when such copies are sent to him".

47.05 Rule 66 [1990]—*Procedure after cancellation of entry pursuant to section 47(3)*

Rule 66 [1990] is rule 67 [1982], renumbered.

47.06 Rule 67 [1990]—*Declaration under paragraph 4A of Schedule 1*

Former rule 67A has been renumbered as rule 67. In paragraph (1) thereof, the words "Patents" and "1977" have been deleted.

COMMENTARY ON SECTION 47

47.08 *Application for cancellation (subss. (1)–(5))*

Rule 65 [1982] has become rule 64 [1990]. The period within which an application for cancellation of the "licences of right" entry has been changed to two months from the date of the register entry, see para. 47.03 *supra*: this period remains inextensible (r. 110(2)).

47.09 *Opposition to cancellation (subs. (6))*

Rule 66 [1982] has become rule 65 [1990], and the opposition period has been reduced to *two* months, see para. 47.04, which remains inextensible (r. 110(2)).

Exception from section 46 for existing patents for certain uses of patented products (Sched. 1, para. 4A)

47.10 *—Relevant dates for patents affected by the exception (para. 4A(6)(a))*

Former rule 67A has become rule 67, see para. 47.06 *supra*. It is irrelevant that the patent had not been sealed by January 15, 1989 (*Research Institute's Patent*, SRIS O/98/90, *noted* IPD 13194).

47.12 *—When declaration for exception may not be filed (sub-paras. 4A(5) and (6))*

Despite the statement in the Main Work, there does not appear to be a prohibition against filing PF 58/77 even before commencement of the 15th year of the patent, perhaps as a precaution against forgetting to do so later, though its declaration can have no effect before the beginning of the 16th year of the patent.

PRACTICE UNDER SECTION 47

Application under subsection (1) by proprietor for cancellation of entry under section 46 **47.15**

Rule 64 [1982] has become rule 63 [1990].

Application under subsection (3) by interested party for cancellation of entry under section 46 **47.16**

Rules 62 and 65 [1982] have become, respectively, rules 61 and 64 [1990]. The period for applying for cancellation of the "licences of right" entry has been reduced to two months, see para. 47.03 *supra*, and remains inextensible (r. 110(2)).

Opposition to cancellation of "licences of right" entry **47.17**

The period for lodging opposition has been reduced to two months, see para. 47.66 *supra*, and remains inextensible (r. 110(2)). Any counter-statement must now be filed within two months from receipt of the opposition statement.

Effecting the cancellation of "licences of right" entry **47.18**

Rule 67 [1982] has become rule 66 [1990], see para. 47.04 *supra*.

Filing of declaration under schedule 1, paragraph 4A **47.19**

Former rule 67A has become rule 67, see para. 47.06 *supra*.

SECTION 48—RELEVANT RULES

Rule 68 [1990]—*Application under section 48(1) for compulsory licence* **48.02**

After each of the words "statement" (first occurrence) and "evidence" the words "in duplicate" have been added.

Rule 70 [1990]—*Procedure on receipt of application under section 48 or 51* **48.03**

The rule title has been slightly changed to that given above.

COMMENTARY ON SECTION 48

General **48.05**

CPCaa. 46–48, referred to in the Main Work, have been renumbered as CPCaa. 45–47 [1989], see para. 86–03 *infra*.

Grounds for application (subs. (3)) **48.07**

Monsanto's Patent (No. 2) (SRIS O/91/89), cited in paras. 48.09, 48.12 and 48.13 of the Main Work, has also been noted at IPD 13033.

48.08 *—Effect of EEC law on these grounds*

The doubt expressed in the Main Work that parts of section 48 (and s.50) may be contrary to EEC law in drawing a distinction between working an invention within the United Kingdom and working it elsewhere within the EEC, is reinforced by the action the E.C. Commission has now taken by seeking from the ECJ a declaration that: "By providing for the grant of compulsory licences where a patent is not worked in the United Kingdom to the fullest extent that is reasonably practicable or where demand for the patented product is being met to a substantial extent by importation, the United Kingdom has failed to comply with its obligations under TRa. 30", that is that some of the provisions of section 48 (and presumably also those in s. 50) are contrary to overriding European law (*E.C. Commission* v. *United Kingdom (ECJ Case 30/90), noted* OJEC 1.3.90, C 50/13; [1990] EIPR D-141). Similar action has been taken against some other EEC countries. Meanwhile the distinction has continued to be applied (*Kaken Pharmaceutical's Patent*, [1990] RPC 72 and *Smith Kline & French's (Cimetidine) Patents*, [1990] RPC 203 (CA)), though in the latter case the question of a refusal to grant a licence of right for importation from elsewhere in the EEC was referred to the ECJ for an opinion under EEC law, the validity of the refusal itself being doubted by the Court of Appeal but nevertheless the decision below was continued pending the ECJ determination, see para. 46.21 *supra*. In *Gebhardt's Patent* (SRIS O/84/90, *noted* IPD 13166 and SRIS C/37/91, *noted* IPD 14115) the Comptroller would (had he not ordered a licence under s. 48(3)(*a*)) have referred the legality of section 48(3)(*b*)(ii) to the ECJ, rather than overturning the *Extrude Hone* decision ([1982] RPC 361, cited in the Main Work) or anticipating the result of the ECJ reference in the *Smith, Kline* case, *supra*, but there was no evidence that the patent did impede imports.

48.09 *—Insufficient domestic wording (subs. (3)(a))*

Monsanto's Patent (No. 2), cited in the Main Work, has been reported as *Monsanto's CCP Patent* ([1990] FSR 93), see para. 48.14 *infra*. A compulsory licence was granted under this provision in *Gebhardt's Patent* (SRIS O/84/90, *noted* IPD 13166 and SRIS C/37/91, *noted* IPD 14115) because a United Kingdom licensee had ceased trading and no other licence had been granted: working in Germany was not considered under subsection (3)(*a*), see also para. 48.08 *supra*.

48.10 *—Failure to meet demand for patented product (subs. (3)(b))*

The "demand on reasonable terms" is that which exists under the prevailing conditions, so that it is irrelevant that price cutting by a licensee might increase the existing demand (*Research Corp.'s (Carboplatin) Patent*, [1990] RPC 663).

48.12 *—Refusal to grant licence on reasonable terms (subs. (3)(d))*

Monsanto's Patent (No. 2), cited in the Main Work, has been reported as *Monsanto's CCP Patent* ([1990] FSR 93), see para. 48.14 *infra*.

48.13 *—Prejudice due to imposed licence conditions (subs. (3)(e))*

Monsanto's Patent (No. 2), cited in the Main Work, has been reported as *Monsanto's CCP Patent* ([1990] FSR 93), see para. 48.14 *infra*.

Cases decided under the 1977 Act **48.14**

CPCaa. 47 and 82, referred to in the Main Work, have been renumbered as CPCaa. 46 and 77 [1989], see para. 86.03 *infra*.

Monsanto's CCP Patent ([1990] FSR 93) is cited in the Main Work, see paras. 48.09, 48.12 and 48.13 *supra*. Here the application failed because the applicant failed to discharge the onus upon him, partly because the licence was required to allow the applicant's customers to work the invention and there was insufficient evidence that this would be done, there being no evidence from the prospective customer on whose behalf a licence was also sought under section 49, see para. 49.02 *infra*.

The references to "patented invention" and "patented product" in subsection (3) have been taken to mean that the alleged insufficient working, demand or use thereof should be considered in relation to a product as described in the patent, and not in relation to some product which happens to embody, among other features, the claimed invention (*Quantel's Patents (Compulsory Licence Application)*, SRIS O/126/90, *noted* IPD 14010). That case also decided that a mere refusal to grant a licence under the patent is not, in itself, an act of unfair prejudice under subsection (3)(*e*).

When ground for licence is established (Subss. (4)–(7)) **48.15**

In *Gebhardt's Patent* (SRIS O/84/90, *noted* IPD 13166 and SRIS C/37/91, *noted* IPD 14115) the Patentee was not allowed time for re-establishment of United Kingdom working following the demise of the first licensee, it being held that subsection (5) is primarily concerned with allowing time from grant to establish working and here 11 years had passed.

Practice under Section 48

General procedure **48.19**

Richco Plastic's Patent (SRIS O/22/89), cited in the Main Work, has been reported ([1989] RPC 722). In *Quantel's Patents (Compulsory Licence Application)* (SRIS O/126/90, *noted* IPD 14010) the applicant's statement of case was also struck out because this failed to indicate clear and specific evidence which could cause the applicant to be granted the compulsory licence which it sought.

The statement of facts and the accompanying supporting evidence must now be filed in duplicate, see para. 48.02 *supra*.

Commentary on Section 49

General **49.02**

Monsanto's Patent (No. 2), cited in the Main Work, has been reported as *Monsanto's CCP Patent* ([1990] FSR 93), see para. 48.14 *supra*.

Commentary on Section 50

Grant of compulsory licences (subs. (1)) **50.03**

The terms of subsection (1) have been found helpful in settling royalty terms for a licence of right under section 46(3), see para. 46.14 *supra*.

50.04 *Principles for grant of compulsory licences (subs. (2))*

Monsanto's Patent (No. 2), cited in the Main Work with cross-reference (which should have been to para. 49.02), has been reported as *Monsanto's CCP Patent* ([1990] FSR 93), see para. 48.14 *supra*.

SECTION 52—RELEVANT RULE

52.01 **Rule 71 [1990]**—*Opposition under section 52(1)*

In paragraph (1), the words "three months" have been changed to "two months". In paragraph (3), the words "three months of the receipt of such copies" have been changed to "the period of two months beginning on the date when such copies are sent to him".

PRACTICE UNDER SECTION 52

52.07 *Procedure on opposition*

The period for opposition is now only *two* months from the date of the advertisement in the O.J. (r. 71(1), reprinted in para. 52.01 *supra*): this period remains inextensible (r. 110(2)). If the opposition is contested, evidence in reply is now due within *two* months from the date of dispatch of the duplicate copy of the evidence which the proprietor has filed with his opposition statement (r. 71(3)).

COMMENTARY ON SECTION 53

53.03 *Compulsory licences under the CPC (subs. (1))*

CPCaa. 46–48, referred to in the Main Work, have been renumbered as CPCaa. 45–47 [1989], see para. 86.03 *infra*.

54.02

COMMENTARY ON SECTION 54

CPCa. 47, referred to in the Main Work, has been renumbered as CPCa. 46 [1989], see para. 86.03 *infra*.

COMMENTARY ON SECTION 55

55.02 *General*

CPCa. 46, referred to in the Main Work, has been renumbered as CPCa. 45 [1989], see para. 86.03 *infra*.

The term "The Crown" now includes "The Crown in the right of the Government of the Isle of Man" and references to a Government department now include references to a Department of the Government of the Isle of Man, and in relation to such a Department as if references to the Treasury were references to the Treasury of the Isle of Man (Patents Act 1977 (Isle of Man) (Variation) Order 1990, S.I. 1990 No. 2295), see para. 132.05 *infra*.

Principles of Crown use **55.03**

Health authorities apparently exercise functions of the Secretary of State, as devolved through the provisions of the legislation establishing the National Health Service, and any use of an invention thereby is accordingly Crown use (*Dory* v. *Sheffield Health Authority*, [1991] FSR 221).

Retrospective authorisation (subs. (6)) **55.13**

Jacques Dory v. *Stratford Health Authority*, incorrectly named in the Main Work, has been reported as *Dory* v. *Sheffield Health Authority* ([1991] FSR 221).

SECTION 60 **60.01**

Note. The amendment to subsection (6) noted in the Main Work came into effect on January 7, 1991 (S.I. 1990 No. 2168).

COMMENTARY ON SECTION 60

Historical background **60.04**

CPCaa. 29–32, referred to in the Main Work, have been renumbered as CPCaa. 25–28 [1989], see para. 86.03 *infra*.

Application of section 60 **60.05**

The former Common Law test of infringement may still apply when considering infringement of a United Kingdom patent registered in a (former) colony, see *Blackburn* v. *Boon Engineering [Brunei]* ([1991] FSR 391).

Territorial scope of infringement **60.06**

Mars v. *Azkoyen*, cited in the Main Work, is also *noted* [1989] EIPR D–219. In *Intel Corp.* v. *General Instrument (No. 2)* ([1991] RPC 235) the foreign parent company had given the address of its subsidiary as its United Kingdom sales office and the subsidiary distributed the sales literature of the foreign parent company: this was held sufficient to establish the required "good arguable case" of joint tortfeasorship. In *Molnlycke and Peaudouce* v. *Procter & Gamble* (SRIS C/67/91, *noted* IPD 14191 and C/82/91, *noted* IPD 15004 (CA)) a high degree of co-ordination between German and British subsidiaries of a United States company as to what was marketed in the United Kingdom, the products for this being manufactured by the German company, was sufficient to found the required "good arguable case" of joint tortfeasorship to avoid a striking out of the plea even though the British company had the ultimate decision of the products to be marketed in the United Kingdom. In *Lubrizol* v. *Esso* (SRIS C/88/91) joinder of a foreign parent company was permitted on a showing that it appeared to place its worldwide business in the hands of local subsidiaries with research being done in one country for the benefit of others, this indicating a sufficient "common design", it being stated that a plaintiff should be allowed to sue whom he wished provided the reason therefor is not merely vexatious and harassing.

Authorised use of invention **60.07**

If there is to be any restriction on future use or re-sale of a patented article, notice thereof must be given at the time of its sale (*Smith Kline & French* v. *Salim [Malaysia]*, [1989] FSR 407).

60.09 *Laches, acquiescence and estoppel*

Mars v. *Azkoyen*, cited in the Main Work, is also noted [1989] EIPR D–219.

Substantive (or direct) infringement (subs. (1))

60.11 *—Scope of subsection (1)*

CPCa. 29, referred to in the Main Work, has been renumbered as CPCa. 25 [1989], see para. 86.03 *infra*.

60.12 *—Infringement of product invention (subs. (1)(a))*

CPCa. 29, referred to in the Main Work, has been renumbered as CPCa. 25 [1989], see para. 86.03 *infra*.

While applying for permission to sell a patented product is not itself an act of infringement (*Upjohn* v. *Thomas Kerfoot*, [1988] FSR 1), the supply thereof to a Government department to obtain permission under regulatory control to sell that product is likely to be an infringing act (*Smith Kline & French* v. *Douglas Pharmaceuticals [New Zealand]*, [1991] FSR 522).

For forced disclosure of documents identifying a foreign supplier of infringing goods, see also *Société Romanaise* v. *British Shoe Corp.* ([1991] FSR 1).

60.13 *—Infringement of process invention (subs. (1)(b))*

CPCa. 29, referred to in the Main Work, has been renumbered as CPCa. 25 [1989], see para. 86.03 *infra*.

In Germany, a claim to the use of a material in a specified way has been held infringed by importation of the article in which the material had been used in the claimed way (*"Covering sheeting with slits" [Germany], noted* (1991) 22 IIC 395); that seems to arise from the "use" claim being regarded as directed to a process and the imported article being the direct product thereof.

Contributory (or indirect) infringement under subsection (2)

60.14 *—Historical derivation*

CPCa. 30, referred to in the Main Work, has been renumbered as CPCa. 26 [1989], see para. 86.03 *infra*.

60.15 *—Scope of subsection (2)*

CPCa. 30, referred to in the Main Work, has been renumbered as CPCa. 26 [1989], see para. 86.03 *infra*.

A finding of infringement under subsection (2) was made in *Helitune* v. *Stewart Hughes* ([1991] FSR 171) where the Defendant was held to have had the requisite knowledge of the use to which his customer would put the product sold to him.

—Involving supply of a staple product (subs. (3)) **60.16**

CPCa. 30, referred to in the Main Work, has been re-numbered as CPCa. 26 [1989], see para. 86.03 *infra.*

Exhaustion of rights (subs. (4)) **60.17**

CPCaa. 81 and 32, referred to in the Main Work, have been renumbered as CPCaa. 76 and 28 [1989], see para. 86.03 *infra.*

Acts exempted from infringement (subs. (5)) **60.18**

CPCa. 31, referred to in the Main Work, has been renumbered as CPCa. 27 [1989], see para. 86.03 *infra.*

—Acts done for experimental purposes (subs. (5)(b)) **60.20**

CPCa. 31, referred to in the Main Work, has been renumbered as CPCa. 27 [1989], see para. 86.03 *infra.* The carrying out of field trials by a Governmental body at the behest of a third party has been held, in Germany, to be an infringing act (*"Ethofumesat" [Germany], noted* OJEPO 3/1991, 196).

—Acts done on transiently visiting ships, aircraft, etc. (subs. (5)(d)–(f)) **60.22**

CPCa. 31, referred to in the Main Work, has been renumbered as CPCa. 27 [1989], see para. 86.03 *infra.*

Section 60(5)(*d*) gives effect to Art. 5*ter* of the Paris Convention as inserted therein by The Hague revision conference of 1925. However, its true origin is section 26 of the Patent Law Amendment Act, 1852 (15 & 16 Vict., c. 83) which was enacted to amend the decision in *Caldwell* v. *Vanvlissengen* ((1851) 9 Hare 415; 68 E.R. 571), as explained in *Brown* v. *Duchesne* [US] ((1856) 60 U.S. (19 How.) 183). This Art. 5*ter* also provides exceptions to infringement for aerial and terrestrial vehicles, but in somewhat different terms and, hence, these exceptions are the subject of section 60(5)(*e*), but these overlap with the exceptions of section 60(5)(*f*) which arise from the Chicago, rather than the Paris, Convention as explained in the Main Work.

A German court has held that, where the defendant loses control of a vehicle within the jurisdiction, that vehicle has not entered the country temporarily (*"Carrying carts for plants" ("Pflanzen-Transportwagen") [Germany], noted* (1990) 21 IIC 99).

Related acts giving rise to joint tortfeasorship **60.25**

The citation of *Gillette* v. *Unilever* in the Main Work should be to *Unilever* v. *Gillette.*

A case of joint tortfeasorship can be pleaded provided that the necessary "good arguable cause of action" can be demonstrated; and such pleading can stand even if the sole purpose of joining the other defendant is to obtain discovery from him (*Molnlycke and Peaudouce* v. *Procter & Gamble*, SRIS C/67/91, *noted* IPD 14191 and C/82/91, *noted* IPD 15004 (CA)). Otherwise, for the liability of foreign defendants for acts of possible joint tortfeasorship, see para. 60.06 in the Main Work and *supra.*

60.26 *Liability of directors*

It is sufficient to join, as a further defendant to patent infringement proceedings, a director of another defendant if the pleadings show that he *could* have acted in a common design with another defendant (*PLG Research* v. *Ardon*, SRIS C/57/91, *noted* IPD 14159). Where a director has authorised, and been personally involved in his company's infringement, he is also personally liable to pay infringement damages (*Martin Engineering* v. *Nicaro [Australia]*, (1991) 20 IPR 241).

61.02 **Rule 72 [1990]**—*Procedure on reference to comptroller under section 61(3)*

In paragraph (4), the words "three months after receipt thereof" have been changed to "the period of two months beginning on the date when such copy is sent to him". In paragraph (5), the words "three months after receipt of the counter-statement" have been changed to "the period of two months beginning on the date when the counter-statement is sent to him". In paragraph (6), the words "three months after receipt of the counter-statement" have been changed to "the period of two months beginning on the date when the counter-statement is sent to him"; and the subsequent words "three months" have been changed to "the period of two months". In paragraph (7), the words "three months of the receipt of the copy of the plaintiff's evidence" have been changed to "the period of two months beginning on the date when the copy of the plaintiff's evidence is sent to him"; the next subsequent words "three months" have been changed to "two months"; and the words "three months of the receipt of the copy of the defendant's evidence" have been changed to "the period of two months beginning on the date when the defendant's evidence is sent to him".

61.03 **Rule 73 [1990]**—*Procedure where validity of patent in dispute*

In paragraph (3), the words "three months after the receipt thereof" have been changed to "the period of two months beginning on the date when the copy is sent to him". In paragraph (4), the words "three months of the receipt of the plaintiff's counter-statement" have been changed to "the period of two months beginning on the date when the copy of the plaintiff's counter-statement is sent to him". In paragraph (5), the words "three months of the receipt of the copy of the defendant's evidence" have been changed to "the period of two months beginning on the date when the copy of the defendant's evidence is sent to him"; the next subsequent words "three months" have been changed to "two months"; and the words "three months of the receipt of the copy of the plaintiff's evidence" have been changed to "the period of two months beginning on the date when the copy of the plaintiff's evidence is sent to him".

61.04 SECTION 61—BOOKS

S. Gee, "Mareva Injunctions and Anton Piller Relief" (Longman, 2nd ed., 1990).

SECTION 61—ARTICLES **61.05**

D. Alexander, "Controls tighten on *Anton Piller* orders", L.S.Gaz. 6.12.89, p. 20.

COMMENTARY ON SECTION 61

General **61.06**

CPCaa. 36, 74 and 79, referred to in the Main Work, have been replaced by CPCaa. 34, 71 and 74 [1989]; and, as indicated in the Main Work, original CPCa. 76 has been amended, see now CPCa. 72 [1989]. The provisions of the Civil Jurisdiction and Judgments Act 1982 (c. 27) have now been prospectively extended to Portugal and Spain (Civil Jurisdiction and Judgments Act 1982 (Amendment) Order 1991, S.I. 1990 No. 2591) and also to Contracting States to the Lugano Convention (*i.e.* members of the EFTA group of countries) (Civil Jurisdiction and Judgments Act 1991, c. 12).

The forum for infringement proceedings **61.07**

The general rule has been that no court in the United Kingdom has any jurisdiction to entertain proceedings concerning a non-United Kingdom patent. Although this rule was altered, or at least intended to be altered, by section 30 of the Civil Jurisdiction and Judgments Act 1982 (c. 27), as regards tortious acts committed within a Contracting State to the Brussels Convention on Jurisdiction and Enforcement of Judgments, courts have maintained the previous rule that infringement of foreign intellectual property is not a matter justiciable in a United Kingdom court, see: the copyright case of *Tyburn Productions* v. *Conan Doyle* ([1990] RPC 185, citing *Potter* v. *Broken Hill [Australia]* ([1906] 3 CLR 479), and the case comment thereon by R. Arnold ([1990] EIPR 254); *L.A. Gear Inc.* v. *Gerald Whelan & Sons* ([1991] FSR 670), where it was opined that an Irish court (if following English law) ought to decline to entertain proceedings for infringement of a United Kingdom trade mark; and the Scots case of *James Burrough Distillers* v. *Speymalt Whisky Distributors* ([1991] RPC 128), where a Scots court held it had no power to adjudicate on infringement of an Italian trade mark. However, these decisions appear to be contrary at least to the spirit of that Convention; and under this it should be appreciated that foreign courts may well hold themselves to have jurisdiction to decide questions of infringement (but not validity) of United Kingdom patents, see paras. 61.25 and 96.24 in the Main Work.

Relief by injunction (subs. (1)(a))

—Interlocutory injunctions **61.11**

The "balance of convenience" scarcely has to be considered if the defendant is not seen to have an arguable defence, see *Quantel* v. *Electronic Graphics* ([1990] RPC 272) where the patent bore a certificate of validity granted in *Quantel* v. *Spaceward Microsystems* ([1990] RPC 83). However, where another Defendant was prepared to challenge the same patent, it was held that it had an arguable case and, upon the Defendant giving a bank guarantee of £2 million, an interlocutory injunction was refused as causing the least degree of injustice where the Defendant's damages, though not the Plaintiff's, would not be readily quantifiable (*Quantel* v. *Shima Seiki*, [1990] RPC 436).

An interlocutory injunction was refused in *Hilbar Plastics* v. *Panda Plastics* (SRIS C/18/90, *noted* IPD 13187; [1990] EIPR D–75) because damages were an adequate remedy for the Plaintiff, though not for the Defendant, and the Defendant could afford to pay these.

Helitune v. *Stewart Hughes*, cited in the Main Work, is *noted* IPD 13015; and *Mars* v. *Azkoyen*, also cited in the Main Work, has also been *noted* [1989] EIPR D–219.

If there is an unresolved application to amend the patent, the patentee cannot obtain an interlocutory injunction as the status of the patent is then *in limbo*; and, probably, likewise if an interlocutory injunction has been granted and an amendment application is then made, the injunction will be discharged (*Mölnlycke* v. *Proctor & Gamble (No. 2)*, [1990] RPC 487).

Because interlocutory relief is an equitable remedy, undue delay in seeking this urgent form of relief will defeat the application. However, delay is not undue when the plaintiff is under some restraint from commencing proceedings, as for example in *Quantel* v. *Electronic Graphics* (*supra*) where the patentee had had to give an undertaking to the court in other proceedings that further proceedings would not be commenced until its application to amend the patent had been considered. Even if delay does not itself defeat the injunction, this may be a factor in the "balance of justice" with the *status quo* being determined at the date of the motion for interlocutory injunction (*PLG Research* v. *Ardon*, SRIS C/17/91, *noted* IPD 14100).

The injunctive relief obtainable by *Anton Piller* and *Mareva* injunctions is fully discussed in the book by S. Gee listed in para. 61.04 *supra*, see also (1991) 3(6) IPBB 2 where the principles are also discussed for obtaining in urgent cases a short term injunction on an *ex parte* basis.

61.12 *—Injunction after trial*

In *Quantel* v. *Spaceward Microsystems (No. 2)* ([1990] RPC 147) an injunction was stayed pending appeal, but only upon guarantees being given as to costs and damages and with payment of 20 per cent. of sales receipts into a blocked bank account; and, likewise, in *Mentor* v. *Hollister* (SRIS C/65/91) where the Defendant also had to undertake to seek an expedited hearing of its appeal and to procure that a new company recently formed to take over the infringing activities should be liable for damages if the appeal failed and should give discovery on the inquiry into damages.

61.14 *Relief by damages (subs. (1)(c))*

For a discussion of the circumstances in which damages for infringement (of trade mark rights) may come to be calculated on the alternative basis of a notional royalty on lost sales, and the determination of the extent of such sales, see *Dormeuil Frères* v. *Feraglow* ([1990] RPC 449). Guidance on the assessment of damages on a royalty basis can also be obtained by considering the settlement of royalty terms for a "licence of right", for which see paras. 46.25–46.20 in the Main Work and *supra*. Indeed, if damages are to be assessed on a royalty basis, it is difficult to see that there can be a difference between the licence of right settlement and the damages calculation, particularly when attention is paid to the "comparables" approach discussed in para. 46.17.

61.15 *Relief by account of profits (subs. (1)(d))*

In *Dart Industries* v. *Decor Corp. [Australia]* ((1991) 20 IPR 144) it was held that only the expenses solely referable to the obtaining or importation, sale and delivery of the goods could be allowed against the profits made, and that the onus of proving these lay on the Defendant. General overhead costs were then disallowed and no deduction was allowed because only a part of the infringing article formed the subject matter of the patent. The computation of an account of profits has been discussed by Coleen L. Kirby for Canada ([1991] EIPR 367) and for infringement of copyright by L. Bently ([1991] EIPR 5).

Eurodefences **61.17**

Ransburg-Gema v. *Electrostatic Plant Systems*, cited in the Main Work, has been further reported ([1990] FSR 287). Attempts to avoid an interlocutory injunction by raising various Eurodefences also failed in *Quantel* v. *Electronic Graphics* ([1990] RPC 272), it being held that these did not provide an arguable defence.

"There is a strong public interest in allowing anyone to assert what he considers to be his legal rights, provided only that he does so in good faith" (*Pitney Bowes* v. *Francotyp-Postalia*, [1990] FSR 72): therefore, it is not *per se* an abuse of a dominant position (contrary to TRa. 86) for a patentee to enforce his rights, or to threaten to do so—even if such enforcement might strengthen a dominant position and might even make it a monopoly, or to refuse to grant a licence on reasonable terms. However, an intellectual property right must not be used in an abusive manner and, if it is, the primacy of TRa. 86 may over-ride the intellectual property right as it did in the copyright case of *BBC* v. *E.C. Commission (Case T–70/89*, ECFI) ([1991] 4 CMLR 669), see also paras. C17 and C18 *supra*.

Costs **61.18**

Where a party is only partially successful, the court often allows it only a proportion of its taxed costs, thereby avoiding taxing the costs of each side. However, there is no universal rule and, in *Southco* v. *Dzus* ([1990] RPC 581) where the findings were of non-infringement with the validity challenge failing, the Defendant was awarded its costs of the action and the Plaintiff its costs on the dismissed counterclaim.

When a *See* v. *Scott-Paine* Order is sought the court should consider the merits in each case and decide as a matter of discretion whether such order should be made and, if so, from what date it should take effect (*Behr-Thomson* v. *Western Thomson*, [1990] RPC 569): here the order was made to apply from the date of an amended defence, rather than from that of the original defence. In *Helitune* v. *Stewart Hughes (Amendment of Pleadings)* ([1991] RPC 73) the amendment was sought during the trial and allowed but with the *Earth Closet* Order to take effect from an earlier date at which it was held the Defendant had enough information to seek the amendment. The Defendant was then allowed to withdraw its request as otherwise the Plaintiff could have withdrawn its pleas leaving the Defendant to bear the costs of the trial. In *CQR Sewing Systems' Patent* (SRIS C/23/91, *noted* IPD 14118) the date was likewise fixed at that when it was reasonable first for the new validity objection to be pleaded. In this case, this was not necessary until the Patentee had sought to amend its patent.

Where an application for an interlocutory injunction fails or is withdrawn, the defendant may be able to obtain an order for immediate taxation and payment of his costs in relation thereto (*Kickers International* v. *Paul Kettle*, [1990] FSR 436), but each case depends upon its own facts, see the later case of *Burton Mechanical Contractors* v. *Cowells* (SRIS C/40/90, *noted* IPD 13132) where the more conventional order of "Defendant's costs in the cause" was made.

The court has discretion to disallow costs. In *Improver Corp.* v. *Remington* (SRIS C/1/89, *noted* IPD 11048) there were disallowed all costs of accountants' reports providing evidence on the appropriate security to be given in respect of a cross-undertaking in return for an interlocutory injunction; and, in *Pall Corp.* v. *Commercial Hydraulics* ([1990] FSR 329 at 358), costs of experiments were disallowed as these had been of no value to the court.

The position of costs in proceedings before the Patents County Court is likely to be similar to that in the High Court because a County Court has (since July 1, 1991) had the discretionary power to award costs on the same basis as the High Court, and it appears that the normal practice of this Court is to award costs on that scale. However, in a registered design action, this was not done because it was a "relatively simple action between small enterprises" (*Parmenter* v. *Malt House Joinery,* SRIS C/103/91).

While a court may order costs to be paid on an "indemnity basis", it will only do so if satisfied that a party has conducted itself unreasonably in the litigation, see *Strix* v. *Otter Controls* ([1991] FSR 163) where indemnity costs were refused although the action had been struck out as disclosing no arguable case.

61.20 *Infringement proceedings in a Patents County Court*

These are governed by new Order 48A of the County Court Rules, reprinted in Appendix H *infra* and discussed particularly in para. 96.22 *infra.* This Order provides for a more written procedure than has been usual in proceedings before the Patents Court with provisions for interrogatories, notices to admit facts, notices of experiments and discovery more under the control of the patents judge of this new court and with a full pre-trial review ("preliminary consideration") envisaged in place of the "summons for directions" under High Court procedure, see paras. 61.22, 61.28, and 61.34 – 61.36 *infra.*

In the Patents County Court more stringent time limits are in force with time extensions not generally being available by consent (as is the position in the High Court), see CCR Ord. 48A, r. 4(9) (reprinted in para. H48A.04 *infra*). In *Herman Miller Inc.* v. *Calsana* (SRIS C/97/91) the Patents County Court stressed that any application for a time extension under this rule should be in writing, fully reasoned and with the background to the request completely stated.

PRACTICE UNDER SECTION 61

61.21 *General*

All pre-trial matters in proceedings before the Patents Court (other than application for orders by consent or for extensions of time) are now required to be brought before a judge of the Patents Court, a Master of the Chancery Division no longer having power to make orders in such matters (*Practice Direction No. 4 of 1989*, L.S.Gaz. January 17, 1990). For service of pleadings etc. in court proceedings, see RSC Ord. 65, rule 5 reprinted in para. E065.5 in the Main Work with amendments thereto noted *infra*.

In infringement proceedings before the Comptroller the time periods specified in rules 72 and 73 (reprinted at paras. 61.02 and 61.03 *supra*) have each been reduced to two months, these periods now being calculated from the date on which the initiatory document for the subsequent stage is dispatched by the Comptroller. For discretion for the Comptroller to stay proceedings before him where validity of a European patent (United Kingdom) is put in issue under rule 73 and where opposition proceedings have been commenced against that patent in the EPO, see para. 27.15 *supra.*

61.22 *Pleadings*

The Patents Court has refused requests for particularisation of the construction of claim (*Lux Traffic* v. *Staffordshire Public Works*, [1991] RPC 73 and *Mars* v.

Azkoyen, SRIS C/34/91, *noted* IPD 14121), this being regarded as placing an unnecessary burden upon a plaintiff.

Intel v. *General Instrument*, cited in the Main Work, has been reported ([1989] FSR 640).

A plea of ambiguity and lack of unfair basis (of an existing patent) need not be particularised if the patentee has not himself pleaded the construction he places on the claims of his patent (*Raychem* v. *Thermon [Pleadings]*, [1989] RPC 578).

In the patents county courts the pleadings take the form of a detailed statement of case which must set out "all facts, matters and arguments relied on" to establish the case, including detailed allegations of infringement of each claim of the patent-in-suit and an example of each type of infringement alleged, see paras. 96.22 and H48A.04 *infra*. Any defence must be similarly detailed and, where validity of a patent is put in issue, the statement of case must explain the relevance of every citation to each claim. It is not clear whether the plaintiff will be required to commit himself to a particular construction of claim before seeing the evidence against him. Attempts to achieve this before the Patents Court have failed, see *supra*.

Striking out of pleadings **61.23**

An action will not be struck out unless the court is satisfied that it is so "plainly and obviously hopeless that the plaintiff should be denied trial at all" (*Mead Corp.* v. *McLaren Packaging*, SRIS C/51/90, *noted* IPD 14021), see also para. 125.12 *infra*, but to avoid a striking out a plaintiff must put before the court some acceptable evidence that he can succeed at trial, for example by addressing the *Catnic* questions (considered in para. 125.16 in the Main Work and *infra*), see *Anchor Building* v. *Redland Roof* ([1990] RPC 283). Nevertheless, it is inappropriate for the court to conduct a mini-trial on the documents (*Strix* v. *Otter Controls*, [1991] FSR 354 (CA), where the decision in the *Anchor* case was distinguished), see also *Lubrizol* v. *Esso* (SRIS C/88/91). Thus, to obtain a striking out, it seems necessary that the case should be one readily understandable and with little scope for argument as regards the *Catnic* questions, and it seems that any evidence from the patentee that he has an arguable case of infringement will probably defeat a striking out application.

Where the Patents Court held that a case of infringement should go to trial, but that there was no defence to the counterclaim for invalidity as regards some of the patent claims, the Court granted a declaration that these claims were invalid and ordered that a copy of the Order be served upon the Comptroller, though an Order that the Patentee should seek amendment of the patent was refused (*Autopia Terakat* v. *Gwent Auto Fabrications*, [1991] FSR 517).

Richco Plastic's Patent, cited in the Main Work, has been reported ([1989] RPC 722).

An application to strike out for delay in prosecuting the action will fail if the other party is seen to have consented, even by implication, to that non-prosecution, see *Fichera* v. *British Steel* (SRIS C/80/90, *noted* IPD 14096) where 25 years had passed since the date of the patent under challenge.

Hearing of a preliminary point **61.24**

The hearing of a preliminary point has possibly been made easier by a new Ord. 14A of the RSC, as reprinted at para. E014A.1 *infra*.

Application to stay proceedings **61.25**

Pall Corp. v. *Commercial Hydraulics* (cited in the Main Work) has now been fully reported ([1989] RPC 703).

For the prospective extension of the Civil Jurisdiction and Judgments Act 1982 (c.27) to other countries, see para. 61.06 *supra.*

In *Hoechst Celanese* v. *Phillips Petroleum* (SRIS C/93/89, *noted* IPD 13095) infringement proceedings had been commenced after the filing of a petition for revocation, which had itself led to amendment proceedings. The court refused to stay the revocation/amendment proceedings until the trial of the infringement action. The Petitioners were entitled to maintain their procedural advantage, particularly as trial in the parallel United States litigation was scheduled to take place after the date fixed for the revocation trial and because they were apparently foregoing a "squeeze" argument based on the appropriate claim construction.

61.26 *Transfer of proceedings*

Where parties are in agreement that a case should be transferred to the Patents County Court, the Patents Court appears to make the necessary Order automatically on a "consent basis". In contested cases for transfer, the Patents Court has refused a transfer order where the petitioner for revocation was not prepared to undertake not to use counsel before that court (*GEC-Marconi* v. *Xyllyx Viewdata*, [1991] FSR 319). However, where the Defendant stated its intention of using its patent agent (already engaged in parallel proceedings before the EPO) to conduct the proceedings before the Patents County Court, it was held that there was a slight balance in favour of ordering transfer (*Memminger* v. *Trip-Lite*, [1991] FSR 3322), but the Patents Court indicated its hope that this intention would not change: the costs of the transfer application were made "costs in the cause" on the High Court scale and it was pointed out that the Patents County Court would have power to order costs on the High Court scale if this were thought appropriate. For comment on the *Memminger* case, see (1990–91) 20 CIPA 291 and (1991–92) 21 CIPA 112 reporting dismissal of a further appeal to the Court of Appeal.

The High Court and County Courts Jurisdiction Order 1991 (S.I. 1991 No. 724) now regulates (by art. 7 thereof) the general distribution of business between the High Court and county courts by providing that cases which are triable in either jurisdiction shall generally be tried in a county court if the value of the action is less than £25,000 and in the High Court if that value exceeds £50,000. However, it is submitted that these provisions do not apply to matters whereby the only jurisdiction of a county court is by jurisdiction conferred on the "patents county courts" under the 1988 Act. This is because this article 7 refers to proceedings in which "the county courts have jurisdiction" and this wording seems apt only to apply to *all* county courts and not merely such of these courts which have been nominated as "patents county courts".

For the procedure on transfer of a case from the High Court to a county court, see para. 96.19 *infra.*

61.27 *The Anton Piller Order*

For case comment on *Swedac* v. *Magnet & Southerns* ([1989] FSR 243), cited in the Main Work, see J. Hull ([1989] EIPR 382); and, generally, on the tightening up of controls on *Anton Piller* orders, see the paper by D. Alexander listed in para. 61.05 *supra.* There must now be proportionality between the perceived threat to the plaintiff's rights and the remedy granted (*Lock International* v. *Beswick*, [1989] 3 All ER 373). The whole subject of *Anton Piller* relief is also fully discussed in the book by S. Gee listed in para. 61.04 *supra.* This book also includes a specimen order and precedents for the supporting affidavits.

The information obtained on execution of an *Anton Piller* Order can only be used for the purposes of the proceedings in which the Order was made, see *VDU*

Installations v. *Integrated Computer Systems* ([1989] FSR 378), that is as if the documents had been produced on discovery, for which see para. 61.31.

Discovery **61.28**

As explained in *Merrell Dow's Patent* ([1991] RPC 221), the principles governing the extent of discovery are those of the "*Peruvian Guano*" case (*Compagnie Financière* v. *Peruvian Guano Company*, (1882) 11 QBD 55 at 62). These are that documents are discoverable if they "relate" to the issues in the case, and a document so relates if it would, directly or indirectly, advance the case of the other party or damage that of the discovering party, or lead the other party on a train of enquiry which may have either of these consequences, see also *Compania Uruguaya de Fomenta* v. *Mentmore* ((1955) 72 RPC 302). These priniples will, if necessary, be followed in proceedings before the Comptroller, see para. 72.44 in the Main Work and para. 46.33 *supra*.

Further discovery of commercial information, allegedly relevant to the issue of commercial success, was largely refused in *Mölnlycke* v. *Procter & Gamble (No. 3)* ([1990] RPC 498), but documents relating to the selection of material for producing the claimed article (dated prior to the publication of the patent) were ordered to be discovered, as also were documents relating to problems encountered with prior art articles as these could be relevant to the issue of whether a defect in such articles did exist.

Intel v. *General Instrument*, cited in the Main Work, has been reported ([1989] FSR 640).

In *Fuji Photo* v. *Carr's Paper* ([1989] RPC 713) discovery of "all documents relating to the invention" of the patent and of indemnities given in relation thereto were each rejected as being classes of documents too widely defined.

Failure to give discovery in the terms of an Order therefor can lead to the action or defence being struck out, though the first step will probably be an "Unless Order" under which striking out is automatic if the original Order is not obeyed within the time set, see *Bonzel* v. *Intervention*, (SRIS C/15/91).

In the patents county courts discovery is not automatic, but is one of the matters for which directions should be sought from the judge on the "preliminary consideration", for which see paras. 96.22 and H48A.08 *infra*. Under Scots law, discovery is also not automatic and is requested for specified categories of documents.

Limitation on discovery **61.29**

There is no obligation on a party giving discovery of foreign language documents to provide a translation thereof (*Bayer* v. *Harris Pharmaceutical*, [1991] FSR 170), though the position may be different if such translations exist as separate documents.

Application for further discovery **61.30**

The general principles applicable to a request for further discovery were explained in *Berkeley Administration* v. *McClelland* ([1990] FSR 381 (CA)), where it was stressed that the court has an overriding discretion over such requests. However, further discovery will be refused if the request therefor is framed in terms broad enough to cover documents, the contents of which would go beyond anything that could relate to the issues in the action (*Minnesota Mining* v. *Rennicks (No. 2)*, SRIS C/33/91, *noted* IPD 14137).

Where a witness statement provided to the other party in advance of the substantive trial indicates the existence of further documents which could be relevant to the issues to be resolved, an application for further specific discovery can be made, any privilege having been waived once the witness statement has been provided (*Black & Decker* v. *Flymo*, [1991] FSR 93.

61.31 *Limitation on use of documents produced on discovery*

The same principles apply to information obtained on execution of an *Anton Piller* Order as with information gained from discovery (*VDU Installations* v. *Integrated Computer Systems*, [1989] FSR 378), though *Twentieth Century Fox* v. *Tryrare* ([1991] FSR 58) suggests that the information obtained on execution of an *Anton Piller* Order can be used for other purposes.

Jacques Dory v. *Richard Wolf (No. 2)* (SRIS C/38/89), cited in the Main Work, has been reported as *Dory* v. *Richard Wolf* ([1990] FSR 266).

In *Bonzel* v. *Intervention* ([1991] RPC 43), the Patents Court held that an order releasing a party from the "implied undertaking", not to use discovery documents other than in the proceedings in which they have been produced, should only be made in special circumstances and then only where this would not cause injustice to the producing party: the existence of a copending opposition in the EPO on the patent-in-issue was then held not to be such a circumstance, particularly because discovery is not a feature of EPO proceedings.

61.33 *Inspection*

Where information on the nature of materials used in the defendants' process had been disclosed in parallel proceedings (for which see para. 72.44A *infra*), a request for samples thereof was refused (*PLG Research* v. *Ardon,* SRIS C/92/91).

61.34 *Admissions and interrogatories*

It is now possible to administer "interrogatories without order", in addition to "ordered interrogatories" as previously, see para. E026.1 *infra*. Such interrogatories without order may be served upon a party not more than twice (Ord. 26, r. 3(1)). The applicant must stipulate a period for response being more than 28 days and, if addressed other than to a natural person shall specify the person who is required to answer on behalf thereof (Ord. 26, r. 2(1)). The response is to be by affidavit (Ord. 26, r. 2(2)), subject to an application to the court for the variation or withdrawal of the interrogatory without order (Ord. 26, r. 3(2)) or unless the addressee claims privilege (Ord. 26, r. 5(1)). The Court may order amplification of an insufficient answer (Ord. 26, r. 5(2)), but otherwise failure to answer can lead to committal for contempt of court (Ord. 26, r. 6(2)) and the court may make any order thought appropriate in the circumstances, including the striking out of pleadings and judgment accordingly (Ord. 26, r. 6(1)).

Under this new procedure, request was made in *Mentor Corp.* v. *Hollister Inc.* ([1990] FSR 577) that 14 named persons answer whether they were aware of certain prior art documents during their development of the alleged infringement, but the request was rejected as oppressive: also knowledge of these specifications could have been so fragmented that any one skilled addressee of the patent-in-suit would not have fully known their contents and so could have missed the invention.

In proceedings before the patents county courts a notice to admit facts may be served within 14 days of the close of pleadings, see para. H48A.06 *infra*: however, otherwise, such notices, and interrogatories, may only be served with leave of the court to be requested on the "preliminary consideration", see paras. 96.22 and H48A.08 *infra*.

Experiments 61.35

Where a party wishes to perform experiments as a preliminary to adducing the results thereof in evidence, the court is first required to give directions in effect approving the carrying out of the experiments proposed (RSC Ord. 104, r. 12(3), reprinted in para. E104.12 of the Main Work); and, where a party serves a notice of experiments, particulars must be given of the facts which those experiments are intended to establish (*Soc. Français Hoechst* v. *Allied Colloids*, [1991] RPC 245). However, it is difficult for the court to decide whether or not requested experiments will turn out to have probative value and therefore the practice is likely to be that leave will be given to carry out proposed experiments, but with an eventual costs penalty if these turn out not to be helpful to the court (*Minnesota Mining* v. *Rennicks (No. 3)*, SRIS C/60/91, *noted* IPD 14190); and in a further application the Defendant was permitted to perform an experiment on a re-commissioned plant in Japan shortly before the trial date, but with the Plaintiff having its costs in relation to that experiment in any event (*Minnesota Mining* v. *Rennicks (No. 4)*, SRIS C/75/91, *noted* IPD 14207).

If experiments are performed which do not assist the court, the performing party may be deprived of a costs recovery in respect thereof (*Pall Corp.* v. *Commercial Hydraulics*, [1990] RPC 329 at 358).

In proceedings before the patents county courts the "application for directions" should give "full particulars of any experiments the applicant intends to conduct, stating the facts which he intends to prove by them and the date by which he will submit a written report of the results": the judge will then give directions in relation thereto on the "preliminary consideration," see paras. 96.22 and H48A.08 *infra*.

Evidence 61.36

In proceedings before the patents county courts the judge is to consider and (where appropriate) give directions on the "preliminary consideration" of: "the witnesses who may be called"; "whether their evidence shall be given orally or in writing or any combination of the two"; and "the exchange of witness statements", see CCR Ord. 48A, rule 8(5)(*a*)–(*c*) reprinted in para. H48A.08, *infra*.

Security for costs 61.37

There is an increasing tendency not to require security for costs from a plaintiff resident in an EEC country which is subject to the Brussels Convention for reciprocal enforcement of judgments, see *Kickers International* v. *Stylo Barratt Shoes* (SRIS C/21/90), but the discretion to require such security from a plaintiff resident in the EEC has been held not to be contrary to the Treaty of Rome (*Berkeley Administration* v. *McClelland, The Times*, February 20, 1990 (CA)).

Procedure at trial 61.38

RSC Order 38 governs the procedure for a plaintiff to "set down" an action for trial in the High Court and, if this is not done in time, the defendant can seek dismissal of the action (RSC Ord. 34, r. 2, reprinted at para. E034.2 of the Main Work). On "setting down", a defined bundle of documents must be lodged, in duplicate, and the other parties notified of this (RSC Ord. 34, rr. 3 and 8, reprinted at paras. E034.3 and E034.8 *infra*). Shortly before the trial date, there must also be lodged a further bundle of documents containing: copies of exchanged witness statements; other documents central to the plaintiff's case and a defendant's case where there is a counterclaim), and such documents as the defendant wishes to have included; and, possibly, notes by each party summarising the issues involved, propositions of law to be advanced and a list of cases to be cited, and a chronology of relevant events (RSC Ord. 34, r. 10, reprinted at para. E034.10 *infra*).

On setting down a patent case for trial there must now be given to the Patents Court time estimates for both the trial itself and for the "reading time" required by the judge. For this a "Reading Guide" should be supplied which is short, non-contentious and, if possible, agreed; and setting out the issues, the parts of documents to be read on each issue and a convenient order of reading: relevant passages from text books and cases can also be included (*Practice Direction (Chancery: Reading Guide in Patent Actions) No. 5 of 1989*, [1990] RPC 60).

For procedure before the Patents County Court, see para. 96.22 *infra*.

COMMENTARY ON SECTION 63

63.02 *General*

The second decision in *Hallen* v. *Brabantia* (SRIS C/40/89), cited in the Main Work, has been reported ([1990] FSR 134). Relief on a partially valid patent was also allowed in *Quantel* v. *Spaceward Microsystems* (SRIS C/78/89), again after the patent draftsman had given evidence, a patentee not being blameworthy for maintaining a claim if he did not know of the consequences of a prior document even though he was aware of its existence.

63.03 *Effect of section 63*

The decision in *Hallen* v. *Brabantia* (SRIS C/40/89), cited in the Main Work, has been reported ([1990] FSR 134).

63.04 *Direction of amendment as condition of relief on partially valid patent (subs. (3))*

The decision in *Hallen* v. *Brabantia* (SRIS C/40/89), cited in the Main Work, has been reported ([1990] FSR 134).

64.01 SECTION 64

Note. The substitution of section 64 noted in the Main Work came into effect on January 7, 1991 (S.I. 1990 No. 2168).

64.03 SECTION 64—ARTICLES

J. U. Neukom, "A prior right use for the Community Patent Convention", [1990] EIPR 165.

COMMENTARY ON SECTION 64

64.04 *General*

In the paper by J. U. Neukom, listed in para. 64.03 *supra*, the extent of the prior user right provided by section 64 is analysed in relation to the similar rights existing under the laws of other EPC countries. J. C. Boff ((1989–90) 19 CIPA 377) has also discussed apparent deficiencies in the wording of the section if the rationale of *EPO Decision G 2/88*, "*Friction reducing additive/MOBIL III*" (OJEPO 4/1990, 93; [1990] 2 EPOR 73), importing an element of technical purpose into a claim, is adopted into the law of infringement.

Scope of the section **64.05**

In *Helitune* v. *Stewart Hughes* ([1991] FSR 171) the words "that act" in the original form of section 64(2) were construed, *obiter*, as meaning an act of the same type (*i.e.* an act as enumerated in s. 60(2)) as the prior act referred to in the original section 64(1), but the prior act need not necessarily have been an identical act to that alleged to infringe the patent, though on the facts in the *Helitune* case, it was held that the Defendant had not done, or made serious and effective preparations to do, an act of the same type as the alleged infringement, in this case an act of sale. Thus, the section may provide a broader defence than is indicated in the Main Work: for a hypothetical example, see the moot judgment at (1990–91) 20 CIPA 311; and for comment by J. U. Neukom, see [1991] EIPR 350. However, the breadth of the *dictum* in the *Helitune* case was doubted in *Lubrizol* v. *Esso* (SRIS C/88/91) where it was pointed out that it could, anyway, be defeated by an amendment of the patent. It was here opined that the section merely safeguards (projected) commercial activity, but does not allow expansion into other products and processes.

COMMENTARY ON SECTION 65

Grant of certificate of contested validity (subs. (1)) **65.03**

The Comptroller granted such certificates in *Mölynlycke's and Boussac Saint Frères' Patents* (SRIS O/15/90), *Haynes International's Patent* (SRIS O/105/90, *noted* IPD 13196) and *Glaverbel's Patent* (SRIS O/32/91).

PRACTICE UNDER SECTION 65

When the Comptroller grants a certificate of contested validity, the fact is **65.06** advertised in the O.J. under the general power of rule 50 (reprinted at para. 32.08 of the Main Work), see O.J. July 31, 1991.

COMMENTARY ON SECTION 67

Definition of "exclusive licensee" **67.03**

A licence granted other than by a deed or for valuable consideration can be no more than a "bare licence" which estops the proprietor for suing the licensee for infringement; such cannot therefore be an "exclusive" licence entitling the licensee to sue for infringement, see *Gough* v. *Greens Onion Services* (SRIS C/1/92 (PCC)) where a plaintiff was struck from the proceedings for not having this status at the commencement of proceedings.

COMMENTARY ON SECTION 68

68.02 *General*

A notification to the Comptroller of a transaction, instrument or event for the purposes of making an entry in the register has been accepted as giving an exclusive licensee the right to claim damages when notice of the notification had been entered in the register (*Insituform* v. *Inliner,* SRIS C/77/91).

68.03 *Effect of non-registration of assignment or licence*

In *Minnesota Mining* v. *Rennicks* (SRIS C/100/91) relief was curtailed because a written licence was held not to be a mere confirmation of an earlier informal licence.

COMMENTARY ON SECTION 69

69.02 *General*

CPCa. 34, referred to in the Main Work, has been renumbered as CPCa. 32 [1989], see para. 86.03 *infra.*

69.04 *Rights conferred by section 69 (subs. (1))*

In *Pall Corp.* v. *Commercial Hydraulics* (SRIS C/90/89) an inquiry into damages was ordered to run from the date of publication of the application.

COMMENTARY ON SECTION 70

70.04 *What constitutes a threat (subs. (1))*

In *Bowden Controls* v. *Acco Cable Controls* ([1990] RPC 427) a letter addressed to a supplier to car manufacturers which referred to a German court decision, stating that the patentee had corresponding patents in all major European countries and intended to enforce its rights, was held likely to have been regarded as a threat of patent proceedings, even though the patentee argued it would be commercial suicide to sue a potential customer in view of the practice of requiring dual sourcing of car components, see also paras. 70.07 and 70.08 *infra.*

It would seem that, to be actionable under the section, the threat should be one made within the United Kingdom: otherwise, the Act would have extra-territorial effect contrary to general jurisprudence. At least it has been so held in Australia (*Norbert Steinhardt* v. *Meth*, (1960–61) 105 CLR 440).

70.07 *Relief (subs. (3))*

In *Bowden Controls* v. *Acco Cable Controls* (see para. 70.04 *supra*) an interlocutory injunction was granted, together with an order for the patentee to identify the individuals to whom the offending letters had been directed.

70.08 *Exclusion of threats made to primary infringers (subs. (4))*

Line 2 of the entry in the Main Work should more correctly read: "relates to primary infringement, . . . " because action may be brought under section 70 by anyone "aggrieved by the threat" (see subs. (1)) and he need not himself be an infringer. In *Bowden Controls* v. *Acco Cable Controls* (see para. 70.04 *supra*) it was indicated (though not decided) that subsection (4) only protects threats against acts of manufacture (for supply or sale) and therefore does not nullify a threat made against a manufacturer who has existing stock for sale.

PRACTICE UNDER SECTION 70 **70.11**

Proceedings to award relief against unjustified threats may now be brought before the patents county courts, see paras. 96.17, 96.22 and Appendix H *infra*.

SECTION 71—RELEVANT RULE

Rule 74 [1990]—*Procedure on application under section 71* **71.02**

In paragraph (2), the words "three months after receipt of the copy of the statement" have been changed to "the period of two months beginning on the date when the copy is sent to him". In paragraph (3), the words "three months of his receipt of the copy of the counter-statement" have been changed to "the period of two months beginning on the date when the copy of the counter-statement is sent to him". In paragraph (4), the words "three months of the receipt of the copy of the applicant's evidence" have been changed to "the period of two months beginning on the date when the copy of the applicant's evidence is sent to him"; the next subsequent words "three months" have been changed to "two months"; and the words "three months of the receipt of the copy of the proprietor's evidence" have been changed to "the period of two months beginning on the date when the copy of the proprietor's evidence is sent to him".

COMMENTARY ON SECTION 71

General **71.03**

Proceedings for a declaration of non-infringement may now be brought before a patents county court, see paras. 96.17, 96.22 and Appendix H *infra*. Also, in a case where a person will not be carrying out the alleged infringing act himself so that he is not entitled to apply under section 71, the court can grant a declaration under its inherent jurisdiction, see *Filhol* v. *Fairfax* ([1990] RPC 293). Where the patentee provides an acknowledgment of non-infringement during the course of proceedings under section 71, the Comptroller will not then grant a declaration (*Brupat's Patent*, SRIS O/89/90, *noted* IPD 13195).

Use of section 71 in practice **71.06**

Filhol v. *Fairfax*, cited in the Main Work, has been reported ([1990] RPC 293). In *Vax* v. *Hoover* ([1990] RPC 656) the defendant in an infringement action was permitted to amend its counterclaim to seek a declaration of non-infringement in respect of a modified device. The court accepted that, otherwise, the defendant would be in difficulty if faced after trial with an injunction in general terms. It was also appropriate to decide this question at the same time as deciding the issue of infringement as regards the device upon which the writ had been issued, even though strictly speaking the cause of action on the counterclaim had not existed at the date of the writ. The modified device was subsequently found to be non-infringing (*Vax* v. *Hoover*, [1991] FSR 307).

In *Schmersal's Patent* (SRIS O/72/91) the Comptroller would have applied the three *Catnic* questions (for which see para. 125.10 *infra*), but there being no evidence on the first two of these (relating to "variants") passed to the third question to find no infringement by the variant in issue, for which see para. 125.10 *infra*.

PRACTICE UNDER SECTION 71

71.08 *Procedure before the Comptroller*

The period for filing a counter-statement, and each of the successive periods for filing evidence, are now each *two* months, calculated from the date of dispatch of the document which initiates that period, see para. 71.02 *supra*.

71.09 *Procedure before the court*

The court will normally order that costs should follow the event in the normal way, even where the plaintiff became entitled to the requested declaration as the result of the patent having been declared invalid in other proceedings (*Mölnlycke* v. *Procter & Gamble*, [1990] RPC 267). Proceedings before the court under section 71 may not be brought by notice of originating motion (*Wincanton Engineering* v. *Alfa Laval*, SRIS C/10/90, *noted* IPD 13110).

72.01

SECTION 72

Note. The amendment to subsection (1)(*b*), and the repeal of subsection (3), each noted in the Main Work, came into effect on January 7, 1991 (S.I. 1990 No. 2168).

SECTION 72—RELEVANT RULES

72.02 Rule 21 [1990]—*Forms of statements, counter-statements and evidence*

In rule 21 the words "at the Patent Office" have been deleted.

72.03 Rule 75 [1990]—*Procedure on application for revocation under section 72*

In paragraph (3), the words "three months of the receipt of such copies" have been changed to "the period of two months beginning on the date when such copies are sent to him". In paragraph (4), the words "three months of the receipt of the copy of the counter-statement" have been changed to "two months beginning on the date when the copy of the counter-statement".

Paragraph (5) has been reprinted to read:

"(5) Within the period of two months beginning on the date when the copy of the applicant's evidence is sent to him or, if the applicant does not file any evidence, within two months of the expiration of the time within which such evidence might have been filed, the proprietor of the patent may file evidence in support of his case and shall send a copy of that evidence to the applicant; and, within the period of two months beginning on the date when the copy of the proprietor's evidence is sent to him, the applicant may file further evidence confined to matters strictly in reply and shall send a copy of it to the proprietor."

Rule 76 [1990]—*Award of costs* **72.04**

The words "the patent" have been changed to "a patent".

Rule 104 [1990]—*Statutory declarations and affidavits* **72.06**

In subparagraph (b), the words from "or in any state . . . " to " . . . British Nationality Act 1948" have been deleted. In subparagraph (c), the words "or before a" have been added before "notary".

Note. The terms "protectorate" and "protected state" are now obsolete, see the British Nationality Act 1981 (c. 61).

Rule 107 [1990]—*Supporting statements or evidence* **72.09**

Note. In paragraph (2) the rules listed are now: "40(3), 41(1), 43(3), 64(1), 65(2), 71(2), 78(2) and 91(5)".

COMMENTARY ON SECTION 72

Forum for revocation **72.13**

Proceedings for revocation may now be brought before a patents county court. The provisions of CCR Order 48A (reprinted in Appendix H *infra*) apply to the procedure. This is discussed generally in para. 96.22 *infra* and see also paras. 61.22, 61.28 and 61.34–61.36 *supra*. For the prospective extension of the Civil Jurisdiction and Judgments Act 1982 (c. 27) to other countries, see para. 61.06 *supra*.

Grounds of revocation

—Invention is not a patentable invention (subs. (1)(a)) **72.16**

CPCa. 57, referred to in the Main Work, has been renumbered as CPCa. 56 [1989], see para. 86.03 *infra*.

—Patent granted to person not entitled thereto (subs. (1)(b) and (2)) **72.17**

CPCaa. 57, 27 and 56, referred to in the Main Work, have been renumbered as CPCaa. 56, 23 and 55 [1989] respectively, see para. 86.03.

Insufficient description (subs. (1)(c))

72.18 *—General*

CPCa. 57, referred to in the Main Work, has been renumbered as CPCa. 56 [1989], see para. 86.03 *infra.*

Impermissible amendments (subss. (1)(d) and (e))

72.25 *—General*

A pleading under section 72(1)(*e*) is only appropriate where the patent has been amended after grant: improper amendments made pre-grant are actionable under section 72(1)(*d*) (*Liversidge* v. *British Telecommunications*, [1991] RPC 229). It is immaterial to objections under section 72(1)(*d*) whether a pre-grant amendment has broadened or narrowed the scope of protection, provided that the amended claim as a whole does not offend against section 76 (*A. C. Edwards* v. *Acme Signs*, [1990] RPC 62 and SRIS C/80/91 (CA)). An applicant for revocation bears the onus of proof and the application will therefore be dismissed if the applicant fails, on the balance of probabilities, to discharge this, see *Haynes International's Patent* (SRIS O/27/90, *noted* IPD 13145).

CPCa. 57, referred to in the Main Work, has been renumbered as CPCa. 56 [1989], see para. 86.03, *infra.*

The reference in the Main Work five lines from the end of the entry to "rule 91(4)" should be to "rule 91(2)."

The EPO has held that the limitations of section 76 apply also to corrections under EPCr. 88 (*EPO Decision T* 401/88, "*Test piece/BOSCH*", OJEPO 7/1990, 297; [1990] EPOR 690). The Main Work suggests the position is otherwise under the 1977 Act, section 117 being governed neither by section 76 nor by section 130(7).

72.26 *—Effect of subsection (1)(d) and (e) in practice*

A "*squeeze argument*" between non-infringement and invalidity for "added subject matter" was run in *Bonzel* v. *Intervention* (*No. 3)* ([1991] RPC 553). Infringement was found on construing the claims as the skilled man would have done, see para. 125.15 *infra*, but added subject matter was also found based on a different wording of the description in the original application, para. 76.13 *infra.*

72.29 *Referral to the court (subs. (7))*

When the Comptroller declines to deal with a revocation action originally brought before him, the applicant for revocation now has a choice of bringing the matter before a patents county court, rather than before some other court also having jurisdiction, see para. 72.13 *supra*: CCR Ord. 48A, rule 10(2) (reprinted in para. H48A.10 *infra*) then applies.

72.30 *Concurrent proceedings*

Prima facie, a plaintiff has a right to litigate in the forum of his choice (*Ferro Corp.* v. *Escol Products*, [1990] RPC 651). Here the court felt that the *Hawker*

Siddeley case was a special one. In *Ferro*, the parties could afford court proceedings, would anyway be using solicitors and counsel, and would be likely to appeal the Comptroller's decision to the Patents Court. Therefore, the court did not feel that finality would be reached significantly more quickly and cheaply if a stay were ordered. Also, it should be noted that, in *Hawker-Siddeley*, it was important that there was also an application to the Comptroller for a declaration of non-infringement.

Pall Corp. v. *Commercial Hydraulics*, cited in the Main Work, has now been fully reported ([1989] RPC 703).

PRACTICE UNDER SECTION 72

General procedure in applications for revocation made to the Comptroller 72.33

The period for filing a counter-statement, and each of the successive periods for filing evidence, are now each *two* months. These are generally calculated from the date of dispatch of the document which initiates that period, but the procedure in revocation proceedings under rule 75 still calculates the time periods for filing evidence from the date, see para. 72.03 *supra*. For a possible stay of the proceedings where opposition proceedings have been commenced against that patent in the EPO, see para. 27.15 *supra*. Where a solicitor omitted to supply the other party directly with a copy of his party's evidence, the Comptroller termed this a "trivial irregularity" and did not impose any penalty (*Bere's Patent*, SRIS O/84/91), but a less lenient attitude could be shown in other cases.

In *Craig Medical's Patent* (SRIS O/152/90) some parts of a declaration were ordered to be deleted as not being "evidence strictly in reply".

If an applicant for revocation withdraws, the Comptroller will decide the application in the public interest, and this is so even if the patentee indicates his intention to allow the patent to lapse by non-renewal (*N.L. Petroleum's Patent*, SRIS O/112/90, *noted* IPD 14043): this is because revocation has complete retroactive effect.

Time limits and extensions of time 72.34

Rules 65 and 66 [1982] have become, respectively, rules 64 and 65 [1990].

Where one party obtains an extension of time for filing evidence and then fails to file that evidence, the other party will be permitted to file further evidence, but the time for this will run from the date when the first party ought to have filed his evidence subject to such extension as the Comptroller may allow (*Highspire's Patent*, SRIS O/126/90).

Statement of case 72.37

Richco Plastic's Patent (SRIS O/22/89), cited in the Main Work, has been reported ([1989] RPC 722).

An allegation which has not been adequately particularised in the Statement (particularly one of improper amendment under s.72(1)(*d*)) will not be permitted to be raised in argument at the hearing because the patentee will not have had proper notice of it and no proper opportunity of dealing with it in his evidence (*Mölnlycke's and Boussac Saint Frères' Patents*, SRIS O/15/90, *noted* IPD 13111). However, late amendment of the Statement is more likely to be permitted in the public interest if the new allegation is one of self prior use (*Moore's Patent*, SRIS O/116/90, *noted* IPD 14083).

Evidence

72.41 *—Attestation of evidence*

As regards attestation of written evidence outside the United Kingdom, RSC Ord. 41, rule 12 (reprinted at para. E041.12 of the Main Work) appears to be of wider scope than rule 104, but rule 104 appears to be mandatory for proceedings before the Comptroller.

72.42 *—Powers of the Comptroller concerning evidence*

Evidence given in other proceedings is not necessarily evidence in the proceedings in issue and an attempt to exhibit such other evidence has been disallowed (*Coal Industry's Patent*, SRIS O/11/90, *noted* IPD 13081), but where a joint hearing is held on two related patents oral evidence given at that hearing may be considered in respect of both patents (*Mölnlycke's and Boussac Saint Frères' Patents*, SRIS O/15/90).

For increased powers to administer interrogatories in court proceedings, see RSC Ord. 26, r. 1 (reprinted at para. E026.1 *infra*) and para. 61.34 *supra.*

72.44 *—Discovery and power to require production of documents*

Discovery cannot be used to establish a case, the onus for which is on the applicant: there must first be indicated the existence of evidence sufficient to meet that onus (*Richco Plastic's Patent*, [1989] RPC 703). In ordering the Patentee to give discovery in *Merrell Dow's Patent* (SRIS O/32/90, *noted* IPD 13140), for which see para. 46.33 *supra*, the Comptroller indicated that in Patent Office proceedings the principles governing discovery in court proceedings would generally be followed, but on appeal ([1991] RPC 221) the Patents Court pointed out that documents are discoverable if they "relate" to issues, not merely if they are "relevant" to them, though discovery will not be ordered "unless it is necessary so to do in order to dispose fairly of the cause or matter or to save costs", see para. 61.28 *supra.*

72.44A *—Restrictions on disclosure of discovered documents*

An appeal in *Roussel-Uclaf* v. *ICI (No. 2)*, cited in the Main Work, was dismissed, both decisions now having been reported ([1990] RPC 45).

In general, it is not appropriate to impose restrictions on inspection of a discovery document in a manner which would hinder a party in its choice of witnesses, unless the discovering party can demonstrate that the document contains "information relating to a genuine trade secret, which is still in use, or commercial information relating to a product which has yet to be launched" (*Molnlycke and Peaudouce* v. *Procter & Gamble*, SRIS C/47/91, *noted* IPD 14192). However, where discovery documents contain confidential information, a party may be required to nominate an independent expert to examine these documents *in lieu* of being permitted to inspect them itself (*Insituform* v. *Inliner*, SRIS C/14/91, *noted* IPD 14136). Also, where it was agreed that documents contained confidential information, permission was given for inspection by expert witnesses and a single attorney acting for the accepting party each in the USA, but with the safeguard that the documents should only be inspected at the offices of a U.S. attorney nominated by the discovering party with no copies to be taken

(*International Video Disk* v. *Nimbus*, SRIS C/51/91; *noted* (1991) 3(5) IPBB 9). In *PLG Research* v. *Ardon* (SRIS C/92/91) persons who had been permitted to witness an inspection of the Defendants' process in parallel United States litigation were permitted also to be informed of the results of the corresponding inspection for the United Kingdom litigation from which they had initially been excluded, but subject to them signing a copy of the confidentiality order.

—Evidence of experiments **72.45**

In *Craig Medical's Patent* (SRIS O/152/90) experimental evidence was allowed to be filed as reply evidence without opportunity for repetition before the other party's observers in order not to delay the hearing, but the question of admission of the evidence was reserved to the hearing.

Amendments **72.47**

The decision in *Eichoff Maschinenfabrik's Patent*, cited in the Main Work, was followed in *Harding's Patent* (SRIS O/94/90, *noted* IPD 13215).

In *Ricoh's Patent* (SRIS O/58/91, *noted* IPD 14165) amendments were proposed in the counter-statement which the applicant for revocation contested should be disallowed for undue delay as amendment of the corresponding U.S. application had been made some time previously. The Comptroller acceded to a request to decide, as a preliminary point, the issue whether discretion to permit amendment could be exercised, and decided that the amendment should be advertised forthwith.

SECTION 73 **73.01**

Note. The substitution of new subsections (2)–(4), each noted in the Main Work, came into effect on January 7, 1991 (S.I. 1990 No. 2168).

Section 73—Relevant Rule

Rule 77 [1990]—*Revocation and amendment of patents under section 73* **73.02**

Rule 77 now reads:

77.—(1) The opportunity to be given by the Comptroller under subsection (1) or (2) of section 73, to the proprietor of a patent to make observations and to amend the specification of the patent shall be given by the comptroller sending to the proprietor notice informing him that he may make the observations and amend the specification and that, if he wishes to do so, he must do so within three months after the notice is sent to him.

(2) Where the comptroller gives leave under section 73 for the specification of the patent to be amended, he may, before the specification is amended, require the applicant to file a new specification as amended, prepared in accordance with rules 16, 18 and 20.

COMMENTARY ON SECTION 73

73.03 *General*

CPCa. 80, referred to in the Main Work, has been renumbered as CPCa. 75 [1989], see para. 86.03 *infra.*

73.06 *Revocation for double patenting in corresponding European patent (UK) (subs. (2)–(4))*

CPCa. 80, referred to in the Main Work, has been renumbered as CPCa. 75 [1989], see para. 86.03 *infra.*

Any difference in scope between the claims of the patent granted under the Act and the corresponding European patent (UK) must be more than a cosmetic difference (*Marley Roof Tile's Patent*, SRIS O/112/91): here it was recognised that claims to a chemical compound *per se* and to a process for preparing this are different (though with unity of invention), but the product claim in issue was held to contain an inherent process feature so that it was here for "the same invention" as the process claim.

Where revocation is ordered under section 73(2), this must be on the normal *ex tunc* base, relief for infringement prior to revocation being available (under s.69) under the European patent application from its publication (*Thomas (M)'s Patent,* SRIS O/129/91).

73.08 PRACTICE UNDER SECTION 73

Rule 77 (reprinted in para. 73.02, *supra*) has been amended to clarify its wording. The period for response remains at three months, but if amendment is allowed, the Comptroller can now require a new specification to be filed, presented in compliance with rules 16, 18 and 20 (r. 77(2)).

74.01

SECTION 74

Note. The amendment of subsection (6), noted in the Main Work, came into effect on January 7, 1991 (S.I. 1990 No. 2168).

COMMENTARY ON SECTION 74

74.02 *General*

CPCaa. 27 and 56, referred to in the Main Work, have been renumbered as CPCaa. 23 and 55 [1989], see para. 86.03 *infra.*

74.04 *Estoppel against challenge to validity*

Bayer and Süllhöfer's Agreement, cited in the Main Work, has been reported ([1990] FSR 300 (ECJ)), and the validity of the rule of "licensee estoppel" has been questioned and discussed by A. Robertson ([1991] EIPR 373).

74.07 *Stay of proceedings pending determination of opposition at the EPO*

Pall Corp. v. *Commercial Hydraulics*, cited in the Main Work, has now been fully reported ([1989] RPC 703).

SECTION 75—RELEVANT RULE

Rule 78 [1990]—*Amendment of patent in infringement or revocation proceedings* **75.02**

The rule title has been changed to that indicated above. In paragraph 1, the words "three months" have been changed to "two months". A new paragraph (4) has been added reading:

(4) Where the comptroller gives leave under section 75 for the specification of the patent to be amended, he may, before the specification is amended, require the applicant to file a new specification as amended, prepared in accordance with rules 16, 18 and 20.

COMMENTARY ON SECTION 75

General **75.03**

CPCaa. 51, 57 and 59, referred to in the Main Work, have been renumbered as CPCaa. 50, 56 and 58 [1989], see para. 86.03 *infra*.

Discretion **75.06**

Procter & Gamble v. *Peaudouce* (SRIS C/47/89), cited in the Main Work, has been reported [1989] FSR 614; and *Smith Kline & French's (Bavin's) Patent (No. 2)* (SRIS C/49/89), also so cited, has been reported as *Smith Kline & French* v. *Evans Medical* [1989] FSR 561.

Imposition of conditions **75.07**

If terms are to be imposed as a condition of allowing amendment of, or relief on, a partially valid patent, it would appear that the defendant must establish that he received reasonable advice that: (a) the patent was not infringed or was invalid; (b) he acted upon this advice to his detriment; and (c) that advice was in some way based upon the defect to be cured by the amendment, see *Hallen* v. *Brabantia* ([1990] FSR 134) where terms were refused. The public interest should also be taken into account, see further *General Tire (Frost's) Patent* ([1974] RPC 207 (CA)).

Opposition **75.08**

The period for lodging opposition is now only *two* months, see para. 75.02, *supra*: this period remains inextensible (r. 110(2)).

PRACTICE UNDER SECTION 75

Application to the court **75.11**

Where proposed amendments have been advertised the patentee will probably not be permitted to resile from these, but where the eventual amendments are more extensive than those advertised, readvertisement will probably not be necessary (*Quantel* v. *Spaceward Microsystems*, [1990] RPC 83). Also, pending determination of an amendment application to the court, a patentee will normally have to undertake not to threaten or institute any further proceedings under the patent, see *Quantel* v. *Electronic Graphics* ([1990] RPC 272).

For amendment proceedings before a patents county court, RSC Ord. 104, rule 3 also applies, save that the application is made on notice to the patents judge rather than by motion (CCR 48A, r. 10(1), reprinted in para. H48A.10 *infra*).

75.12 *Allowance of amendment by the court*

Rules 79A, 79B and 79F are now respectively paragraphs 1, 2 and 6 of Schedule 4 to the Rules, for which see paras. 77.03, 77.04 and 77.06 *infra*. Rule 78(4) (reprinted in para. 75.02 *supra*) now makes specific provision for the filing of an amended specification of a European patent (UK), should the Comptroller so require.

75.13 *Application to the Comptroller*

The period for lodging opposition is now only *two* months, see para. 75.02 *supra*. If and when amendment is permitted, the Comptroller can now make it a precondition of amendment that a new specification be filed, presented in accordance with rules 16, 18 and 20 (r. 78(4), reprinted in para. 75.02 *supra*).

76.01

SECTION 76

Note. The substitution of section 76, noted in the Main Work, came into effect on January 7, 1991 (S.I. 1990 No. 2168).

76.03

ARTICLES

G. W. Dworkin, "Implied added subject matter: An academic overview", (1990–91) 20 CIPA 340.

COMMENTARY ON SECTION 76

76.04 *General*

The same questions arise under the various parts of section 76 (*Coin Controls' Application*, SRIS O/76/90, *noted* IPD 13212).

76.07 *Effect of breach of subsection (1)*

There is no objection to claims in a main patent and also in one derived from a divisional application both being infringed by the same device, and a device described in the parent application as a distinct concept can properly form the subject of claims in a divisional application (*Quantel* v. *Spaceward Microsystems*, [1990] RPC 83). However, a contention that objection under subsection (1) only arises if the alleged added feature is not an essential feature failed in *Coin Controls' Application* (SRIS O/76/90, *noted* IPD 13212).

Examples of impermissible "additional matter"

—The general principles **76.11**

The paper by G. W. Dworkin, listed in para. 76.03 *supra*, reviewed EPO and British cases on allowability of amendments under EPCa. 123(2) and section 76. The paper considered the history of, and reasons for, the rule against added subject matter and searched (without success) for some underlying rationale between apparently inconsistent decisions.

In *Southco* v. *Dzus* ([1990] RPC 587 and SRIS C/86/91 (CA)) the main claim of the granted patent was worded differently from the application as filed, but both the Patents Court and the Court of Appeal held that the different wording, while (unobjectionably) possibly broadening the claim, did not add "fresh subject matter" to the application, the claim (even as amended) not extending to cover the alleged infringement, for which see para. 125.10 *infra*. This case illustrates the squeeze argument between validity and non-infringement if the claims are given a narrow construction, and infringement but invalidity for added subject matter if the claim is given a broader construction. Also, in *A. C. Edwards* v. *Acme Signs* ([1990] RPC 621 and SRIS C/80/91 (CA)), the Court of Appeal stressed that here the essential question was whether the granted claim *disclosed* the alleged new subject matter, it being immaterial that the granted claim *covered* this, the text of the granted specification, as in the *Southco* case, being substantially unchanged from that of the application as filed. Anyway, the original application and the granted patent must each be (purposively) construed as a whole.

—Adding to the implicit disclosure **76.13**

The court has applied the EPO "novelty test" (for which see para. 76.22 *infra*), though with caution, finding an amendment not objectionable when the amended specification lacks novelty over the description as originally filed, and section 130(3) provides that the claims as filed constitute part of the original disclosure, to be read in context with it: as was done in the *Southco* and *A. C. Edwards* cases referred to in para. 76.11 *supra*. However, to delete the main drawing, stated to illustrate the principle of the invention, is likely to result in implicit addition of new matter, see *Rockwool International's Patent* (SRIS O/63/90, *noted* IPD 13164, decided under s.31(2) [1949]). Also, addition of subject matter was found in *Bonzel* v. *Intervention* (*No. 3*) ([1991] RPC 553) as a consequence of revision of the preamble to a specification during examination rather than as a result of claim revision. Here the test for added subject matter was stated to involve ascertaining through the eyes of the skilled addressee the explicit and implicit disclosure of both the application as filed and the patent as granted, with subject matter having been added if this is not found to have been clearly and unambiguously disclosed in the application either explicitly or implicitly.

The possibility of claim broadening during prosecution **76.16**

It is immaterial whether a pre-grant amendment has the effect of widening (or narrowing) the monopoly claimed, provided that the invention in the amended claims is disclosed in the original application (including its claims by virtue of s.130(3)), when this is read as a whole (*Southco* v. *Dzus* [1990] RPC 587 and SRIS C/86/91 (CA)); and see *A. C. Edwards* v. *Acme Signs* ([1990] RPC 621 and SRIS C/80/91 (CA)) where a distinction was drawn between the *disclosure* in a claim and the *cover* which a claim provides.

76.17 *Extending scope of granted patent (subs. (3)(b))*

Where a patent was amended to leave only an omnibus claim, it was successfully contended that deletion of any of the descriptive matter must necessarily have the effect of broadening the scope of the claim (*Shoketsu's Patent (No. 3)*, SRIS O/60/91, *noted* IPD 14142).

Prohibition of amendments under the EPC

76.19 *—Effect of EPC on section 76*

The EPO does not allow amendments during the opposition phase unless these are necessitated by the pleaded grounds of opposition (*EPO Decision T* 127/85, "*Blasting compositions/IRECO*," OJEPO 7/1989, 271; [1989] 6 EPOR 358).

The EPO regards the case law developed under EPCa. 123(2) as also applicable to the permissible relationship of a divisional application to its parent (*EPO Decision T* 527/88, "*Interconnected bags/WAVIN*", [1991] EPOR 184): this seems to be the position also as regards the relationship between subsection (1) and subsections (2) and (3) of section 76.

76.21 *—Permissible addition of well-known matter (EPO Guidelines C–VI, 5.6, 5.7)*

Applicants are, apparently, permitted to amend claims to cover embodiments which would be obvious to the skilled person from reading the original description (*EPO Decision T* 192/88, "*Homogenising immiscible fluids/GEC Alsthom*", [1990] 4 EPOR 287).

76.22 *—Relation of test for additional subject-matter to tests of novelty and priority (EPO Guidelines C–VI, 5.4, 5.5)*

EPO Decision T 133/85 ("*Amendments/XEROX*"), cited in the Main Work, is also reported (*abridged* OJEPO 12/1988, 441).

The EPO has now stated that the test for additional subject-matter corresponds to the test for novelty *only in so far* as both require assessment of whether information is directly and unambiguously derivable from that previously presented, in the originally-filed application or in a prior document respectively (*EPO Decision T* 194/84, "*Cellulosic fibres/GENERAL MOTORS*", OJEPO 3/1990, 59; [1989] 6 EPOR 351): therefore, the "lack of novelty test" is to be applied to the change in content of the amended claim and not to the amended claim *per se*. For example, an attempt to import a negative feature (the absence of internal fittings) from the drawing has been rejected because such absence did not make it "unequivocally inferable that such feature is to be excluded" (*EPO Decision T* 170/87, "*Hot-gas cooler/SULZER*", OJEPO 11/1989, 441; [1990] 1 EPOR 14). Alternatively, the subject-matter generated by the amendment must be novel over the specification as filed (*EPO Decision T* 265/88, "*Diffusion device/LUNDIA*", [1990] 5 EPOR 399). Also, care must be taken in construing words, such as "and", used somewhat ambiguously in the original text (*EPO Decision T* 171/89, "*Vaccine/BAYER*", [1990] 2 EPOR 126). (*EPO Decision T* 194/84, "*Cellulosic fibres/GENERAL MOTORS*", *supra*).

It is possible to overcome an objection of alleged added subject matter by construing the claim wording in a restrictive way (*EPO Decision T* 164/90, "*Authenticator device/LIGHT SIGNATURES*", [1991] EPOR 289).

The EPO Enlarged Board of Appeal has allowed an appeal in *EPO Decision T* 59/87, "*Friction reducing additive/MOBIL II*," cited in the Main Work), see *EPO Decision G* 2/88, "*Friction reducing additive/MOBIL III*" (OJEPO 4/1990, 93; [1990] 2 EPOR 73), as discussed in paras. 2.10 and 2.13 *supra* and 125.08 *infra* and at (1989–90) 19 CIPA 111 and 171). In this decision it was stated that a post-grant change of category of claims can be allowed if the extent of protection (when considered in the light of the Protocol to EPCa. 69) is not extended, but in this regard national laws relating to the question of infringement should not be considered. Likewise, claims could be changed from being directed to "a compound" to "a composition including such compound", or to "the use of that compound in a composition for a particular purpose", without offending EPCa. 123(2).

—Addition of subject-matter by excision of text (EPO Guideline C–VI, 5.8) **76.23**

EPO Decision T 260/85, "*Coaxial connector/AMP*" has also been published at [1989] 7 EPOR 403, and *EPO Decision T* 133/85, "*Amendments/XEROX*", also cited in the Main Work, is further reported (*abridged* OJEPO 12/1988, 441). The principle of these cases is that removal of a claim feature does not violate EPCa. 123(2), provided that the skilled person would directly and unambiguously recognise that: (1) the feature was not explained as essential to the disclosure; (2) it is not, as such, indispensable for the function of the invention in the light of the technical problem it seeks to solve; *and* (3) the removal requires no real modification of the feature to compensate for the change, see: *EPO Decision T* 331/87, "*Removal of feature/HOUDAILLE*" (OJEPO 1–2/1991, 22; [1991] EPOR 194); *EPO Decision T* 467/90, "*Spooling process.../THOMSON-CSF*" ([1991] EPOR 115); and *EPO Decision T* 212/87, "*Sterilising pouch/LMG*" ([1991] EPOR 144), in each of which a feature was allowed to be deleted from a claim because the skilled man would have perceived this as an inessential limitation. However, a disclosure of a vague and general character will not satisfy this three point test (*EPO Decision T* 527/88, "*Interconnected bags/WAVIN*", [1991] EPOR 184), this being a case where a divisional application was not permitted as not being in conformity with its parent. Also, removal of a claim feature is not permissible if that feature has been presented as essential, or if it is indispensable for solving the technical problem in issue, or if its removal requires modification of other features (*EPO Decision T* 514/88, "*Infusor/ALZA*", [1990] 2 EPOR 157 and *EPO Decision T* 24/88, "*Unacceptable generalisation/SGS*", [1990] 4 EPOR 274).

The silence of a claim as to the presence of a particular feature does not necessarily mean that this must be absent: thus to specify such absence could amount to addition of new matter, see *EPO Decision T* 170/87, "*Hot gas cooler/SULZER*" (OJEPO 11/1989, 441; [1990] 1 EPOR 14).

PART II

PROVISIONS ABOUT INTERNATIONAL CONVENTIONS

SECTION 77 **77.01**

Note. The amendments to section 77, noted in the Main Work, came into effect on January 7, 1991 (S.I. 1990 No. 2168).

SECTION 77—RELEVANT RULES

77.02A **Rule 80 [1990]**—*European patents and applications (UK): translations*

New rule 80 reads:

80. Schedule 4 shall have effect in cases where translations are required by the Act to be filed in connection with applications for, and with, European patents (UK).

Note. The individual paragraphs of Schedule 4 correspond to previous rules 79A–79F and are dealt with respectively in paras. 77.03–77.06, 78.03 and 80.02 *supra*.

77.03 **Schedule 4, paragraph 1 [1990]**—*Translations of European patents (UK) filed under section 76*

This rule corresponds to previous rule 79A. Subparagraph (1) thereof now reads:

1.—(1) A translation filed under section 77(6) shall be filed in duplicate and shall be accompanied by—

(a) Patents Form 54/77 in duplicate, in the case of a translation filed under section 77(6)(a), or
(b) Patents Form 55/77 in duplicate, in the case of a translation filed under section 77(6)(b)

In subparagraph (2), "77(6)(*a*)" has been changed to "77(6)"; and, after the word "patent", "(including the claims)" has been added. In subparagraph (3)(h), after "free from" have been added the words "extraneous matter and also"; and at the end "and" has been added. In subparagraph (5), "paragraph (2)" has been changed to "subparagraph (2)".

77.04 **Schedule 4, paragraph 2 [1990]**—*Periods prescribed under section 77(6)*

This rule corresponds to previous rule 79B, and remains unaltered except that, in subparagraph (2), "an amendment to" has been changed to "the specification as amended of".

77.05 **Schedule 4, paragraph 5 [1990]**—*Verification of translation*

This rule corresponds to previous rule 79E, and otherwise has been altered; by substituting semi-colons at the end of subparagraphs (a)–(c); deleting the formal "or" from each of subparagraphs (a) and (b); and, in subparagraph (b), replacing "the amendment" by "the specification as amended".

77.06 **Schedule 4, paragraph 6 [1990]**—*Inspections of translations*

This rule corresponds to previous rule 79F, and otherwise remains unaltered.

COMMENTARY ON SECTION 77

Effect of European patent (UK) (subs. (1)) **77.09**

The authentic text of a European patent (UK) is that on file in the EPO on which the grant was made. Therefore, misprints in a published version have no effect and the EPO can correct these, the printed text having no binding character (*EPO Legal Advice 17/90*, OJEPO 6/1990, 260).

The printed version of a European patent now indicates any applications which were divided out of it and which may therefore mature into individual patents.

Registration of European patents (UK) in other countries **77.10**

For an updated position on the acceptability of European patents (UK) for registration in other countries in the same way as patents granted under the Patent Acts, see (1991–92) 21 CIPA 93.

Translation of European patents (UK) (Subss. (6)–(9)) **77.12**

Rules 79A, 79B, 79E and 79F are now respectively paragraphs 1, 2, 5 and 6 of Schedule 4, see paras. 77.03–77.06 *supra*. This paragraph 1(2) now applies also in the case of amendment of a European patent (UK), for example in opposition proceedings before the EPO, and more expressly stipulates that the claims must be translated as part of the specification. This is so even though claims a translation of the claims in the English language will be included in the publication of the specification of the European patent as granted, or as amended, see also para. 77.16 of the Main Work. Where the European patent (UK) is amended, Schedule 4. paragraph 2(2) now requires a translation to be provided of "the specification as amended", rather than a "translation of the amendment" as under the former rule 79B [1982].

General obligations on proprietor of European patent (UK) **77.14**

Note. This para. should have been preceded by the heading:

"PRACTICE UNDER SECTION 77"

Translations **77.16**

For further comment on the authentic text of a European patent (UK), see para. 77.09 *supra*.

Because the translation is published as such, it must be presented in compliance with the formal requirements of Schedule 4, paragraph 1 (for which see para. 77.03 *supra*) (O.J. August 22, 1990). Also, a verification of the translation of the European patent (UK) must identify this patent by its publication number. If a translation is permitted to be filed late (under the provisions of rule 110(4)), and after the patent has already been advertised in the O.J. as having become void, its re-instatement is also advertised in the O.J., see *e.g.* O.J. August 28, 1991.

Amendment **77.18**

Rules 79A and 79E are now respectively paragraphs 1 and 5 of Schedule 4, see paras. 77.03 and 77.05 *supra*. The amendment of former rule 79A(2), consequent on the amendment of section 77(6)(*b*), now makes it necessary to translate the whole of an amended specification under the substituted Schedule 4, paragraph 1(2), and Schedule 4, paragraphs 2(2) and 5 now so require, see paras. 77.04 and 77.05 *supra*. The filing of an amended translation is advertised in the O.J., see O.J. January 31, 1990.

78.01 SECTION 78

Note. The amendments to section 78, noted in the Main Work, came into effect on January 7, 1991 (S.I. 1990 No. 2168).

SECTION 78—RELEVANT RULES

78.03 Schedule 4, paragraph 3 [1990]—*Translations of claims of applications for European patents (UK) filed under section 78(7)*

Previous rule 79C has been reworded in the substituted paragraph 3 of Schedule 4 to read:

3.—(1) A translation of the claims of an application for a European Patent (UK),—

(a) in the case of an application which has been published by the European Patent Office, may be filed under subsection (7) of section 78 after the application has been so published; and
(b) in the case of an application which has not been so published but which is the subject of proceedings before the European Patent Office by virtue of Article 150 of the European Patent Convention, may be filed under that subsection after the application has been published under Article 21 of the Patent Co-operation Treaty.

(2) A translation filed by virtue of subparagraph (1) above shall be filed in duplicate and shall be accompanied by Patents Form 56/77, also filed in duplicate.

(3) The translation shall comply with the requirements contained in paragraph 1(3) above.

PRACTICE UNDER SECTION 78

78.10 *Translation of claims*

The new paragraph 3 of Schedule 4 to the Rules (reprinted in para. 78.03 *supra*), which has replaced former rule 79C, also now expressly provides (in paragraph 1(1)(b)) for the submission of a translation of the claims of a Euro-PCT application as described in para. 79.04 of the Main Work, but the filing of any translation under section 78(7) of the claims of a European or Euro-PCT application (UK) is now explicitly prohibited before publication of such application. Rule 79A is now paragraph 1 of Schedule 4.

It is not clear that the intention of paragraph 3(1)(b) has been fully achieved, *i.e.* it can be questioned whether this provision enables a translation of the claims of a Euro-PCT application to be filed before entry into the European phase. This is because EPCa. 150 is of quite general application, enabling the EPO to be an international authority under the PCT, a designated office and an elected office. Because EPCa. 150(2) prescribes that the provisions of the PCT shall prevail, PCTaa. 22 and 39 prevent proceedings taking place before the EPO as designated or elected office before expiry of the prescribed 20 or 30 months' period, as the case may be. If the EPO is not the receiving office, the application is not the subject of proceedings before the EPO until the expiry of the prescribed 20 or 30 months' period and the translation (if required) into an EPC official language has been filed. The obvious intention of this paragraph 3(1)(b) is that it should relate to an application to which section 79 refers, *i.e.* a Euro-PCT application for which the EPO is a designated office pursuant to EPCa. 152.

COMMENTARY ON SECTION 79

Provisional protection arising from Euro-PCT application (subs. (3)) **79.04**

Paragraph 3(1)(b) of Schedule 4 to the Rules (reprinted in para. 78.03 *supra*) now expressly provides for the filing of a translation of the claims of a Euro-PCT application designating the United Kingdom. This provision is discussed in para. 78.10 *supra*.

If the Euro-PCT application has not entered the European phase when the translation of the claims is filed, the international publication ("WO") number must be inserted on PF 56/77 which must also contain a declaration that the United Kingdom has been designated in the international application. Whilst the filing of the translation is advertised in the O.J., there can be no entry in the register since the register entry for a Euro-PCT application is not established until after the application has entered the European phase. The European filing number should be notified to the Patent Office as soon as it is known (O.J. December 28, 1989).

SECTION 80 **80.01**

Note. The amendment to section 80, noted in the Main Work, came into effect on January 7, 1991 (S.I. 1990 No. 2168).

SECTION 80—RELEVANT RULE

Schedule 4, paragraph 4 [1990]—*Corrected translations filed under section 80(3)* **80.02**

This rule corresponds to previous rule 79D, and remains unaltered except for the replacement in sub-paragraph (2) of "rule 79A(3) and (4)" by "paragraph 1(3) and (4) above".

COMMENTARY ON SECTION 80

Correction of translation (subs. (3)) **80.06**

Rule 79D has become paragraph 4 of Schedule 4 to the Rules, see para. 80.02 *supra*.

PRACTICE UNDER SECTION 80

80.10 *Filing of corrected translation (Rules, Sched. 4, para. 4)*

Former rules 79A–79F are now paragraphs 1–6 of Schedule 4 to the Rules. For former rule 79D, see para. 80.02 *supra*.

SECTION 81—RELEVANT RULES

81.04 **Rule 82 [1990]**—*Procedure where section 81(2)(b)(ii) applies*

In paragraph (2), the words "two months" have been changed for "four months".

PRACTICE UNDER SECTION 81

Procedure for conversion

81.11 *—Initiation of conversion*

As predicted in the Main Work, the period within which the translation, when required, and PF 40/77 must be filed (together with PF 7/77, if required, and PF 9/77) has been extended to four months from the date when the Comptroller is notified by the foreign patent office of the applicant's request for conversion to an application under the Act. This gives the applicant more time to make the translation when the European application was filed in French or German. This period remains extensible under present rules 110(3) and (4). However, the 20 month period for the foreign patent office to make that notification (specified under r. 82(1)) remains inextensible under rule 110(2).

82.01

SECTION 82

Note. Subsections (5) and (6) have each been prospectively amended to substitute for the words "proper law of" therein the words "law applicable to" (Contracts (Applicable Law) Act 1990 (c. 36, Sched. 4, para. 3).

COMMENTARY ON SECTION 82

82.06 *—Jurisdiction under section 82 where there is no prior agreement between the parties*

Even in an uncontested case concerning a European application, the Comptroller requires to satisfy himself that he has jurisdiction under section 82 but, if satisfied that jurisdiction arises under either subsection (4) or (5), then he need not decide which of these subsections applies (*Travenol Laboratories' Application*, SRIS O/45/90, *noted* IPD 13141).

84.01

SECTION 84 [Repealed]

Note. The repeal of section 84 took effect from August 13, 1990 (S.I. 1990 No. 1440).

SECTION 85 [Repealed] 85.01

Note. The repeal of section 85 took effect from August 13, 1990 (S.I. 1990 No. 1400).

COMMENTARY ON SECTION 86

General **86.03**

At a further diplomatic conference in December 1989, also held in Luxembourg, the CPC was further revised with revisions also being made to the proposed Implementing Regulations. The "Agreement" and "Protocol", each referred to in the Main Work, were also formally signed. All four of these documents have been published (OJEC L.401, 31.12.89), but they await ratification before coming into force. The revised form of the CPC replaces the original form signed in 1975. Unfortunately, the revisions have the effect of changing most of the numbers of the CPC articles. All these revised numbers are noted in this Supplement against the paras. to which reference was made in the Main Work to articles of the 1975 CPC form. Thus, CPCa. 91 referred to in this para. 86.03 of the Main Work now becomes CPCa. 84 [1998].

Basis for giving effect to Community patents under United Kingdom law **86.04**

In the references to CPC articles contained in para. 86.04 of the Main Work: CPCa. 93 has been deleted from the 1989 form of the CPC; CPCaa. 29–36 have become CPCaa. 25–34 [1989], with CPCaa. 30 and 31 [1989] being new articles following original CPCa. 33; CPCaa. 39–49 have become CPCaa. 38–48 [1989]; CPCaa. 69, 70 and 72 have become CPCaa. 67, 68 and 70 [1989]; CPCaa. 74, 76 and 79 have become CPCaa. 71, 72 and 74 [1989], with original CPCa. 75 having become CPCa. 35 [1989]; and CPCa 89 has become CPCa. 83 [1989], see para. 86.03 *supra*.

COMMENTARY ON SECTION 87

General **87.03**

The revisions for litigation of Community patents, mentioned briefly in the Main Work, have now been embodied in a formal "Protocol for the Settlement of Litigation of Community Patents". This was formally signed at the 1989 Luxembourg diplomatic conference and then published (OJEC L.401/34–44, 31.12.89).

The present provisions of section 87 **87.04**

Original CPCaa. 63 and 73, referred to in the Main Work, have now been deleted, but corresponding provisions are present in the Protocol on litigation, for which see para. 87.03, *supra*.

SECTION 88 [Repealed] 88.01

Note. The prospective repeal of section 88, noted in the Main Work, came into effect on January 7, 1991 (S.I. 1990 No. 2168).

COMMENTARY ON SECTION 88 [Prospectively repealed]

88.04 *Reasons for repeal of section 88*

CPCa. 69, referred to in the Main Work, has become CPCa. 67 [1989], see para. 86.03, *supra*.

Schedule 1 to the CJJA has been replaced with a new version thereof consequent on the accession of Greece to the Brussels Convention (Civil Jurisdiction and Judgments Act 1982 (Amendment) Order 1989 (S.I. 1989 No. 2346); and a further revision of this Schedule has provided for the eventual accession of Portugal and Spain thereto (Civil Jurisdiction and Judgments Act 1982 (Amendment) Order 1990 (S.I. 1990 No. 2591)), this becoming effective for Spain from December 1, 1991 though still prospective as regards Portugal. Provision has also been made for the eventual extension of the CJJA to Contracting States to the Lugano Convention, *i.e.* to the EFTA group of countries (Civil Jurisdiction and Judgments Act 1991 (c. 12)). When this Act comes into force, Schedule 1 of the CJJA will once more be replaced with a modified version in order to accommodate the new accessions to the Brussels and Lugano Conventions.

89.01 **SECTION 89**

Note. The prospective substitution of section 89, noted in the Main Work, took effect from January 7, 1991 (S.I. 1990 No. 2168).

SECTION 89—RELEVANT RULE

89.03 **Rule 85(8)–(13) [1990]**—*International applications for patents: section 89*

Former rule 85(4)–(6) has been replaced by rule 85(8)–(13) which reads:

(8) Where, in relation to an international application for a patent (UK), the applicant desires that section 89(1) shall not cease to apply to the application by virtue of the operation of section 89(3), application shall be made to the comptroller on Patents Form 44/77, accompanied by a statement of the facts upon which the applicant relies.

(9) An international application for a patent (UK) shall not be treated as withdrawn under the Act if it, or the designation of the United Kingdom in it, is deemed to be withdrawn under the Patent Co-operation Treaty where, in the same or comparable circumstances in relation to an application under the Act (other than an international application)—

(a) the comptroller could have directed that an irregularity be rectified under rule 100 or that an extension be granted under rule 110; and
(b) the comptroller determines that the application would not have been treated as withdrawn under the Act.

(10) Where under section 89(3) an application is not to be treated as withdrawn and the applicant wishes to proceed—

(a) the comptroller may amend any document received by the Patent Office from the receiving office or the International Bureau and alter any period or time which is specified in the Act or these Rules upon such terms (including payment of any appropriate prescribed fee) as he may direct; and
(b) the fee prescribed under section 89A(3) shall not be payable.

(11) Where the applicant satisfies the comptroller that,—

(a) because of an error made by the receiving office, an international application for a patent (UK) has been accorded a date of filing which is not correct; or
(b) the declaration made under Article 8(1) of the Patent Co-operation Treaty has been cancelled or corrected by the receiving office or the International Bureau because of an error made by the Office or the Bureau,

the comptroller may amend any document received by the Patent Office from the receiving office or the International Bureau or alter any period or time which is specified in the Act or these Rules as if the error were an error on the part of the Patent Office.

(12) Where—

(a) an international application for a patent (UK) purports to designate the United Kingdom; and
(b) the applicant alleges that he has been refused a filing date under the said Treaty on account of an error or omission in any institution having functions under the said Treaty,

The applicant may apply to the comptroller for it to be treated as an application under the Act by filing Patents Form 44/77, accompanied by a statement of the facts upon which he relies; and the comptroller may amend any document filed by the applicant and alter any period or time which is specified in the Act or these Rules upon such terms as he may direct.

(13) In this rule "receiving office" has the same meaning as in the Patent Co-operation Treaty.

Note. Paragraphs (8) and (11)–(13) of rule 85 [1990] are derived respectively from paragraphs (4), (4A), (5) and (6) of rule 86 [1982]. Paragraph (9) is new in terms but derived from the final clause of section 89(3) and paragraph (10) makes consequent provisions for dealing with the situation where this subsection applies. Paragraphs (1)–(7) of rule 85 [1990] are dealt with in para. 89A.02 *infra*.

RELEVANT RULES FOR INTERNATIONAL APPLICATIONS

89.05 Rule 118 [1990]—*Transmittal, international and search fees*

The rule title has been changed. In paragraph (1), the word "prescribed" has been inserted before "transmittal". Paragraphs (1A) and (2) have been renumbered as (2) and (3) respectively and, in the first of these, "or" (between paragraph (1A)(*a*) and (*b*) in the Main Work) has become "and".

It seems likely that this rule will have to be amended from July 1, 1992 because of changes in the PCT Regulations which will then come into effect. There will be need either for the rule to refer to the fees for confirmation of a designation, late payment, and the making of fee refunds, or to limit the rule to payment of the transmittal fee (which is determined by the receiving office) leaving the other fees to be governed by the PCT Regulations themselves.

89.07 Rule 120 [1990]—*Fees for international preliminary examination*

This rule has been reworded and now reads:

120. Where an applicant makes a demand to the Patent Office, as International Preliminary Examining Authority, for international preliminary examination under Article 31 of the said Treaty, he shall—

(a) in accordance with rule 58 of those Regulations, pay the appropriate prescribed preliminary examination fee;
(b) in accordance with rule 57 of those Regulations, pay the handling fee therein referred to; and
(c) upon request by the Patent Office, pay to it an amount which is the equivalent in sterling of the search fee referred to in rule 118(3).

It seems likely that, because of changes in the PCT Regulations coming into effect from July 1, 1992, rule 120(*b*) will then either have to be amended to refer to possible refund of the handling fee or be deleted, and rule 120(*c*) may also need to be deleted.

89.08 Rule 121 [1990]—*Additional fees for further inventions*

The comma after "complied with" has been deleted; and the word "international" (final occurrence) has been changed to "appropriate prescribed".

Because of changes in the PCT Regulations coming into effect from July 1, 1992, rule 121 will then require amendment if the Patent Office should then wish to charge a fee for hearing a protest, as these Regulations will then permit.

COMMENTARY ON SECTION 89

89.13 *General*

The definition of "receiving office", previously in rule 85(6) [1982], is now in rule 85(13) [1990], see para. 89.03 *supra*. Contrary to what was assumed when compiling the Main Work, rule 85 [1990] does not use the terms "international phase" and "national phase". The discussion of the international phase in *EPH* (2nd edition) is in Chapter 16, not Chapter 15 thereof as stated in the Main Work. Amendments to the PCT Regulations come into force on July 1, 1992, details of which were published, with a commentary, in the PCT Gazette No. 20/1991 (September 5, 1991), see also the paper by C. Jones ((1991–92) 21 CIPA 54). Some of the consequential amendments to the Patents Rules 1990, which would seem necessary or desirable, are noted in paras. 5.07, 89.24, 89.26, 89.27, 89A.18 and 89B.07 *infra,* see also further comment in para. 89B.07 *infra.*

Advantages of the PCT **89.15**

Sub-rules 110(3A) and (3C) have become sub-rules 110(4) and (6) respectively.

Patent Office as an international authority

—Transmittal, international and search fees (r. 118) **89.24**

From July 1, 1992 the PCT Regulations will be amended with fees then being introduced for confirmation of country designations (PCTr. 15.5) and for late payment (PCTr. 16 *bis,* 1), and fee refunds will be made available (under PCTrr. 15.6, and 16.2) when timely withdrawals are made. If rule 118 is then retained, it should be amended to refer to these matters.

—Handling and preliminary examination fees (r. 120) **89.26**

Rule 120 (reprinted in para. 89.07 *supra*) has been revised to remove the unenforceable requirement that the international preliminary examination fee may accompany the demand, but omits to prescribe the *due date* for payment of this to which the Main Work refers in relation to PCTr. 58.1(*b*). When this fee is changed, the amount payable is determined by the Fees Rules in force at the due date, and not that at the date of payment where this is later (*PCT Applicant's Guide*, Vol. 1, para. 145, *mutatis mutandis*, see also paras. 222 and 234(iii) thereof).

Sub-rule 85(11) [1990], whose application is not restricted to a review under subsections 89(3) and (5) (pursuant to PCTa. 25), is discussed further in para. 89B.13 *infra*. Sub-rule 85(12) [1990] relates to a review under subsection 89(5) of a refusal to accord an international filing date, for which see para. 89.37 *inffra*.

When the PCT Regulations are amended from July 1, 1992, a refund of the handling fee will become available (under PCTr. 57.6). If rule 120 is then retained, it will require amendment to reflect this change. In any event rule 120(*c*) should then be deleted as an international preliminary examination authority will no longer be required to examine any claims excluded from the international search.

—Additional fees for further inventions (r. 121) **89.27**

When the PCT Regulations are amended from July 1, 1992, the Patent Office will have the power to charge a fee for considering a protest against a requirement to pay an additional fee for international preliminary examination under PCTr.

68.3(*e*). That would presumably require an addition to rule 121 and a further item in the Schedule to the Patents (Fees) Rules.

89.29 —*Delay or loss in mail (PCTr. 81.1)*

Note that European mail now requires an airmail sticker unless of minimal weight.

89.32 —*No appeal*

An example of the Patent Office acting as an international authority, and affording the applicant a hearing on his request for amendment of the Request Form, is *Henderson's Application* (SRIS O/17/90).

89.35 *Patent Office review of deemed withdrawal (subs. (3))*

Paragraphs (4), (4A) and (5) of rule 85 [1982], each cited in the Main Work, have become respectively paragraphs (8), (11) and (12) of rule 85 [1990], see para. 89.03 *supra*. New rule 85(9) enables the Comptroller to exercise discretionary powers (as he has under rules 100 and 110), discussed in paras. 123.20–123.22 and 123.30 and 123.36 in the Main Work and *infra*) in order to reinstate an application under the Act, even though it (or the United Kingdom designation for it) has been deemed to have been withdrawn in the international phase. New rule 85(10) then provides the Comptroller with further powers which he could exercise to give practical effect to the operation of rule 85(9). Thus, sub-rules 85(8)–(11) provide a substratum of rules which should enable a greater flexibility for the Comptroller to alleviate the consequences of errors or omissions occurring during the international phase, particularly where these have occurred inadvertently or due to no fault of the applicant or his agent.

The new rule pursuant to the last part of section 89(3) is sub-rule 85(9) [1990]. Disappointingly, this new sub-rule does not refer to rule 97 (reprinted at para. 119.02 in the Main Work), nor to rule 101 (as amended, for which see para. 123.08 in the Main Work and *infra*), or to rule 111 (as amended, for which see para. 123.11 in the Main Work and *infra*). Thus, it appears that the Comptroller does not have general discretion to apply any provisions of the Act and Rules which are pertinent pursuant to PCTa. 48(2) and PCTr. 82*bis*, other than those of rules 100 [1990] and 110 [1990].

It is also disappointing that new paragraph (9) is confined to the operation of subsection (3) and specifically to an irregularity in procedure or non-observed time limit attributable wholly or in part to an error, default or omission on the part of the international authority which has resulted in the application being deemed withdrawn. Thus, paragraph (9) is not applicable to a loss of rights which does not result in the application being deemed withdrawn (a matter discussed in para. 89B.14 of the Main Work). It is therefore still questionable whether the United Kingdom has yet met its obligations under PCTa. 26 and 48(2) and PCTr. 82*bis*. In practice, the only real advantage of rule 85(9) [1990], made pursuant to the last provision of section 89(3), is that rule 100 may be applied to grant a discretionary extension to a term specified by the receiving office for removal of a formalities objection when the non-compliance with this specified term resulted in an international application being declared withdrawn.

The purpose of rule 85(10)(a) [1990] is to enable the Comptroller to give the applicant time to do things which he may not have had the opportunity to do in a curtailed international phase, such as to file a copy of the priority document. It also enables the Comptroller to shorten time limits, as well as extend them. In particular, he may require PF 9/77 to be filed well in advance of the 22 months' period prescribed by rule 85(7) [1990] in order that publication under section 16 will not be delayed unduly (see para. 89B.15 of the Main Work).

The purpose of rule 85(10)(b) [1990] is to make it clear that the fee on PF NP 1 is not payable in addition to the fee on PF 44/77. Rule 85(11) [1990] replaces rule 85(4A) [1982].

The two months' time limit for filing PF 44/77 prescribed by PCTr. 51.3 is not mentioned in rule 85(8) [1990] which replaces rule 85(4) [1982], or in rule 85(12) [1990] which replaces rule 85(5) [1982]. Rule 85(12) [1990] is brief. However, the Comptroller's wide discretion under this paragraph does not extend to enable him to review a refusal to accord an international filing date: it applies only to subsequent events, as described *supra* in connection with rule 85(10)(a) [1990]. The Comptroller can only accord a United Kingdom filing date under section 89(5) when he has determined that the application in fact has met PCT requirements for according an international filing date (PCTa. 11).

International application designating the EPO (subs. (4)) **89.36**

The commentary in the Main Work states that there is no official way for the United Kingdom Patent Office to be supplied with a copy of the international application when the designation of the United Kingdom is coupled with a request for a European patent. However, the applicant can authorise the Office to obtain a copy of the international application from the International Bureau under PCTr. 94. It is not known whether the International Bureau would oblige when no international filing date has been accorded.

The review of PCTa. 25, referred to in the Main Work, is now at *EPH* (2nd ed.), Section 17.6.

Patent Office review of refusal to accord international filing date (subs. (5)) **89.37**

The rule under which a review by the Comptroller of refusal to accord an international filing date is sub-rule 85(12) [1990], which replaces sub-rule 85(5) [1982]. The period for filing PF 44/77 is two months from the date of the letter from the receiving office notifying the applicant that the application will not be treated as an international application (PCTrr. 20.7, 51.3). Sub-rule 85(12) [1990] gives the Comptroller discretion to amend the papers of an international application and alter time limits as necessary similar to the power afforded by sub-rule 85(10) [1990], for which see para. 89.35 *supra*. An application of this type was *Secretary of State for Defence's Application* (SRIS O/72/90, *noted* IPD 14013) where the evidence was deemed insufficient, but the International Bureau would be asked to publish a warning as the Applicant intended to pursue the matter before the Bureau and the designated or elected offices.

PRACTICE UNDER SECTION 89

International phase **89.43**

Telephone enquiries concerning the filing of international applications (and the fees payable in respect thereof) should now be made to 0633 814611 or 071–438 4724. Any queries on PCT formalities and objections on them can be made to 0633 814586.

No filing certificate for an international application is issued by the United Kingdom Patent Office until the documents have been checked and forwarded to the International Bureau. This may take some time. If an applicant, or agent, wishes to receive confirmation that his communication to the Office has been received, he may file a duplicate of his covering letter and request that this be returned to him as confirmation of receipt (O.J. February 7, 1990 and (1989–90) 19 CIPA 130), but this procedure is no confirmation that the papers filed meet the PCT requirements.

When ordering a certified copy to be made by the Patent Office in support of a claim to priority in an international application, the fee payable on PF 24/77 is that for a certificate sealed and attached to documents.

When amendments are filed to an international application filed with the United Kingdom Patent Office as receiving office, these should be filed in triplicate.

89.44 *Request for review (subss. (3) and (5))*

Notwithstanding the comment in the Main Work, it seems that there will be little change in practice under these subsections. The only change in the rules relating thereto is a slight relaxation in the circumstances in which these provisions may be invoked, for which see para. 89.35 *supra*.

89A.01

SECTION 89A

Note. The prospective addition of section 89A, noted in the Main Work, took effect from January 7, 1991 (S.I. 1990 No. 2168).

SECTION 89A—RELEVANT RULE

89A.02 **Rule 85 [1990]**—*International applications for patents: Section 89*

Paragraphs (1)–(3) of former rule 85 have been amended to form new paragraphs (1)–(7) reading:

85.—(1) Subject to the provisions of this rule, in relation to an international application for a patent (UK) which is, under section 89, to be treated as an application for a patent under the Act, the prescribed periods for the purposes of section 89A(3) and (5) are—

(a) the period of twenty months calculated from the date which, by virtue of section 89B(1)(b), is to be treated as the declared priority date or, where there is no declared priority date, the date of filing of the international application for a patent (UK); or

(b) in a case where the United Kingdom has been elected in accordance with Chapter II of the Patent Co-operation Treaty—

  (i) before the expiry of nineteen months calculated from the declared priority date, the period of thirty months calculated from the declared priority date; or

  (ii) where there is no declared priority date and the United Kingdom has been so elected before the expiry of nineteen months calculated from the date of filing of the international application for a patent (UK), the period of thirty months calculated from the date of filing of that international application.

(2) Where, in accordance with paragraph 1 of Schedule 2, the information specified in subparagraph (2)(a)(ii) of that paragraph is added to an international application for a patent (UK), rule 113(1) shall not apply in respect of that information; and where the translation of the information, the filing of which is required to satisfy the relevant conditions of section 89A(3), has not been filed at the Patent Office before the end of the relevant period referred to in paragraph (1) above,—

(a) the comptroller shall give notice to the applicant at the address furnished by the applicant in accordance with rule 30 requiring the applicant to file the translation within the period of two months commencing on the day on which the notice is sent; and
(b) the relevant period shall be treated in respect of the translation as not expiring until the end of the period specified in the notice given under subparagraph (a) above.

(3) In the case of an international application for a patent (UK),—

(a) rule 5(1) shall not apply if the applicant, on filing the application, states in writing to the receiving office that the invention has been displayed at an international exhibition;
(b) rule 5(2) may be complied with—
    (i) where subparagraph (a) of paragraph (1) above applies, at any time before the end of the period of twenty-two months, or
    (ii) where subparagraph (b) of paragraph (1) above applies, at any time before the end of the period of thirty-two months,

  after the declared priority date or, if there is no declared priority date, the date of filing of the international application for a patent (UK);
(c) rule 6(6) shall have effect with the substitution, for the reference to the period of twenty-one months after the declared priority date, of a reference to the period of twenty-two months after that date;
(d) where the United Kingdom has been elected in accordance with Chapter II of the Patent Co-operation Treaty before the expiry of the nineteenth month after the declared priority date, rule 6(6) shall have effect with the substitution, for the reference to the period of twenty-one months after the declared priority date, of a reference to the period of thirty-two months after that date; and
(e) where a translation into English of a document or part of a document is required by the Act or these Rules to be filed—

(i) before the end of the relevant period referred to in paragraph (1)(a) above, verification of the translation, as required by rule 113(1), may be given to the comptroller at any time before the end of the period of twenty-two months, or

(ii) before the end of the relevant period referred to in paragraph (1)(b) above, verification of the translation, as required by rule 113(1), may be given to the comptroller at any time before the end of the period of thirty-two months,

after the declared priority date or, if there is no declared priority date, the date of filing of the international application for a patent (UK).

(4) Where the relevant period referred to in paragraph (1) above has been extended under rule 100 or rule 110 so as to expire later than one month before the end of a period prescribed by paragraph (3) above or (7) below, paragraphs (3) above and (7) below shall have effect with the substitution for the period so prescribed of a period ending one month later than the relevant period referred to in paragraph (1) above as so extended.

(5) For the purposes of section 89A(3) and (5), to the extent that the application and any amendment as published under the Patent Co-operation Treaty and any amendment annexed to the international preliminary examination report under Chapter II of the Treaty are not in English, a translation into English of the application as originally filed or, as the case may be, of the application as originally filed and of the amendment is necessary; however, the translation—

(a) shall exclude the request and abstract unless—

(i) the applicant expressly requests the comptroller to proceed earlier than the expiry of the period prescribed in paragraph (1) above; and

(ii) a copy of the application published by the International Bureau has not yet been sent to the Patent Office in accordance with the Treaty; and

(b) shall include any textual matter in the drawings in a form which complies with rule 49.5(d) of the Patent Co-operation Treaty.

(6) The comptroller shall publish any translation supplied in accordance with section 89A(3) or (5) following the filing of Patents Form 43/77 and payment of the prescribed fee.

(7) In the case of an international application for a patent (UK) in respect of which the conditions specified in section 89A(3)(a) are satisfied, the period prescribed,—

(a) for the purposes of sections 13(2), 15(5)(b) and 17(1),—

(i) where subparagraph (a) of paragraph (1) above has effect, shall be the period which expires twenty-two months; or
(ii) where subparagraph (b) of paragraph (1) above, has effect, shall be the period which expires thirty-two months; and

(b) for the purposes of section 18(1)—
(i) where subparagraph (a) of paragraph (1) above applies, shall be the period which expires two years; or
(ii) where subparagraph (b) of paragraph (1) above applies, shall be the period which expires thirty-two months,

after the declared priority date or, if there is no declared priority date, the date of filing of the international application for a patent (UK).

Notes. 1. Paragraphs (1), (2) and (3) of rule 85 [1990] are derived respectively from paragraphs (1), (1A) and (2A) of rule 85 [1982]. Paragraphs (6) and (7) of rule 85 [1990] are likewise derived respectively from paragraphs (2) and (3) of rule 85 [1982]. The proviso to rule 85(1) [1982] was no longer needed. Paragraphs (4) and (5) of rule 85 [1990] are new in terms, paragraph (4) being consequent on the possibility of extensions of time limits under rules 100 and 110, and paragraph (5) modifying in most cases the need to provide full translations of all the documents forming part of a PCT application.

2. Rule 85(13) [1990] (reprinted in para. 89.03 *supra*) supplies a definition of the term "receiving office" used in these sub-rules.

3. Changes in the PCT Regulations which become effective from July 1, 1992 may result in some amendment of at least rule 85(5) (*content of translation*).

OTHER RELEVANT RULES **89A.03**

Rule 102(1)(*b*) [1982] has been renumbered as rule 102(1)(a) [1990].

COMMENTARY ON SECTION 89A

Valid entry into the United Kingdom phase (subss. (2) and (3)(a))

General **89A.08**

The entry into force of section 89A(3), which accords with PCTaa. 22 ad 39 and PCTr. 47.1(*c*), has enabled the complex proviso to rule 85(1) [1982] to be dropped. Time limits for actions to be taken after entry into the United Kingdom phase are now nearly all measured from the declared priority date (or from the international filing date) so that the problems of aggregate time limits (described at para. 89A.36 of the Main Work) are avoided. Also, time limits have been rationalised so that there is a single period, usually of about two months, following entry into the United Kingdom phase, for meeting nearly all conditions which have to be met and for which the applicant must be given time after entry into the United Kingdom phase. These include: filing PF 9/77 (for which see para. 89A.24); PF 7/77, when required (for which see para. 89A.28); verification of the translation of the international application, when required (for which see para. 89A.21); and a verified translation of the priority document, when required (for which see para. 89A.27). For the period for filing PF 10/77, see para. 89A.25 *infra*.

89A.09 —*Payment of the national fee*

Rule 85(1) [1990] replaces rule 85(1) [1982]. Rule 85 [1990] does not define the national fee, nor does it prescribe the fee payable under section 89A(3), the latter being prescribed only in the current Fees Rules (for which see para. 144.01).

89A.10 —*Filing of translation of the international application*

Rule 85(2A)(*c*) [1982], cited in the Main Work, has become rule 85(3)(e) [1990], see para. 89A.02 *supra*.

89A.11 —*Time limits*

Sub-rules 85(1) and 110(3A) [1982] have been respectively replaced by sub-rules 85(1) [1990] and 110(4) [1990].

Where the period for entering the national phase under rule 85(1) [1990] (for paying the national fee; and, if necessary, filing translation of the international application, for which see para. 89A.02 *supra*) is extended under rule 100 or 110, then the later time periods under rules 85(3) and (7) [1990] (for filing: declaration of priority; certified copy of priority application; translation thereof; verification of translation of the international application; verification of translation of the priority application; and PF 7/77, 9/77 and probably 10/77), are (if necessary) each extended automatically to one month after the expiry of the extended period under rule 85(1) (r. 85(4) [1990]) if this expires later than the prescribed 22 or 32 months' period. Entry into the United Kingdom phase is, in effect, delayed in the event of the applicant being invited to file a translation of information concerning the deposit of a micro-organism pursuant to rule 85(2)(a) [1990], for which see para. 89A.16. However, this does not postpone any other time limits so that the applicant may find it necessary to file PF 7/77, 9/77, probably 10/77 and the other documents mentioned above before filing the translation of information concerning the deposit of a micro-organism. The provisions of rule 85(2) [1990] are thus a vestige of the inelegant, but ingenious, proviso to former rule 85(1) [1982].

89A.14 *Amendments in the international phase (subss. (5) and (6))*

The filing of a translation of amended claims published in a language other than English is now regulated by rule 85(5) [1990].

Rule 85(2A)(*c*) [1982], cited in the Main Work, has become rule 85(3)(e) [1990], see para. 89A.02 *supra*.

89A.15 *Copy and translation of priority document*

Rule 85 [1990] does not require that a verified translation of the priority document shall be accompanied by an uncertified copy of the priority document itself. The filing of such verified translation is now regulated by rule 85(3(c) and (d) [1990].

89A.16 *Further formalities after entry into the United Kingdom phase*

Rule 85(7) [1990] has replaced rule 85(3) [1982]. The new rule shortens the period for filing PF 10/77 when PCT Chapter II has been invoked so that PF 10/77 must now be filed within 32 (formerly 33) months from the declared priority date (or from the date of filing the PCT application if no priority is claimed therefor). However, where there is no international preliminary examination, the period for filing PF 10/77 remains at two years from such date. The periods for filing PF 7/77 (if required) and 9/77 remain unchanged, but are now specified as being 22 or 32 months from the declared priority (or filing) date, the longer period applying when PCT Chapter II has been invoked. Thus, though the filing of PF 10/77 can be delayed by two months *when PCT Chapter II is not invoked*, it remains prudent to file PF 7/77, 9/77 and 10/77 at the same time within the 22 or 32 month period as the case may be.

The period for filing a translation of the information concerning the deposit of a micro-organism is now prescribed by rule 85(2) [1990], which has been substituted for rule 85(1A) [1982], and is two months from the date of a request to furnish such translation. This translation need not be verified because rule 113(1) does not apply. Rule 85(2) [1990] seems to entail the Patent Office issuing such invitation even if the translation has already been received but after expiry of the relevant 20 or 30 months period. Otherwise, the period for filing the translation of the information concerning the deposit of a micro-organism is not postponed beyond expiry of the relevant 20 or 30 months period. A consequence of rule 113(1) not applying is that the heavy sanction remains of the application being deemed to be withdrawn upon failure to file such a translation.

The period for filing verification of the translation of the international application and any amendments is now measured from the declared priority date, or from the international filing date when there is no declared priority date (r. 85(3)(e) [1990], which has been substituted for r. 85(2A)(*c*) [1982]). This period is now identical to that prescribed for filing PF 9/77 and for filing a verified translation of the priority document, as discussed at para. 89A.08 *supra*.

PRACTICE UNDER SECTION 89A

Translation of the international application **89A.19**

Section 89A(3) and (4) continues to require that any required translation of the international application must be filed before the end of the "prescribed period", that is the 20 or 30 months' period prescribed in rule 85(1) [1990]. The commentary in paras. 89A.11 and 89A.19 in the Main Work therefore remains applicable as regards time limits. However, it is now expressly provided that the translation of the international application need not include the application "request" or the abstract (unless the applicant has expressly requested the Comptroller to proceed with the application before the end of the 20 or 30 months' period prescribed in rule 85(1), and before publication of the application by the International Bureau and communication of the application to the United Kingdom Patent Office under PCTa. 20), but must always include textual matter appearing in the drawings (r. 85(5) [1990]).

The amendments to the PCT Regulations, which become effective on July 1, 1992, will provide liberalised requirements for the filing of translations. This may result in some amendment of rule 85(5).

Verification of translation of application **89A.21**

The time limit for verifying a translation of the application (previously in r. 85(2A)(c) [1982]) is now set out in rule 85(3)(e) [1990]. This time limit effectively remains at about two months after entry into the United Kingdom phase, but the calculations described in para. 89A.36 of the Main Work no longer apply.

89A.24 *Request for preliminary examination and search (PF 9/77)*

Rule 85(7)(a) [1990] (reprinted in para. 89A.02 *supra*, which has replaced r. 85(3)(a) [1982]) now measures the period for filing PF 9/77 from the declared priority date, or from the international filing date when there is no declared priority date. The complications described in para. 89A.36 of the Main Work therefore no longer occur, but the period for filing the PF 9/77 remains at about two months from the entry into the United Kingdom phase.

89A.25 *Request for substantive examination (PF 10/77)*

Rule 85(3)(*b*) [1982], cited in the Main Work, has been replaced by rule 85(7)(b) [1990], see para. 89A.02 *supra*. Under this, the period for filing PF 10/77 remains unchanged at two years from the priority date when the Patent Office is *not* an elected office, but is reduced by one month to be the same 32 month period described in para. 89A.24 *supra* for filing PF 9/77 when the Patent Office has been elected within 19 months of the priority date for the purposes of international preliminary examination under PCT Chapter II. This period remains extensible as of right for one month under rule 110(3), and further with the Comptroller's discretion under rule 110(4) (formerly r. 110(3A)).

89A.26 *Priority document*

It is understood that, if the priority document is filed late in the international phase, *i.e.* after 16 months from the declared priority date, the International Bureau does not automatically transmit a copy of the priority document to the United Kingdom Patent Office. This is relevant to the operation of rule 110(3) and (4) [1990] (for which see para. 89B.07 of the Main Work and *infra*).

89A.27 *Translation of priority document*

The period for filing a verified translation of a priority document is now as stated in the Main Work, but the requirement stems from a modification of rule 6(6), see rule 85(3)(c) and (d) [1990] reprinted in para. 89A.02 *supra*, and see para. 5.02 *supra*. However, the period is now measured as 22 (or 32) months from the declared priority date, which is the same as the period prescribed for filing PF 9/77 and the period remains extensible by one month under rule 110(3) [1990].

89A.28 *Statement of inventorship (PF 7/77)*

Rule 85(3(a) [1982], cited in the Main Work, has been replaced by rule 85(7)(a) [1990], see para. 89A.02 *supra*. There is, therefore, now a uniform period for filing PF 7/77 and 9/77. This is 22 months after the declared priority date (or after the PCT filing date if no priority is claimed), extended to 32 months if an election has been made for substantive examination under Chapter II of the PCT. This period is extensible as stated in the Main Work. If the period under rule 85(1) [1990] is extended under rule 100 or rule 110, then, if necessary, the periods under rules 85(3) and (7) [1990] are automatically extended to expire one month after the extended rule 85(1) period (r. 85(4) [1990]). The aggregate time limits described in para. 89A.36 of the Main Work, are no longer relevant.

89A.29 *Inventions concerning micro-organisms*

The title to this para. is incorrectly stated in the Main Work. Rules 17(1)(*a*)(iii) [1982] and 85(1A), each cited in the Main Work, have become respectively

Schedule 2, paragraph 1(2)(a)(ii) [1990] and rule 85(2) [1990], see para. 89A.02 *supra*. Any translation of information concerning the deposit of a micro-organism no longer needs to be verified because rule 113(1) does not here apply.

International exhibition certificate **89A.30**

Rule 85(2A)(*a*) [1982], cited in the Main Work, has become rule 85(3)(a) [1990], see para. 89A.02 *supra*. Because the period for filing a certificate of an international exhibition is now measured from the declared priority date (or from the international filing date), the aggregate time limits described in para. 89A.36 of the Main Work, are no longer applicable.

Refunds and remission of fees **89A.33**

Rule 102(1)(*b*) [1982], referred to in the Main Work, has been renumbered as rule 102(1)(a) [1990].

Placing application in order **89A.34**

Rule 85(3)(*c*) [1982], cited in the Main Work, has been deleted as such, but without change in effect. Thus, the time for placing an international application in compliance with the Act and Rules is now governed (as for applications under the Act) by rule 34, for which see paras. 18.03 and 18.10 in the Main Work and *supra*, where the possibilities for extension of that period are discussed. This rule 34 period is, in the normal case, a period of four-and-a-half years from the declared priority date (or the date of filing the international application if no priority is claimed therefor), if necessary extended to 18 months from actual filing in the case of a replacement application filed under section 8(3), 12(6) or 37(4). The possibility of extending the rule 34 period is dealt with in para. 18.10 *supra*.

Extensions of time **89A.35**

Periods which were formerly measured as two months after entry into the United Kingdom phase are now measured as 22 or 32 months from the declared priority date (or from the international filing date if there is no declared priority), the longer period applying when Chapter II of the PCT has been invoked. The same 32 months period is now also applicable to the filing of PF 10/77 when PCT Chapter II has been invoked. These periods, which are now also the same for the filing of the verified translation of the priority document, can all be extended, as of right, by one month by filing a single PF 50/77. Also, a single PF 52/77 can now be used to seek discretionary extensions of time for filing all the documents and forms and for paying the national fee for entering and prosecution in the United Kingdom phase, provided that the desired extensions expire on the same date for all such documents, forms and fees.

The aggregate time limits described in para. 89A.36 of the Main Work no longer occur.

Aggregate time limits **89A.36**

Rule 85(3)(*a*) [1982], cited in the Main Work, has been assimilated into rule 85(7) [1990]. The wording of the new rule, and of sub-rules 85(3)(b) (c) and (e), no longer describe the time limits as an extension of two months running from the expiry of the rule 85(1) period, but measures the period for filing: certificate of an international exhibition; a verified translation of the priority documents; verification of a translation of the international application; PF 9/77 (as well as PF 7/77 and 10/77) from the earliest declared priority date (or filing date of the international application if no priority is claimed). This revision removes most, if not all, of the complications over aggregate time limits indicated in the Main Work.

89B.01 **SECTION 89B**

Note. The prospective addition of section 89B, noted in the Main Work, took effect from January 7, 1991 (S.I. 1990 No. 2168).

COMMENTARY ON SECTION 89B

89B.07 *Effect of late filing or non-filing of priority document in the international phase*

Neither of rules 85 or 110 [1990] contains any explicit provisions to enable PF 50/77 or 52/77 to be filed in respect of a time limit prescribed under the PCT and expiring in the international phase. Thus, the remarks in the Main Work on seeking an extension of time for filing the priority document remain speculative. Had the discretion given to the Comptroller in rule 85(9)(a) to apply rules 100 and 110 to a review under PCTa. 25 been extended to any time limit applicable in the international phase, and to the case wherein the missed time limit did not result in the application being deemed withdrawn, the situation might have been rather clearer.

With effect from July 1, 1992, it will be possible to obtain copies of the priority documents from the International Bureau (PCTr. 17.2(c)). Also, the date for calculating the relevant 20 or 30 months period will then be displaced if the declaration of priority is withdrawn at any time during the international phase, even after publication of the application has occurred (PCTr. 90*bis*.3(a)).

89B.09 *Effect of international publication (subs. (2))*

An application will also have entered the United Kingdom phase before international publication in the event of a favourable review under PCTa. 25, for which see para. 89.35 in the Main Work.

89B.11 *Provisional protection arising on publication (subs. (3))*

Rule 85(2) [1982], cited in the Main Work, has become rule 85(6) [1990], see para. 89A.02 *supra*.

89B.13 *Correction of errors arising in international phase*

This paragraph is only concerned with the correction of errors which did *not* result in the international application, or the designation of the United Kingdom, being deemed withdrawn or which did not result in the international application being refused an international filing date. These matters, to which sub-rules 85(8), (9), (10) and (12) relate exclusively, are discussed in paras. 89.35 and 89.37 *supra*.

Rule 85(4A) [1982], cited in the Main Work, has become rule 85(11) [1990], see para. 89A.02 *supra*, but its effect is unchanged. Whereas rule 85(11) [1990] applies to all international applications for a patent (UK), sub-rules 85(9) and (10) [1990], which give the Comptroller discretionary power to rectify errors and grant extensions, only apply in the case of a review under PCTa. 25 following filing of PF 44/77, as described in paras. 89.35 and 89.37 *supra*. It would seem that sub-rule 85(11) effectively extends some of the powers which the Comptroller has under rule 100 (for which see para. 123.07 *infra*) to a case where an irregularity in procedure occurs within an international authority.

On reflection, and contrary to the inference in the Main Work, correction would not have been possible in the *Vapocure* case even if section 123(3A) had then been in force because here the request for correction was received by the International Bureau too late for the Bureau itself to allow a correction in country designation. Errors which have resulted in the international application, or the designation of the United Kingdom therefor, being deemed withdrawn or the application being refused an international filing date are discussed in paras. 89.35 and 89.37 of the Main Work.

The authorisation of rectification of errors under PCTr. 91 by international authorities and the effect or otherwise of such corrections are outside the scope of this Work. For example, the decision of the United Kingdom Patent Office acting as the PCT receiving office in *Henderson's Application* (SRIS O/17/90) (in which the Office refused to authorise the correction of the designation "KP" for North Korea to read "KR" for South Korea), has no relevance to practice under the Act and, furthermore, is not even binding on the Patent Office of South Korea in the latter's capacity of designated office. Another similar case is *R.* v. *Comptroller-General* ex p. *Celltech* ([1991] RPC 475) where judicial review was denied in respect of a refusal to allow amendment of the designations for a PCT application because these did not meet the stringent condition of PCTr. 91.1 that both the error and the manner of its correction must be apparent from the documents filed.

More favourable law and excusing delay (PCTaa. 26, 27 and 48) **89B.14**

Rule 85(4A) [1982], cited in the Main Work, has become rule 85(11) [1990], see para. 89A.02 *supra*. The same remarks apply here as stated in para. 89B.13 *supra*.

Publication and re-publication **89B.15**

In the interval between valid entry into the national UK phase and re-publication, the file of the international application can be inspected at the Patent Office, see para. 118.20 *supra*.

Examination in the United Kingdom phase (subs. (5)) **89B.17**

Rule 113(3), cited in the Main Work, has been amended so that the Comptroller is now entitled to ask for a translation of all or a part of a document first cited in the international preliminary examination report. The Main Work is incorrect in stating that he could not call for a translation of any document cited in the international *search* report.

Compliance with Act and Rules **89B.21**

Rule 85(3(*c*) [1982], cited in the Main Work, has been deleted as such, but without change in effect, see para. 89A.34 *supra*.

COMMENTARY ON SECTION 90

90.03 *Countries designated as "convention countries"*

The entry for "German Democratic Republic (East Germany)" should now be deleted, as well as the words "(West Germany)" after "German Federal Republic". Lesotho acceded to the Paris Convention with effect from September 28, 1989 ([1989] EIPR D–188), but does not yet appear to have been designated as a "convention country" under the Act. Bangladesh has also acceded to the Paris Convention (O.J. January 23, 1991).

COMMENTARY ON SECTION 91

91.03 *Application of section 91 in practice*

In *Asahi's Application* ([1991] RPC 485) the House of Lords decided specifically to follow EPO decisions, as did the Court of Appeal in *Gale's Application* ([1991] RPC 305). However, the Comptroller will primarily follow decisions of United Kingdom courts, even if these may conflict with EPO decisions (*Sharp K.K.'s Application*, SRIS O/75/91, *noted* IPD 14171).

93.01

SECTION 93

In section 93(*b*) the words "a recorded decree arbitral" have been replaced by "an extract registered decree arbitral bearing a warrant for execution issued by the sheriff court of any sheriffdom in Scotland" (Debtors (Scotland) Act 1987 (c. 18, Sched. 6).

SECTION 94—RELEVANT RULE

94.02 Rule 87 [1990]—*Communication of information to European Patent Office*

The final word "below" has been deleted.

COMMENTARY ON SECTION 94

94.03 *General*

Section 94 only makes lawful that which a statutory enactment prevents and does not apply to the use of documents disclosed on discovery (*Bonzel* v. *Intervention*, [1991] RPC 43).

94.05 *Disclosure by the Patents Court*

Documents produced to the opposing party by way of discovery under the Rules of Court are not documents "in the files of the court" and section 94 is, therefore, inapplicable thereto (*Bonzel* v. *Intervention* [1991] RPC 43).

PART III

MISCELLANEOUS AND GENERAL

SUPREME COURT ACT 1981 (c. 54)

Section 6: The Patents, Admiralty and Commercial Courts 96.02

Note. To the Chancery Division are assigned all causes and matters relating to ". . . patents, trade marks, service marks, registered designs, design rights or copyright" (Supreme Court Act 1981 (c. 54) Sched. 1, para. 1): other Divisions of the High Court therefore have no jurisdiction in respect of these matters.

SECTION 289 [1988] 96.08

Note. Section 289 [1988] refers to sections 40 to 42 of the County Courts Act 1984. These sections 40 and 42 have been prospectively substituted by new wording, and section 41 prospectively amended, by section 2 of the Courts and Legal Services Act 1990 (c. 41).

SECTION 290 [1988] 96.09

Note. This section has been prospectively repealed by the Courts and Legal Services Act 1990 (c. 41, Sched. 20).

SECTION 96 [Repealed]—ARTICLES 96.13

Judge Peter Ford, "The Patents County Court", (1989–90) 19 CIPA 361; "Patent litigation: A better deal for litigants", [1990] EIPR 435; and "The first year of the Patents County Court", (1991–92) 21 CIPA 82.

P. R. B. Lawrence, "The Patents County Court Rules", (1990–91) 20 CIPA 14;

A. Webb, "Patent litigation in the UK: The new Patents County Court", [1991] EIPR 203.

COMMENTARY ON SECTION 96 [Repealed]

General 96.14

A Patents Court Users' Committee has been set up as a forum in which users of the Court can discuss anything affecting them, including procedure, practice and the facilities available (*Practice Note (Summonses in Patent Actions*, [1990] RPC 45.

Patents County Courts

—Nature and jurisdiction (s. 287 [1988]) 96.17

The Edmonton County Court has been designated as the first Patents County Court, operative from September 3, 1990, with general jurisdiction over matters relating to patents or designs throughout England and Wales, see S.I. 1990

No. 1496, reprinted in para. 96.11A *supra*. The address of this Court is: Woodall House, Lordship Lane, Wood Green, London N22 6LF (tel. 081–881 1400; fax. 081–881 4802; DX 35650—Wood Green 1). This court has the power to sit elsewhere in England and Wales should this be appropriate or more convenient.

The power provided by section 287 [1988] to designate a county court as a "Patents County Court" has been subsumed into a more general power under which the Lord Chancellor may, by Order and after consultation with other senior judges, confer jurisdiction on all or designated county courts for all proceedings (other than those for judicial review) for which the High Court presently has jurisdiction, and allocate proceedings to the High Court or to county courts, perhaps exclusively, and either with or without the meeting of specified criteria (Courts and Legal Services Act 1990 (c. 41, s. 1). However, this power has not been specifically exercised in relation to intellectual property litigation and the Patents County Court remains as designated under section 287 [1988]. While county courts do not have power themselves to make *Anton Piller* Orders or grant *Mareva* injunctions, but must transfer the case to the High Court for consideration of this type of relief, this prohibition has been dis-applied to Patents County Courts (County Courts Remedies Regulations 1991 (S.I. 1991 No. 1222), r. 3).

96.18 *—Financial limits to jurisdiction (s. 288 [1988])*

The Patents County Court (Designation and Jurisdiction) Order 1990 (S.I. 1990 No. 1496 (reprinted in para. 96.11A *supra*) contains no restriction on jurisdiction as adumbrated in section 288 [1988].

96.19 *—Transfer of proceedings between Patents Court and a patents county court (s. 289 [1988])*

Sections 40–42 of the County Courts Act 1984 have been replaced by new provisions which empower the Lord Chancellor to make orders for mandatory transfer of cases from the High Court to a County Court, and *vice versa*, when these fall within categories specified in the order (Courts and Legal Services Act 1990 (c. 41, s. 2). However, the Orders so far made under the new provisions are thought not to alter the position concerning patent proceedings and their potential transfer to the Patents County Court, see para. 61.26 *supra*.

The procedure when the Patents Court does order transfer to the Patents County Court is governed generally by RSC Ord. 107, rule 2(1A) (reprinted at para. E107.2 *infra*). It is understood that, upon such transfer, the Patents County Court has not insisted upon the existing pleadings being modified into the more detailed form normally required under CCR Order 48A (for which see para. 96.22 *infra*).

96.20 *—Limitation on costs (s. 290 [1988])*

No Order has been made fixing the "prescribed amount" envisaged by section 290 [1988] and, indeed, the section has been prospectively repealed, see para. 96.09 *supra*, consequent upon County Courts being given a general discretion as to awards of costs (Courts and Legal Services Act 1990 (c. 41, s. 4).

96.21 *—Judges in the Patents County Courts (s.291 [1988])*

The appointed judge of the first Patents County Court (for which see para. 96.17 *supra*) is His Honour Judge Ford. His views on the procedure of this new court and of its workings have been outlined in the paper listed in para. 96.13 *supra*. Under Order 48A, rule 2 of the County Court Rules (reprinted at para. H48A.02 *infra*), all proceedings in the Patents County Court are to be dealt with by the patents judge, except that urgent interlocutory matters may be dealt with by another judge. Certain Queen's Counsel of the Patent Bar have been appointed to sit as deputy judges in the Patents County Court should the need arise.

—Procedure in the Patents County Courts **96.22**

A new Order 48A has been inserted in the County Court Rules by S.I. 1990 No. 1495. This is reprinted *infra* in a new Appendix H to the Main Work. This Order generally follows RSC Order 104 (reprinted at paras. E104.01–E104.22 of the Main Work), but has some significant differences. Thus, all proceedings are generally to be conducted personally by the judge. Every summons (which should be on Form N4P obtainable from the Patents County Court, for which see para. 96.17 *supra*) is to be endorsed or accompanied by a statement of case and, unlike pleadings before the High Court, this statement must, in the case of an infringement allegation, set out which of the claims of the patent are alleged to be infringed and, in respect of each such claim, the grounds relied on in support of these allegations together with "all facts, matters and arguments relied on as establishing those grounds, including at least one example of each type of infringement alleged". Where validity is put in issue, the statement of case is, likewise, to give particulars of the objections relied on and "explain the relevance of every citation to each claim, with identification of the significant parts of each citation, and shall give all facts, matters and arguments which are relied on for establishing the invalidity of the patent", see para. H48A.04 *infra*. However, note that the defendant's defence statement does not require him to detail the facts and arguments on which he contends that there is no infringement.

Interrogatories and notices to admit facts may only be served with the leave of the court, except for such notices served within 14 days of the close of pleadings, see para. H048A.06 *infra*, and there is no automatic right of discovery. At the end of this 14-day period, all parties are required to file and serve an "application for directions". This will be on Form N.244 and has to summarise the outstanding issues, and the further steps necessary to prove the applicant's contentions and prepare his case for a hearing; and give full particulars of: desired experiments; what these intend to prove; and the date by which a written report thereof can be submitted; as well as setting out all pre-trial orders and directions desired, see para. H048A.08(1), (2) *infra*. For further discussion on these matters, see paras. 61.21–61.38 *supra re*. "Practice under Section 61".

There is then to be a "preliminary consideration" of the case by the judge who has wide powers to strike out points raised in the pleadings, and is required to consider and (where appropriate) give directions in respect of:

(*a*) the witnesses who may be called;
(*b*) whether their evidence should be given orally or in writing or any combination of the two;
(*c*) the exchange of witness statements;
(*d*) the provision of Patent Office Reports [see paras. 99A.02–99A.04 in the Main Work];
(*e*) the use of assessors at the hearing [see para. 96.25 *infra*];
(*f*) transfer to the High Court [see para. 61.26 in the Main Work];
(*g*) reference to the Court of Justice of the European Communities [see para. 61.26 in the Main Work];

(*h*) applications for discovery and inspection [see para. 61.28 *supra*];
(*i*) applications for leave to serve interrogatories and notices to admit facts [see para. 61.34 in the Main Work]; and
(*j*) written reports of the results of any experiments of which particulars have previously been given [see para. 61.35 *supra*],

see CCR Ord. 48A, rule 8(5), reprinted in para. H48A.08 *infra*. The way in which the first Patents County Court judge, Judge Peter Ford, envisages this procedure operating in practice was explained in his talk, the report of which is listed in para. 96.13 *supra*, see also his paper and the articles by P. R. B. Lawrence and A. Webb, each likewise listed.

Thus, the aim is that the Patents County Court achieves a simpler, and therefore quicker, procedure than obtains in the Patents Court. However, the apparent restrictions on discovery, etc., may make it significantly harder for a party to proceedings before a Patents County Court to establish its allegations, and easier for a party to conceal the weaknesses of its own position. Thus, while a party is required (by CCR Order 48A) to set out in its initial pleading all "facts, matters and arguments relied on", a party's perception of its case will inevitably change as its investigations continue and as facts emerge from the other party's pleadings, etc. For example, the attitude of the Patents County Court to requests for amendments of pleadings will be an important factor in indicating whether the court adopts a "user-friendly" attitude. Thus, although it is expected that Requests for Further and Better Particulars of a party's pleadings will be discouraged, it is hoped that the court will require amendment thereof so that each party may know precisely the case which it has to meet. It will be factors such as these which will indicate whether it is appropriate for those seeking to litigate in a Patents County Court to accept the increased difficulties which face it in establishing its case in return for a speedier, more written, and hopefully a cheaper, type of procedure. Time, coupled with the attitude of the Court of Appeal to appeals from Patents County Court decisions, will show whether these aims are achieved.

The judgment in the first patent infringement case decided by the Patents County Court was that of *Daily* v. *Établissements Fernand Berchet*, ([1991] RPC 587), see para. 125.10 *infra*.

96.23 *—Representation in the Patents County Courts*

In the first paragraph, line 5, of para. 96.23 in the Main Work, the reference to "section 280 [1988]" should be to "section 292 [1988]"; and, in the penultimate line of para. 96.23, "102.04" should read "102.05".

No regulations have so far been made under section 292(2) and, consequently, it is not clear whether in fact registered patent agents are to be regarded as officers of the court in the same way as solicitors and, therefore, whether the court has disciplinary powers over patent agents as it does over solicitors engaged in litigation before it: nevertheless, it should not be assumed that such disciplinary power is lacking.

The Courts and Legal Services Act 1990 (c. 41) [the "1990 Act"] now regulates rights of audience before a court (s. 27) and the right to conduct litigation (s. 28). Such persons can be, *inter alia*, those having such a right "granted by or under any enactment". Consequently, the right of patent agents to represent litigants before the Patents County Court and to appear therebefore (as conferred by section 292 [1988]) is preserved. However, a patent agent is not an "authorised advocate" or an "authorised litigator" (as defined in s. 119 of the 1990 Act) because these definitions apply only where the "right" has been granted by an authorised body in accordance with that Act. This appears to have the following consequences: (1) that a patent agent providing advocacy or litigation services before the Comptroller or Patents County Court does not obtain legal professional privilege (other than perhaps under s. 280 [1988], for which see paras. 104.02 and 104.08 in the Main Work) for communications made to or by him in the conduct of litigation, see s. 63 of the 1990 Act; (2) legal aid cannot be granted for such representation, see Sched. 18, paras. 60 and 63(4) of the 1990 Act; (3) patent agents have not become excused from jury service, as is enjoyed in each case by an authorised advocate or litigator so acting, see s. 63 and Sched. 18, paragraph 5 of the 1990 Act; and (4) there is no entitlement to administer oaths and hence use the title "Commissioner for Oaths" (s. 113 of the 1990 Act). However (by s. 62 of the 1990 Act), a patent agent, when acting as an advocate, will enjoy immunity from actions in negligence or for breach of contract to the extent that a barrister would have a like immunity.

A Patent Litigators Association has been formed (restricted to members of the Chartered Institute of Patent Agents) to encourage litigation in the Patents County Court ((1990–91) 20 CIPA 156).

Jurisdiction of various United Kingdom courts **96.24**

For the prospective extension of the Civil Jurisdiction and Judgments Act 1982 (c. 27) to other countries, see para. 61.06 *supra*.

Appointment of scientific advisers **96.25**

It is perhaps significant that, despite its side-note, section 70 of the Supreme Court Act 1981 provides only for the appointment of "scientific advisers", and not "assessors" to assist the Patents Court, whereas section 291(3) [1988] provides for the appointment of both types of persons to assist the Patents County Court with CCR Ord. 48A, rule 8(5)(*e*) (reprinted in para. H48A.08 *infra*) only providing for the use of "assessors". Such persons can take part in the decision of the court, whereas the rôle of a scientific adviser is more limited, as indicated in the Main Work.

Commentary on Section 97

Right of appeal from Comptroller (subs. (1)) **97.04**

Rule 93(6) now prevents any appeal from a decision of the Comptroller under rule 93(5)(a)(i) (*refusal to make available for public inspection a document containing damaging disparaging statements*).

The judicial review procedure has also been used in respect of a decision of the Comptroller acting as a PCT receiving office, for which there is no statutory right of appeal (*R.* v. *Comptroller-General* ex p. *Celltech*, [1991] RPC 475).

Further appeals from the Patents Court (subs. (3)) **97.06**

In *American Cyanamid's Patent* ([1991] RPC 415) the Court of Appeal observed that in licence of right cases that court should only be asked to intervene when there is truly an issue of law of general importance to be decided.

Principles affecting exercise of appellate jurisdiction

97.09 *—By the Court of Appeal*

Because further appeals of decisions of the Comptroller to the Court of Appeal are often allowable on points of law only, that Court will generally feel itself bound by decisions on facts reached by the Patents Court, even though the Patents Court hearing will have been a complete rehearing of the case before the Comptroller, see para. 99.02. Accordingly, the Court of Appeal will not, on such appeals, exercise a separate discretion and so will only reverse an exercise of discretion by the Patents Court if that court has exercised its discretion with error of law (*Smith, Kline & French's (Cimetidine) Patents*, [1990] RPC 203 (CA)).

97.11 *Proceedings in Scotland (subss. (4) and (5))*

While further appeal of a Comptroller's decision in Scotland to the Inner House of the Court of Session is subject to the same limitations as for England and Wales under subsection (3), subsection (5) does not require such further Scottish appeal to have leave for this from the Outer House of the Court of Session.

PRACTICE UNDER SECTION 97

Appeals from the Comptroller to the Patents Court

97.12 *—Lodging and service of notice of appeal*

The administrative offices of the Chancery Division have moved to the Thomas More Building at the Royal Courts of Justice. Fees for appeals from the Comptroller should now be paid in Room 204 and notices of appeal now lodged in Room 211, with appeals being listed in Room 413, each of that Building. The telephone number for listing inquiries is 071 936–6690.

97.14 *—Hearings and representations thereat*

The certificate of estimated length of the appeal hearing should now be lodged in Room 413 in the Thomas More Building, see para. 97.12 *supra*.

97.16 *—Admission of new evidence on appeal*

The Patents Court has refused to allow evidence of common general knowledge to be added for an appeal against rejection of an application for revocation made to the Comptroller (*Shoketsu's Patent*, SRIS C/26/91, *noted* IPD 14078); and has also refused new evidence in an appeal from the Comptroller (*Gebhardt's Patent*, SRIS C/37/91, *noted* IPD 14115), it not being sufficient that the new evidence was important if it could have been presented previously, the *Ladd* v. *Marshall* rules (cited in the Main Work) being applicable. Also, the Court of Appeal refused to allow submission of new evidence in *Strix* v. *Otter Controls* ([1991] FSR 354), though the availability of that evidence seems to have influenced the eventual decision in that case, see para. 61.23 *supra*.

Appeals from the Patents Court to the Court of Appeal

97.23 *—Skeleton arguments*

The timetable for submission of skeleton arguments has been relaxed so that these must now be produced 14 days before the hearing date, but relief from this, now general, requirement will rarely be given (*Practice Direction (Court of Appeal: Skeleton Arguments: Time Limits)*, [1990] 1 WLR 794; [1990] 2 All ER 318 (CA)).

SECTION 98—RELEVANT RULE

Rule 108 [1990]—*Proceedings in Scotland* **98.02**

In paragraph (4), "three months of" has been changed to "two months after"; and, after "notification of the request" the words "is sent to him" have been added.

COMMENTARY ON SECTION 98

General **98.03**

Strictly speaking, proceedings under the 1949 Act remain governed by section 103 [1949], see para. A103 *infra*.

PRACTICE UNDER SECTION 98

Proceedings before the Court **98.09**

The "Patent Judge" in the Court of Session is now Lord Cullen. The rules of court for patent proceedings in Scotland have been extensively revised and now more closely correspond to the current form of RSC Order 104, see Act of Sederunt (Rules of the Court of Session Amendment No. 7) (Patents Rules) 1991 (S.I. 1991 No. 1621).

Hearings by the Comptroller in Scotland **98.10**

An objection to a hearing in Scotland must now be lodged within *two* months, see para. 98.02 *supra*.

COMMENTARY ON SECTION 99A

Opinion from the European Patent Office **99A.05**

The term "Patent Office" in sections 99A and 99B does not include the EPO and, as no rules have been made (either under the RSC or the CCR) to provide for either the Patents Court or the Patents County Court to seek an opinion from the EPO under EPCa. 25, there appears to be no power whereby this provision of the EPC could be implemented, even if this were to be desired.

COMMENTARY ON SECTION 100

General **100.02**

CPCa. 75, referred to in the Main Work, has become CPCa. 35 [1989], see para. 86.03 *supra*.

100.04 *Protection of confidential information (subs. (2))*

CPCa. 75(2), referred to in the Main Work, has become CPCa. 35(2) [1989], see para. 86.03 *supra*.

An appeal in *Roussel-Uclaf* v. *ICI*, cited in the Main Work, was dismissed and both decisions have been reported ([1990] RPC 45).

SECTION 101—RELEVANT RULES

101.02 **Rule 88 [1990]**—*Comptroller's discretionary powers*

Rule 88 has been amended to read:

88.—(1) Before exercising any discretionary power vested in him by or under the Act adversely to any party to a proceeding before him, the comptroller shall, unless the party concerned consents to shorter notice, give that party at least fourteen days' notice of the time when he may be heard.

(2) If, in *inter partes* proceedings, a party desires to be heard, he shall give notice in writing to the comptroller; and the comptroller may refuse to hear any party who has not given such notice before the day appointed for the hearing.

(3) In *inter partes* proceedings, any party who intends to refer at the hearing to any document (other than a report of a decision of any court or of the comptroller) not already mentioned in the proceedings shall, unless the comptroller consents and the other party agrees, give at least fourteen days' notice of his intention with details of, or a copy of, the document to the comptroller and the other party.

(4) After hearing the party or parties desiring to be heard or, if no party so desires, without a hearing, the comptroller shall decide the matter and shall notify all parties of his decision and, if any party so desires, shall give his reasons for the decision.

101.03 **Rule 89**—*Admittance to hearings before Comptroller*

Rule 89 has been amended to read:

89.—(1) Subject to the following provisions of this rule, where a hearing before the comptroller of any dispute between two or more parties relating to any matter in connection with a patent or an application for a patent takes place after the publication of the application under section 16, the hearing of the dispute shall be in public.

(2) After consulting those parties to the dispute who appear in person or are represented at a hearing to which paragraph (1) above applies, the comptroller may direct that the hearing be not held in public, but without prejudice to paragraph (3) below.

(3) A member of the Council on Tribunals or of its Scottish Committee may, in his capacity as such, attend such a hearing or any other hearing before the comptroller under these Rules.

Procedure for hearings 101.05

Under the revised rule 88 [1990], PF 46/77 has been abolished, and the rule is now limited to situations where the Comptroller is being asked to exercise a discretionary power "vested in him by or under the Act". If a party wishes to be heard in an *inter partes* hearing, prior written notice should be given to the Comptroller, failing which there is power not to hear that party (r. 88(2)). There is now power for the prior 14 days' notice of a hearing to be waived by consent (r. 88(1)); and, while 14 days' prior notice is still required of documents to which it is intended to refer at the hearing, this requirement no longer applies to papers already mentioned in the proceedings nor to reports of decisions of (United Kingdom) courts or of the Comptroller: again there is power for these requirements to be waived, though only with the consent of the Comptroller *and* with the agreement of other parties (r. 88(3)). Such consent and agreement should therefore only be sought in genuinely unexpected circumstances.

Communication of decisions 101.06

Rule 88(4) now permits the Comptroller not to give a written decision in *inter partes* proceedings, but he must do so if *any* party so desires.

Public access to hearings and decisions 101.07

Under the revised form of rule 89 (reprinted in para. 101.03 *supra*) a member of the Council on Tribunals (or of its Scottish equivalent), acting as such, may attend any hearing of the Comptroller, even if he decides to hold such hearing *in camera*. It is not clear whether any invitation for such attendance is required.

SECTION 102 [Repealed] 102.01

Note. The prospective amendments and repeals noted in the Main Work took effect from August 13, 1990 (S.I. 1990 No. 1400), thereby bringing into effect the substituted section 102, new section 102A and sections 274–286 [1988].

SECTION 102 [Substituted] 102.02

The substituted section 102 came into force on August 13, 1990, see para. 102.01 *supra*. A further subsection (5) was later added, by the Courts and Legal Services Act 1990 (c. 41; Sched. 18, para. 20(1)), effective from January 1, 1991, reading:

(5) Nothing in this section shall be taken to limit the right to draw or prepare deeds given to a registered patent agent by section 68 of the Courts and Services Act 1990 [c. 41].

SECTION 102A 102.03

The new section 102A came into force on August 13, 1990, see para. 102.01 *supra*. A further subsection (6) was later added, by the Courts and Legal Services Act 1990 (c. 41; Sched. 18, para. 20(2)), effective from January 1, 1991, reading:

(6) Nothing in this section shall be taken to limit the right to draw or prepare deeds given to a registered patent agent by section 68 of the Courts and Services Act 1990 [c. 41].

102.08 **SECTION 278 [1988]**

Note. In the application of the section to the Isle of Man: in subsection (1), the references to "solicitor" and "solicitors" are substituted by "advocate" and "advocates" respectively; subsection (2) is rewritten to read:

"(2) No offence is committed under section 1 of the Legal Practitioners Registration Act (an Act of Tynwald) (which restricts the use of certain expressions in reference to persons not qualified to act as advocates)";

and subsection (3) is omitted (S.I. 1990 No. 1505).

102.10 **SECTION 285 [1988]**

Note. In the application of the section to the Isle of Man, subsection (2)(*b*) is omitted (S.I. 1990 No. 1505).

COMMENTARY ON SECTIONS 102, 102A AND 274–279, 285 AND 286 [1988]

102.13 *The basis of the new provisions*

Sections 274–286 [1988] came into force on August 13, 1990, together with the substitution of new section 102 and the addition of new section 102A (S.I. 1990 No. 1400), see paras. 102.02–102.11 in the Main Work.

Commentary on substituted section 102

102.14 *—General*

A registered patent agent who is not also a person on the "European List" is not a "duly qualified legal practitioner" under EPCa. 134 (*EPO Decision J* 19/89, "*Legal practitioner*", OJEPO 8/1991, 425).

Persons entitled to carry on business as a patent agent (s.274 [1988])

102.19 *—Agency under the EPC*

It is no longer necessary for a person on the "European list" of authorised representatives to file an authorisation with the EPO when an application or opposition is first filed, but authorisations continue to be required upon a change of representation or when representation is to be by a person not on the "list", *i.e.* by a general lawyer or by an employee of the applicant or opponent (OJEPO 9/1991, 489).

102.23 *—Obstacles to practice by unqualified person*

The Rules of Professional Conduct of the Chartered Institute of Patent Agents, referred to in the Main Work, are amplified by "Guidelines" concerning the observance of these Rules. These were amended by the Council of the Chartered Institute in June 1990. These Rules and amended Guidelines are now reprinted in Appendix G *infra* at paras. G13 and G14 respectively. The Chartered Institute can take disciplinary action against its members even if a complaint to the Comptroller under section 115 or 281 [1988] (for which see para. 115.05) has previously failed, but its Council must not act both as accusers and judges (*Law* v. *Chartered Institute of Patent Agents*, [1919] 2 Ch. 276).

—General liability **102.24**

The liability of patent agents in negligence is the subject of a paper by T. Z. Gold ((1990–91) 20 CIPA 120).

—Offences relating to document preparation **102.25**

Section 22 of the Solicitors Act 1974 was amended by the Courts and Legal Services Act 1990 (c. 41, s. 68) so as to insert in subsection (2) thereof (persons exempt from subsection (1)) the following subparagraphs, effective from January 1, 1991:

(aa) a registered trade mark agent drawing or preparing any instrument relating to any design, trade mark or service mark;
(ab) a registered patent agent drawing or preparing any instrument relating to any invention, design, technical information, trade mark or service mark.

Corresponding provisions were likewise inserted in sections 102 and 102A of the 1977 Act, see paras. 102.02 and 102.03 *supra*, but none of these provisions themselves extend to Scotland, Northern Ireland or the Isle of Man. It is, therefore no longer an offence (at least in England and Wales) for "patent agents" to prepare deeds or other instruments, provided that these relate to the subjects as listed above.

The register of patent agents (s. 275 [1988])

—The Register of Patent Agents Rules (subss. (2)–(4)) **102.27**

Pursuant to section 275 [1988], the Register of Patent Agents Rules 1990 (S.I. 1990 No. 1457) have been made effective from August 13, 1990, revoking the Register of Patent Agents Rules 1978 (S.I. 1978 No. 1093 and S.I. 1982 No. 1428). These new Rules are reprinted in Appendix F *infra*. They provide that the register kept under the former Rules shall be maintained and continued under the new Rules as previously, that is by a Registrar appointed annually by the Chartered Institute of Patent Agents (rr. 3(1) and 7), but subject to possible direction from the Comptroller (r. 21). This register contains at least the name of each person entitled to be registered under the rules, together with his business address, date of registration, and qualifications for registration (r. 3(2)). The Register is generally open to public inspection (r. 5) and the Chartered Institute is required to publish by April 1 annually an alphabetical list of the entries in the register as at the end of the previous year (r. 6), and to submit an annual report to the Comptroller (r. 22).

The Chartered Institute continues to have delegated responsibility for the regulations for the examinations which qualify persons for entry in the register (after a period of supervised practice in, or experience of, patent agency work) and for the conduct of those examinations, but now must make these in consultation with the Institute of Trade Mark Agents, as well as with the approval of the Comptroller (rr. 8–10). An appeal lies to the Comptroller from any decision of the Chartered Institute or Registrar made under the Rules (r. 19).

The Chartered Institute is empowered by the Rules to levy fees for: examinations (on a generally non-profit-making basis); entry into the register; an annual practice fee; and a fee for amendment of the Register (r. 20). The entry fee and the annual practice fee have been fixed at £60 (O.J. October 1990). Failure to pay any annual practice fee can lead to erasure of that person's name from the register either permanently or for a designated period (r. 12). There is provision for inquiry by the Secretary of State into misconduct by a registered agent which, after due hearing, can also lead to erasure of the registration of that person (rr. 14–17), but with possible subsequent restoration (r. 18). The erasure of a name from the register under rule 14 results in publication of a notice accordingly, see O.J. May 8, 1991.

Rather similar Rules have been made governing the new Register of Trade Mark Agents, with responsibility for the qualifying examination for entry thereto delegated to the Institute of Trade Mark Agents, see Register of Trade Mark Agents Rules 1990 (S.I. 1990 No. 1458).

102.29 *—The Chartered Institute and "Chartered Patent Agent"*

By a Third Supplemental Charter granted September 13, 1991, a Fellow of the Chartered Institute may now alternatively style himself as a "Chartered Patent Attorney", abbreviated (as for the alternative designation of "Chartered Patent Agent") as "C.P.A." ((1990–91) 20 CIPA 484). The Chartered Institute has submitted an application that those of its members suitably qualified should have certain rights as "authorised litigators" under the Courts and Legal Services Act 1990 (c. 41, s. 29). This submission contained much useful background information on the rights and duties of patent agents, see (1991–92) 21 CIPA 59).

102.30 *—Examinations for entry into the Register of Patent Agents*

The new form of the Register of Patent Agents Rules (S.I. 1990 No. 1457, reprinted in Appendix F *infra*), continues to delegate to the Chartered Institute of Patent Agents responsibility for the examinations for entry into this Register, but see para. 102.27 *supra* for the need to consult with the Institute of Trade Mark Agents and the requirement that the examination fees should be at a general non-profit-making level. Before entry to the register there is also required a period of practice in the field of intellectual property, including substantial experience in patent agency work, in the United Kingdom, which is not less than two years if supervised by a qualified practitioner *or* not less than four years of such practice and experience if not so supervised (r. 9), but there is now no qualifying period of experience before the examinations can be taken. The Examination Regulations made under rule 8 of the Register of Patent Agents Rules 1991 are reprinted in Appendix G *infra*.

The titles of "patent agent" and "patent attorney" (s. 276 [1988])

102.33 *—Improper use of titles of "patent agent" and "patent attorney" and analogous expressions*

The Chartered Institute has set up a "Protected Titles Committee" to monitor, and take action in respect of, any improper use of these protected titles ((1990–91) 20 CIPA 417) and has taken action against a directory entry by solicitors under the heading "Patent Agents" and also against use by the same firm of the description "patent agency" ((1991–92) 21 CIPA 149).

The European Patents Institute or "EPI" **102.45**

The Main Work incorrectly prints, for the EPI Secretariat, the address of the EPO: the EPI address is "Postfach 26 01 12, D–8000 München 26, German Federal Republic.

SECTION 104 [Repealed] **104.01**

Section 104 was repealed from August 13, 1990 (S.I. 1990 No. 1440).

SECTION 280 [1988] **104.02**

Note. In the application of the section to the Isle of Man: in subsection (2) the words "England, Wales or Northern Ireland" are replaced by "The Isle of Man"; the word "solicitor" is replaced by "advocate"; and subsection (4) is omitted (S.I. 1990 No. 1505).

Article **104.02A**

A. J. Webb, "Patent agents: The new privilege", (1990–91) 20 CIPA 477.

Commentary on Sections 104 [Repealed] and 280 [1988]

General **104.03**

Section 280 [1988] came into effect on August 13, 1990 (S.I. 1990 No. 1440).

The nature of privilege

—General and the grounds of privilege **104.06**

For the general nature of "legal professional" and "legal advice" privilege and the possible limitation of privilege for patent agents, see A. J. Webb ((1989–90) 19 CIPA 279), with comment thereon by J. C. H. Ellis ((1989–90) CIPA 380) and the further paper by A. J. Webb listed in para. 104.2A *supra*. While it is well settled that, where trade secrets are involved, a court may restrict inspection of discovered documents, the discovering party has the onus of seeking a special order in this regard and of justifying it (*Roussel-Uclaf* v. *ICI (No. 2)*, [1990] RPC 45).

Legal professional privilege arising from actual or contemplated proceedings **104.08**

The proceedings which give rise to the privilege can be foreign proceedings, for example documents created in the course of United States litigation and subject to a "Protective Order" prohibiting their use outside those proceedings (*Minnesota Mining* v. *Rennicks*, [1991] FSR 97); and privilege has been accorded to an analytical report prepared on advice from a British patent agent after samples of a defendant's product had been seized in French litigation (*Société Française Hoechst* v. *Allied Colloids*, SRIS C/91/91; [1992] FSR 66), it there being opined that it is immaterial who commissioned such a report provided that it was brought into existence for the purposes of litigation. For a doubt whether patent agents enjoy a litigator's privilege when acting before a patents county court, see para. 96.23 *supra*.

104.09 *Limitations on privilege*

For a discussion on privilege under United States law, see [1991] EIPR 54. Privilege for a British patent agent, as a non-lawyer, was denied by a U.S. court in *Chubb* v. *National Bank of Washington* ((1985) USPQ 1002).

105.01

SECTION 105

Note. The prospective amendment of section 105 took effect from August 13, 1990 (S.I. 1990 No. 1440).

107.01

SECTION 107

In section 107(3) the words "a recorded decree arbitral" have been replaced by "an extract registered decree arbitral bearing a warrant for execution issued by the sheriff court of any sheriffdom in Scotland" (Debtors (Scotland) Act 1987 (c. 18, Sched. 6)).

COMMENTARY ON SECTION 107

Awards of costs

107.03 *—Basis of awards*

In *Haynes International's Patent* (SRIS O/105/89, *noted* IPD 13196) a special award of costs was made where the unsuccessful applicant for revocation required a witness from the United States to attend for cross-examination.

107.05 *Security for costs (subs. (4))*

The current practice is only to require security for costs to be given by an applicant in *ex parte* proceedings before the Comptroller if that person neither lives nor resides within the EEC (*Kokta's Applications*, SRIS O/16/90).

COMMENTARY ON SECTION 109

109.02 *General*

The term "statutory maximum" in relation to fines for criminal offences is now defined (variously for: England and Wales; Scotland; and Northern Ireland) in amended Schedule 1 to the Interpretation Act 1978 (c. 30) (Criminal Justice Act 1988 (c. 33), Sched. 15, para. 58).

COMMENTARY ON SECTION 110

Penalties **110.03**

The term "standard scale" in relation to fines for criminal offences is now defined (variously for: England and Wales; Scotland; and Northern Ireland) in amended Schedule 1 to the Interpretation Act 1978 (c. 30) (Criminal Justice Act 1988 (c. 33), Sched. 15, para. 58).

Patented product **110.05**

The ECJ has ruled that it is contrary to TRa. 30 to found an offence of false marking that a trade mark is registered when the mark is registered in other EEC countries (*Pall Corp.* v. *Dahlhausen*, (*ECJ Case* 238/89), *The Times*, February 4, 1991, *noted* (1991) 3(2) IPBB 8).

SECTION 114 [Repealed] **114.01**

Note. The repeal of section 114 took effect from August 13, 1990 (S.I. 1990 No. 1400).

SECTION 115 [Repealed] **115.01**

Note. The repeal of section 115 took effect from August 13, 1990. The section was then replaced by section 281 [1988] (S.I. 1990 No. 1400).

RELEVANT RULES

Rule 90 [1990]: *Agents* **115.03**

Note. Paragraphs (3) and (4) of rule 90 [1982] were deleted by S.I. 1990 No. 1455 and replaced by a new rule, for which see para. 115.03A *infra*.

THE PATENT AGENTS (NON-RECOGNITION OF CERTAIN AGENTS BY COMPTROLLER) RULES 1990 (S.I. 1990 No. 1454) **115.03A**

1. These Rules may be cited as the Patent Agents (Non-recognition of Certain Agents by Comptroller) Rules 1990 and shall come into force on 13th August 1990.

2. In these Rules—

"the Act" means the Copyright, Designs and Patents Act 1988 [c. 48];
"the Comptroller" means the Comptroller-General of Patents, Designs and Trade Marks;
"the register" means the register of patent agents required to be kept pursuant to rules made under section 275 of the Act [see the

Register of Patent Agents Rules, S.I. 1990 No. 1457 (reprinted at para. F01–F23 *infra*)].

3. The Comptroller is hereby authorised to refuse to recognise as agent in respect of any business under the Patents Act 1949 [c. 87], the Registered Designs Act 1949 [c. 88] or the Patents Act 1977 [c. 37]—

(a) a person who has been convicted of an offence under section 88 of the Patents Act 1949, section 114 of the Patents Act 1977 or section 276 of the Act;
(b) an individual whose name has been erased from and not restored to the register on the ground of misconduct;
(c) a person who is found by the Secretary of State to have been guilty of such conduct as would, in the case of an individual registered in the register, render him liable to have his name erased from the register on the ground of misconduct;
(d) a partnership or body corporate of which one of the partners or directors is a person whom the Comptroller could refuse to recognise under paragraph (a), (b) or (c) above.

COMMENTARY ON SECTION 281 [1988]

115.05 *Rules for recognition of agent (subss. (2)–(4))*

The Patent Agents (Non-recognition of Certain Agents by Comptroller) Rules 1990 (S.I. 1990 No. 1454, reprinted in para. 115.03A *supra*) have been made upon the bringing into force of section 281 [1988], the concomitant repeal of section 115 and omission of rule 90(3) and (4), for which see paras. 115.01 and 115.03 *supra*. Rule 3 of these new Rules mirrors the terms of section 281(2). However, no rule has been made (under s. 281(3) [1988]) to prescribe circumstances of deemed misconduct.

A disciplinary case before the Comptroller is referred to in *Law* v. *Chartered Institute of Patent Agents* ([1919] 2 Ch. 276). Here an accusation of "disgraceful professional conduct" was not upheld.

115.06 *Residence or place of business of agent*

No rule has been made in support or amplification of section 281(5) [1988] and, as rule 30 has not been amended to permit an address for service outside the United Kingdom (for which see para. 32.16 *supra*), it appears to follow that, while the Comptroller must refuse to recognise an agent who neither resides in, nor has a place of business in, the EEC (or Isle of Man), there is a discretion to recognise other agents, but these must provide an address for service which is within the United Kingdom (or Isle of Man).

SECTION 117—RELEVANT RULE

117.02 Rule 91 [1990]—*Correction of errors in patents and applications*

Paragraph (1) has been replaced by:

91.—(1) Except where rule 45(3) or paragraph 4 of Schedule 4 has effect, a request for the correction of an error of translation or transcription or of a clerical error or mistake in any specification of a patent, in an application for a patent or in any document filed in connection with a patent or such an application shall be made on Patents Form 47/77 and shall be accompanied by a document clearly identifying the proposed correction; and the comptroller may, if he thinks fit, require that the correction be shown on a copy of the document of which correction is sought.

In paragraph (4), the words "three months" have been changed to "two months". In paragraph (5), the words "three months of the receipt of the copies" have been changed to "the period of two months beginning on the date when the copies are sent to him".

COMMENTARY ON SECTION 117

General **117.04**

Rule 91 no longer applies to alteration of an address or address for service, for which rule 45(3) (discussed in paras. 32.23 and 32.24 *supra*) now applies, nor to the correction of a translation of a European patent (UK) under section 80(3), for which see para. 80.10.

Nature of permissible correction (r. 91(2)) **117.06**

The Main Work does not discuss to whom the correction has to be "immediately evident", but it is thought that this has to be to the notional addressee of the specification upon him reading that document, rather than to its draftsman, *i.e.* the test is objective rather than subjective: otherwise that addressee cannot be in a position to judge whether a specification really means what it appears to him to mean.

There is a high evidentiary burden to be met before correction can be permitted (*Tragen's Application*, SRIS O/96/90), where a discrepancy between the specification and its priority document did not establish an error in the specification because the discrepancy could have arisen from an error of judgment by its draftsman.

EPO decisions on correction **117.07**

The EPO has ruled that EPCaa. 123(2) and 138(1)(*c*) override EPCr. 88 so that a correction is not allowed if it would have the effect of introducing new subject-matter or extend the scope of protection (*EPO Decision T* 401/88, "*Test piece/BOSCH*", OJEPO 7/1990, 297; [1990] EPOR 640), but the EPO Enlarged Board of Appeal is considering whether correction can be allowed if this would extend the subject-matter of the document as originally filed; and also whether evidence is admissible after the date of filing to show that nothing else would have been intended than the offered correction (*EPO Case G* 3/89, *noted* OJEPO 4/1990, 187). Meanwhile, the EPO has also held that correction is retrospective, while amendment is not; and that, while the existence of an error can be demonstrated subjectively by any evidence, the requested correction must be determinable objectively from the entire text of the patent in isolation, see *EPO Decision*

T 200/89 *"Obvious error/BOEING"* ([1990] 5 EPOR 407), where this was possible because the claims and description were inconsistent and the error was identifiable in the claims since otherwise all of the examples would have been outside their scope. However, the Comptroller has refused to follow EPO decisions on correction as section 117 is not mentioned in section 130(7) (*Alps Electric's Application*, SRIS O/12/90, *noted* IPD 13083).

117.08 *"Correction" as contrasted with "Amendment"*

If *EPO Decision T* 401/88, *"Test piece/BOSCH"*, OJEPO 7/1990, 297; [1990] EPOR 640) discussed in para. 117.07 *supra*, is applicable under the Act, then "correction" would be aligned with "amendment", contrary to the position indicated in the Main Work, with consequences for possible revocation under section 72(1)(*d*) or (*e*).

The EPO has allowed correction of an erroneous withdrawal of designation of a Member State (*EPO Decision J* 10/87, *"Retraction of withdrawal/INLAND STEEL"*, [1989] 7 EPOR 437, *abridged* OJEPO 8/1989, 323), see para. 14.39 *supra*.

PRACTICE UNDER SECTION 117

117.13 *Request for correction*

Mere alteration of an applicant's address can now be made in writing without PF 47/77 under rule 45(3) discussed in paras. 32.23 and 32.24. Rule 91 also does not apply to correction of a translation of a European patent (UK) or application therefor: such is governed by section 80(3), see paras. 80.02 and 80.10. The correction sought must be clearly identified, though it is not now necessary to show the correction on a copy of the document to be corrected unless the Comptroller should so require.

117.14 *Opposition to correction*

The period for lodging opposition is now only *two* months from advertisement in the O.J. (r. 91(4)), and remains inextensible (r. 110(2)). Any counter-statement to such opposition is now due within *two* months, calculated from the date of dispatch of the statement by the Comptroller to the applicant for correction (r. 91(5)).

118.01 **SECTION 118**

Note. The amendment to section 118, noted in the Main Work, came into effect on January 7, 1991 (S.I. 1990 No. 2168).

SECTION 118—RELEVANT RULES

118.04 **Rule 92 [1990]—***Request for information under section 118*

In paragraph (1), subparagraph (c) now reads:

(c) as to when an application for a patent has been withdrawn, has been taken to be withdrawn, has been treated as having been withdrawn, has been refused or has been treated as having been refused;

in subparagraph (g), "an" has been added before "application"; the word "and" has been inserted after subparagraph (h); and "below" has been deleted from the end of subparagraph (i). After subparagraph (2)(b), "and" has been added. A new subparagraph (4) has been added reading:

(4) In this rule, "existing patent" means a patent mentioned in section 127(2)(a) and (c) and "existing application" means an application mentioned in section 127(2)(b).

Rule 93 [1990]—*Inspection of documents under section 118* **118.05**

In paragraph (1), the references to paragraphs "(6)" and "(5)" have been changed to "(5)" and "(4)" respectively; "prescribed" has been added before "fee"; and "to" has been deleted before "any patent". In paragraph (2) "below" has been deleted after "rule 96." Subparagraph (3), having previously been revoked, subparagraphs (4)–(6) have been renumbered as (3)–(5). In what is now sub-rule (4)(e), the comma after "52(2)" has been replaced by "or"; and "below" has been deleted from sub-rule 93(4)(f). Present paragraph (5) has had all words after "inspection" replaced by:

(a) any document or any part of a document—
 (i) which in his opinion disparages any person in a way likely to damage him; or
 (ii) the publication or exploitation of which would in his opinion be generally expected to encourage offensive, immoral or anti-social behaviour; or
(b) the file (but not the report) of the international preliminary examination of an international application under the Patent Cooperation Treaty; or
(c) any document filed with or sent to the Patent Office before 1st June 1978.

A new paragraph (6) has been added, reading:

(6) No appeal shall lie from a decision of the comptroller under paragraph (5)(a) above not to make a document or part of a document available for public inspection.

Rule 95 [1990]—*Bibliographic data for purposes of section 118(3)(b)* **118.07**

The word "and" has been added after sub-rule (d); sub-rule (e) now reads:

> if the application has been withdrawn, has been taken to be withdrawn, has been treated as having been withdrawn, has been refused or is treated as having been refused, that fact.

COMMENTARY ON SECTION 118

118.11 *General*

Under section 47(3) [1988], the Comptroller has authorised the copying of United Kingdom patent applications and patent specifications laid open to public inspection pursuant to statutory requirements, and also English translations of European patents (UK) filed at the Patent Office under section 77, "for the purpose of disseminating information about matters of general scientific, technical, commercial or economic interest" (O.J. March 6, 1991).

The files of the Patents County Court are, as with High Court files, not normally open to public inspection ((1990–91) 20 CIPA 412). To obtain access to court files when there is no entitlement to do so is a contempt of court (*Dobson* v. *Hastings, The Times,* November 18, 1991).

Access to register and to documents filed at Patent Office (subs. (1))

118.13 *—Documents available concerning "existing patents"*

Rule 93(6) [1982] has become rule 93(5)(c) [1990], see para. 118.05 *supra*.

118.16 *Documents not available (r. 93(5))*

Despite what is stated in the Main Work, new rule 93(5)(a) (reprinted in para. 118.07 *supra*) has now provided the Comptroller with power to exclude from inspection, and (by new r. 52(3), reprinted in para. 32.10, *supra*) also refuse to supply a copy, any document which: (i) "in his opinion disparages any person in a way likely to disparage him"; or (ii) of which the publication or exploitation would "in his opinion be generally expected to encourage offensive, immoral or anti-social behaviour". Moreover, a decision under the first of these provisions has been made unappealable (r. 93(6)), made under the authority of s.97(1)(*d*)).

118.17 *Confidentiality*

The Comptroller has refused an order for confidentiality in respect of filed evidence where that evidence had previously been before the Patents Court without request for confidentiality in those proceedings (*Coal Industry's Patent*, SRIS O/11/90, *noted* IPD 13081).

PRACTICE UNDER SECTION 118

118.20 *Inspection of register and file*

Rule 93(5)(e) [1982] has become rule 93(4)(e) [1990].

Now that the Patent Office has moved to Newport, see para. 123.16 *infra*, all files are stored there. However, a public search room has been established at 25 Southampton Buildings, London WC2A 1AY at which register and file inspections may be made, though it is unlikely that files can be made available until at least 48 hours after request because of the need to transport these from Newport. Prior application should therefore be made by telephone (071–438 4707). Files and register entries can also be inspected at Newport (tel. 0633 814560 or 814657).

Inspection is also possible of PCT applications between valid entry into the national phase and republication ((1990–91) 20 CIPA 414).

Although no fee is now payable on filing PF 23/77, photocopy charges remain for copies of documents requested on that form (O.J. July 24, 1991). Moreover, the London search room will normally only be prepared to copy documents from files inspected there if the total does not exceed 20 pages: otherwise, the file is returned to Newport and the requested copies dispatched by post from there.

PF 23/77 (for register and file inspection) has been revised (see para. 141.23 *infra*). Request for information concerning renewal is now made by completing section 3 of that form. As the register is now computerised for patents in force, a request for inspection of the register will normally be met by providing a copy of the entry from the Patent Office OPTICS database: this automatically contains the date when the last renewal fee was paid if the patent remains in force.

If an application has not yet been published under section 16, Forms 23/77 and 24/77 (the latter for obtaining copies of documents from the file) will only be accepted if filed by the applicant or his *previously authorised* agent, this being a consequence of rule 93(2) (reprinted in para. 118.05 in the Main Work, with amendment thereof noted in para. 118.05 *supra*).

COMMENTARY ON SECTION 119

Service in the ordinary course of the post (r. 97) 119.04

It is understood that the Comptroller does not recognise as "post" anything sent to him by other than a Royal Mail service: *i.e.* he does not recognise courier services such as the "Red Star" service of British Rail.

SECTION 120—RELEVANT RULE

Rule 99 [1990]—*Excluded days* 120.03

After subparagraph (1)(c) "and" has been added.

COMMENTARY ON SECTION 121 121.03

As a consequence of the Patent Office acquiring "Trading Fund" status from October 1, 1991 (for which see para. B04 *infra*), the Comptroller's Annual Report is now prepared for each financial year ending March 31st and has to be presented to Parliament before November 30th, the 1991 Report covering the extended period to March 31, 1991 (S.I. 1991 No. 1796).

SECTION 123 123.01

Note. The repeal of subsection (2)(*k*) took effect from August 13, 1990 (S.I. 1990 No. 1400).

RELEVANT RULES 123.02

The Patents Rules 1982 (as amended) have been wholly replaced by the Patents Rules 1990 (S.I. 1990 No. 2384), effective from January 7, 1991. These constitute a consolidation of the previous rules but with further changes, particularly in stipulating a reduced and uniform period of two months (if appropriate, from the date a communication is *sent* from the Patent Office, rather than from its date of receipt, as formerly) for time periods in the Rules governing oppositions and other *inter partes* proceedings. However, time limits which had already commenced to run under the 1982 Rules are not affected by these changes (see r. 123(4), reprinted in para. 127.02 *infra*).

For the most part the 1990 Rules retain the rule numbering of the replaced 1982 Rules, but see the "Important Notice" on the inside cover of this Supplement. Throughout the new Rules the forms are now referred to as "Patents Form x/77" and not as "Patents Form No. x/77" as formerly. However, for simplicity, this change has been ignored.

123.03 Rule 1 [1990]—*Citation and commencement*

Rule 1 now reads:

1. These Rules may be cited as the Patents Rules 1990 and shall come into force on 7th January, 1991.

123.04 Rule 2 [1990]—*Interpretation*

In the preamble the words ", unless the context otherwise requires" have been deleted. In the definition of "the Act" the words after "1977" no longer appear (but see para. 123.05 *infra*). In definition (*c*) of "declared priority date", "section 8(1)" in the Main Work should read "section 81(1)"; and, in the following definition (d), "the priority for which" has been changed to "the priority of which". The definitions of "existing patent" and "existing application" have been deleted.

Notes. 1. The definitions of "existing patent" and "existing application" are now to be found in rule 92(4), but are then only applicable to the operation of rule 92 (*Request for information under section 118*).

2. The definition of "declared priority date" in rule 2(*d*) will probably need some amendment in 1992 consequent upon revision of the PCT Regulations from July 1, 1992: it will then be possible to withdraw a priority declaration for an international application during expiry of the international phase, that is possibly after publication of the international application has already occurred.

123.05 *Fees*

Rule 3 of the Patents (Fees) Rules 1986, reprinted in the Main Work) has now been replaced by rule 3 of the Patents (Fees) Rules 1991 (S.I. 1991 No. 1627) with different wording but similar effect, except that there has been added to the end of the rule the words:

> "or, where payment may be made within a prescribed period of time after the form has been filed, the fee so specified shall be paid within that period".

Rule 3 [1990]—*Construction* **123.05A**

3. In these Rules, save where otherwise indicated,—

(a) references to a section are references to that section of the Act;
(b) references to a rule are references to that rule in these Rules;
(c) references to a Schedule are references to that Schedule in these Rules;
(d) references to a form are references to that form as set out in Schedule 1;

and references to the filing of a form or other document are references to filing it at the Patent Office.

Note. This is an entirely new Rule 3 (divided out of previous rule 1) in order to take the place of an already repealed rule so as to preserve the numbering of subsequent rules.

Rule 4 [1990]—*Forms* **123.06**

Rule 4 [1990] now reads:

4.—(1) The forms of which the use is required by these Rules (except those mentioned in rule 123(1)) are those set out in Schedule 1.

(2) A requirement under these Rules to use a form set out in Schedule 1 is satisfied by the use either of a replica of that form or of a form which is acceptable to the comptroller and contains the information required by the form set out in that Schedule.

Note. The forms under the rules have been moved from Schedule 2 to Schedule 1. Most of these have been reprinted, for which see paras. 141.01–141.58 *infra*.

Rule 100 [1990]—*Correction of irregularities* **123.07**

Paragraph (2) has been re-set to read:

(2) In the case of an irregularity or prospective irregularity—

(a) which consists of a failure to comply with any limitation as to times or periods specified in the Act or the 1949 Act or prescribed in these Rules or the Patents Rules 1968 as they continue to apply which has occurred, or appears to the comptroller is likely to occur in the absence of a direction under this rule;
(b) which is attributable wholly or in part to an error, default or omission on the part of the Patent Office; and
(c) which it appears to the comptroller should be rectified,

the comptroller may direct that the time or period in question shall be altered but not otherwise.

In paragraph (3), "or 111" has been added after "110".

123.08 Rule 101 [1990]—*Dispensation by comptroller*

In line 4, "that that document" has been changed to "that document".

123.09 Rule 102 [1990]—*Remission of fees*

In paragraph (1), subparagraph (a) having previously been deleted, subparagraphs (b) and (c) have been redesignated as (a) and (b), and "and" has been inserted between them. In paragraph (3), the reference to "paragraph (1)(c)" is now to "paragraph (1)(b)".

123.10 Rule 110 [1990]—*Alteration of time limits*

Paragraph (1) has been reworded to read:

> (1) The times or periods prescribed by these Rules for doing any act or taking any proceeding thereunder, other than times or periods prescribed in the provisions mentioned in paragraph (2) below, and subject to paragraphs (3) and (4) below, may be extended by the comptroller if he thinks fit, upon such notice to the parties and upon such terms as he may direct; and such extension may be granted notwithstanding that the time or period for doing such act or taking such proceeding has expired.

In paragraph (2), the rules therein specified are now: rules 6(1), 26 (so far as it relates to rule 6(1)), 39(1) and (2), 40(2), 41(1), 43(2), 59(2), 64(1), 65(1), 71(1), 78(1), 81(1), 82(1) and 91(4) and paragraph 4(2) of Schedule 2.

Paragraph (3) now reads:

> (3) A time or period prescribed in rules 6(2) and (6) (including the period therein prescribed as substituted by rule 85(3)(c) and (d)), 15(1), 23, 25(2) and (3) (except so far as it relates to the filing of claims for the purposes of the application and filing of the abstract), 26 (except so far as it relates to rule 6(1)), 33(2), (3) and (5), 34, 41(4), 81(2) and (3), 82(2) and (3), 83(3) and 85(1) and (7), paragraph (6) below, paragraph 1(3) of Schedule 2 and paragraph 2 of Schedule 4 shall, if not previously extended, be extended for one month upon filing Patents Form 50/77 before the end of that month; and where in any proceedings more than one such time or period expires on the same day (but not otherwise), those times or periods may be extended upon the filing of a single such form.

Paragraph (3A) has been renumbered as paragraph (4) and amended to read:

(4) Without prejudice to paragraph (3) above, a time or period (other than any time or period expiring before 24th March 1987) prescribed in

the rules referred to in that paragraph may, upon request made on Patents Form 52/77, be extended or further extended if the comptroller thinks fit, whether or not the time or period (including any extension obtained under paragraph (3) above) has expired; and the comptroller may allow an extension, or further extension, under this paragraph on such terms as he may direct and subject, unless he otherwise directs, to the furnishing of a statutory declaration or affidavit verifying the grounds for the request.

Paragraphs (3B)–(4) are now renumbered as (5)–(7) respectively: in new paragraph (5) (formerly paragraph (3B)), "paragraph (3A)" has been changed to "paragraph (4); and "made" has been added after "extensions are to be". In new paragraph (6) (formerly paragraph (3C), "paragraph (3A)" and "paragraph (3B)" have been respectively changed to "paragraph (4)" and "paragraph (5)"; after "invite him" the words "within two months after the notification is sent to him" have been inserted; and a proviso has been added reading:

"Provided that, in a case where a notification under this paragraph is sent to the applicant before these Rules come into force, this paragraph shall have effect as if the words "within two months after the notification is sent to him" were omitted." In new paragraph (7) commas have been inserted before and after the words "or any further".

Rule 111 [1990]—*Calculation of times or periods* **123.11**

In paragraph (6)(c)(iii), after "application" the words "and the day on which the declaration specifying that application" were omitted from the Main Work.

Rule 113 [1990]—*Translations* **123.12**

In paragraph (1), "80" has been deleted and "40" inserted at the same place; and the words "and paragraph (3) below" have been changed to "paragraph (3) below and paragraph (5) of Schedule 4". Paragraph (3) has been amended to read:

(3) Where any document which, or any part of which, is in a language other than English—

(a) is referred to in a search report drawn up under Article 18 of the Patent Co-operation Treaty; or
(b) is cited in the statement contained in an international preliminary examination report established under Article 35 of that Treaty,

and any such report is filed at the Patent Office in relation to the provisions of section 89A, a translation into English of that document or part verified to the satisfaction of the comptroller as corresponding to the original text thereof shall, if the comptroller so directs, be filed within two months of the date on which such direction is given.

In paragraph (4) the words "unless such a translation has already been filed under section 77(6)" have been changed to read:

"unless—
(a) such a translation has already been filed under section 77(6); or
(b) the comptroller determines that it is not necessary".

123.15 Rule 116—*Reports of cases*

Rule 116 has been rephrased to read:

116. The comptroller shall from time to time publish reports of—

(a) cases relating to patents, trade marks, registered designs and design right decided by him; and
(b) cases relating to patents (whether under the Act or otherwise), trade marks, registered designs, copyright and design right decided by any court or body (whether in the United Kingdom or elsewhere),

being cases which he considers to be generally useful or important.

PATENT OFFICE (ADDRESS) RULES

123.16 The address of the Patent Office was altered (with effect from April 28, 1991) to "The Patent Office, Cardiff Road, Newport, Gwent NP9 1RH" with an alternative address of "25 Southampton Buildings, London WC2A 1AY" (Patent Office (Address) (Amendment) Rules 1991, S.I. 1991 No. 675). The latter address is merely a filing office (with telephone number 071–438 4700), all correspondence being dealt with in the Newport office, which has the telephone number 0633 814000. Some useful individual telephone numbers for enquiries to the Newport Office for various matters were published at (1990–91) 20 CIPA 414.

To protect against the possible (though considered remote) possibility of documents and fees going astray between London and Newport, it is possible to supply *additional* copies of the forms and documents by facsimile transmission to 0633 814814 on the same day as the primary documents and fees are filed, though these will only serve to provide *prima facie* evidence of original filing: enquiries concerning this facility can be made by telephone to 0633 814570 (O.J. July 10, 1991).

COMMENTARY ON SECTION 123

Definitions for Patents Rules (r. 2) **123.18**

The definitions of "existing patent" and "existing application" have been removed from rule 2 to rule 92(4). These definitions, however, now apply only for the purpose of rule 92 (*Request for information under rule 118*), for which see para. 118.12 in the Main Work.

Form and content of documents (subs. (2)(a)) **123.19**

The use of replica or modified forms is now officially sanctioned, provided that it contains the information required by the official form and is otherwise also acceptable to the Comptroller (r. 4(2) [1990], reprinted in para. 123.06 *supra*). If such a form fails to satisfy the Comptroller, presumably time would be permitted (at least under r. 110(4) [1990]) to rectify the deficiency, *but this cannot be guaranteed if necessary information has been omitted from the form*. To assist the completion of forms, the Patent Office has made available a computer software program, to be run from a personal computer and an HP Laserjet III printer, whereby the following forms may be printed out and completed in a single operation, *viz*. PF 1, 7, 9–12, 14, 16, 20, 21, 23, 24, 28, 43, 47, 49–51, 53, 54, 56, 57 and NP 1, see O.J. August 28, 1991. Thus, although the official forms are printed on coloured paper, for which see para. 140.02 *infra*, black/white replicas would appear to be acceptable.

Procedure before the Comptroller (subs. (2)(b) and r. 100)

General **123.20**

The revision of rule 100(2) (noted in para. 123.07 *supra*) clarifies its wording, but does not seem to make any substantive change.

Since the move of the Patent Office to Newport, Gwent (for which see para. 123.16 *supra*) all filing receipts emanate from there and documents sent to, or hand delivered to, the London address are merely date-stamped and then forwarded, unopened, to Newport. However, for documents taken by hand to the London office between 10 a.m. and 4 p.m., it is possible for the agent to provide a check list listing the documents delivered in an unsealed or resealable package. For this purpose, the Patent Office has introduced a four-part carbonless copy check list (O.J. October 30, 1991). When this is done, the package is opened at the London office, its contents checked against the check list, and the first page of each document or form date-stamped. All the documents are then replaced in the package which is then sealed and given an identification number. This number is endorsed on a separate receipt, the receipt and check list are date-stamped, and one copy of the checklist and receipt is handed back to the person lodging the package. However, no check can be made whether cheques contained in the package are for the total of the sums due in respect of the documents so lodged. The receipt, but not the check list, is issued for all documents filed by hand in London. If the documents are filed outside the hours of 10 a.m. and 4 p.m., the receipt can be collected the next day from the London filing office. One of the other of the copies of the check list is eventually returned to the agent after the formal checking procedure in Newport (which would otherwise be as described above); and the other copies are retained respectively in London and Newport.

When documents are filed by post, or filed sealed or open for checking, the outside of the envelope should be marked with the sender's name and address and an identifying number added to assist in tracing envelopes in the case of later queries on the filing date.

Applications for reinstatement of an application under rule 100 are now advertised in the O.J., see *e.g.* O.J. May 30, 1990. Presumably, the Comptroller would take notice of any representations made to him by another party, although there is no procedure for formal opposition to such an appliction. There was a further advertisement on the outcome of that application, see O.J. June 13, 1990.

123.21 *—Irregularity in procedure*

In *Aiskin Seiki's Application* (SRIS O/74/90, *noted* IPD 13139) the Comptroller refused self-certification by the patent agent that a priority document had been filed when no trace of this, or a receipt therefor, could be found in the Patent Office, and pointed out that the agent's evidence did not go beyond an intention to file the document, not that it had been filed: reinstatement of the claimed priority was, however, allowed under rule 110(3A) (now r. 110(4)).

In *Harding's Patent* (SRIS O/94/90, *noted* IPD 13215) an error, default or omission by the Patent Office was acknowledged because the allowability of amendments had been decided without consideration of observations by a proper party.

The Comptroller also has limited powers under rule 85(11) to rectify irregularities in procedure which occur during the international phase of an international application for a patent (UK), for which see para. 89B.13 of the Main Work and *supra*.

123.22 *—Relief under rule 100 is discretionary and may be conditional*

Because relief under rule 100 is discretionary, the delay in seeking this is a factor to be considered (*Jovanovic's Patent*, SRIS O/115/90, *noted* IPD 14028), an extreme case where the patent sought to be restored, if rule 100 could be invoked, had lapsed 13 years previously.

When there is a reinstatement under rule 100, this fact is now advertised in the O.J., see *e.g.* O.J. August 15, 1990.

123.23 *—Dispensation by Comptroller (r. 101)*

Rule 101 cannot be used to dispense with the explicit requirements of the Act or Rules and therefore cannot be used to dispense with the payment of a required fee (*Commissariat à l'Energie's Patent*, SRIS O/143/90, *noted* IPD 14027).

Fees and remission of fees (subss. (2)(c) and (4))

123.24 *—Fees*

Fees may now be paid by direct bank tansfer to the Account of "The Patent Office" at the Bank of England, Threadneedle Street, London EC2R 8AH (A/C 25011006), but a reference should be quoted in order that the payment becomes linked with forms sent separately to the Patent Office (O.J. October 9, 1991).

The Department of Trade and Industry (Fees) (Amendment) Order 1990 (S.I. 1990 No. 1473) amended S.I. 1988 No. 93, cited in the Main Work, to enable the

Secretary of State to take into account, in fixing the level of Patent Office fees, "any other function of the Secretary of State and the Comptroller in relation to patents", including work done on legislative proposals and developments and of any EC institution or international convention.

When fees are increased, care needs to be taken to ascertain whether the fee revision takes effect from the date when the fee is actually tendered (as is normally the case, *e.g.* see notice in O.J. November 6, 1991), or whether (when an extension of time for fee payment is permitted), exceptionally, the previous fee remains applicable if the due date preceded the payment date.

—Remission of fees (r. 102) **123.25**

Sub-rules 102(1)(b) and (c) have become sub-rules 102(1)(a) and (b) respectively, see para. 123.09 *supra*.

Advertisements (subs. (2)(e)) **123.27**

Rules 62 and 66 [1982] have become, respectively, rules 61 and 65 [1990].

Time limits (subs. (2)(h) and rr. 110 and 111)

—General **123.30**

Paragraphs (3A)–(4) have become respectively paragraphs (4)–(7), see para. 123.10, *supra*.

—The inextensible time periods under rule 110 (r. 110(2)) **123.31**

To the list of inextensible time periods has now been added the period for applying for restoration under section 28, this now being the 19-month period prescribed in rule 41. Otherwise the specified inextensible periods were mainly of three months permitted for various kinds of oppositions. However, these periods have generally been reduced to only *two* months. Rules 60, 65 and 66 [1982] have become respectively rules 59, 64 and 65 [1990].

—Automatic limited extension of certain time periods (r. 110(3)) **123.32**

Rules 79B and 85(3) [1982], each cited in the Main Work, have become respectively Schedule 4, paragraph 2 and rule 85(7) [1990]; and there have been added to the list of rules covered by rule 110(3) rule 41(4) (*paying fees after restoration has been allowed*) and rule 123(6) (*payment of additional fee when reinstatement allowed under rule 110(4), formerly rule 110(3C))*. Also, it is now stipulated that PF 50/77 must be filed *before* the end of the month for which the extension is required, thereby making statutory the decision in *Konishiroku's Application*, cited in the Main Work.

—Further discretionary extension of the time periods covered by rule 110(3) (r. 110(4)–(6)) **123.33**

Sub-rules 110(3A)–(3C) have become respectively sub-rules 110(4)–(6), see para. 123.10 *supra*. Extension under rule 110(4) is now possible "whether or not the time or period (including any extension obtained under rule 110(3) has expired", this being made possible by new section 123(3A). Rule 110(4) now also provides for the Comptroller to call for evidence (by statutory declaration or affidavit) verifying the request for discretionary extension, and such request can be expected to be made in most cases under sub-rule 110(4). Where reinstatement is permitted, sub-rule (6) now requires PF 53/77 to be filed within two months after the notification of reinstatement is sent to the applicant (unless this was before January 7, 1991), but this period is extensible by one month under rule 110(3), see para. 123.32 *supra*.

Although the same considerations do not apply to the grant of a discretionary extension under rules 110 and 111 as apply to patent restoration under section 28, nevertheless there is an analogy in that a loss of rights should not be suffered through unforseen circumstances and an underlying intention to proceed with the application or patent is a necessary requirement in both cases: consequently, discretion should not be exercised under rule 110 where there has been a change of mind by whoever had the responsibility for deciding whether the required action should be timely taken (*Heatex Group's Application*, SRIS O/132/90). This case also held that a lack of care in making the decision not to proceed is not a determining factor under rules 110 and 111.

Where a patent (or application) is reinstated under this sub-rule after advertised lapsing, a notice now appears in the O.J., see, *e.g.* O.J. October 20, 1990.

123.36 —*Extension after lapsing (subs. (3A))*

In accordance with new subsection (3A), rule 110(4) now specifically provides for extension to be granted thereunder even though, without the extension, the application or patent has already lapsed, see para. 123.33 *supra*. However, it is not seen that the operation of new subsection 123(3A) has any effect in a case where no application for a patent under the Act ever came into existence, as distinct from one deemed to have lapsed. For the possible correction of errors occurring in the international phase of an international application for a patent (UK), see paras. 89.35 and 89.37 in the Main Work and *supra*.

As an example of the application of these rules, Application No. 2,129,502 can be noted: this was revived some years after it had erroneously been abandoned by failure to respond to a substantive examination objection.

123.37 —*Calculation of time limits*

Rule 110(4) has become rule 110(7), see para. 123.10 *supra*.

123.39 —*Extensions arising from postal dislocation or interruption in Patent Office operations (r. 111(1), (2) and (4)–(6))*

The EPO has held that a general interruption in the postal service is a question of fact and it accepted letters from the United Kingdom Patent Office that such interruption had occurred and such would have been certified if a request therefor had been made (*EPO Decision J* 11/88, "*Postal strike/LELAND STANFORD*", OJEPO 11/1989, 433; [1990] 1 EPOR 50), and a "general" disruption can be a local, rather than national, one provided that this is of general effect in that locality (*EPO Decision J* 3/90, "*Postal strike/FISHER SCIENTIFIC*", OJEPO 11/1991, 550 and *EPO Decision J* 04/90, "*Postal strike/MARELLO*", [1990] 7 EPOR 576).

Further general interruptions in the postal service have been certified to have occurred from February 8 to 20, 1991 (O.J. March 20, 1991).

Translations (subs. (2)(j) and r. 113) **123.41**

Rule 113(3) has been amended, see para. 123.32 *supra*, but without apparent change in effect, other than that rule 113(1) no longer applies to the proposed advertisement in the O.J. of an amendment to a European patent (UK) which is in the French or German language, rule 40 [1990] (for which see para. 27.02 in the Main Work and *supra*) no longer being made subject to rule 113(1). Rules 79A–79F are now respectively paragraphs 1–6 of Schedule 4 to the Rules, for which see paras. 77.03–77.06, 78.03 and 80.02 *supra*.

The Journal (subs. (6)) **123.47**

Since January 30, 1990 the O.J., in listing the filing of translations of European patents (UK), and the claims of applications therefor, has included also details of the application number and proprietor thereof: lists of such applications which have become void are also now listed, see O.J. January 31, 1990.

Patent law reports (subs. (7)) **123.48**

Rule 116 is mandatory in terms, but subsection (7) is in broader terms giving, for example, discretion for publication of reports of decisions relating to service marks, passing off, copyright, mis-use of confidential information or competition law.

COMMENTARY ON SECTION 125

General **125.06**

The Main Work refers (third paragraph) to the "extent of protection" being defined by reference to "an invention for a patent". More accurately, however, the "extent of protection" is defined by reference to "an invention", that invention being one for which either a patent has been granted or an application for a patent has been filed. The question then is to determine what that "invention" is; and that, in turn, then determines the extent of the protection conferred.

Meaning of "invention" **125.08**

The special rule of construction cited in the Main Work for claims which specify a purpose for which the claimed article or process is to be used (namely that such purpose has no effect on the scope of the claim), must now be in doubt following the decision by the EPO Enlarged Board of Appeal (*EPO Decision G 2/88, "Friction reducing additive/MOBIL III"*, OJEPO 4/1990, 93; [1990] 2 EPOR 73), discussed in para. 2.13 *supra* and at (1989–90) 19 CIPA 111 and 171). In this decision it was held that novelty can be conferred on a claim by inclusion therein of a mere, but novel, statement of purpose for obtaining a technical effect. If adopted into United Kingdom law, this decision ought to have the effect of narrowing the scope of a claim when considering this in the context of alleged infringement, as well as regards its novelty, by including the stated purpose as a claim-limiting feature, *i.e.* by treating it as a claim to a method of using the article or process for that specified (technical) use.

125.10 *Infringement test of "purposive construction"*

An important part of the decision in *Catnic* v. *Hill and Smith* ([1982] RPC 183 (HL)), discussed in the Main Work, is now seen to be the three questions which Lord Diplock there stated should be asked in cases where infringement by a variant of the literal wording of a claim is to be considered. These questions were paraphrased in *Improver Corp.* v. *Remington* ([1990] FSR 181) as follows:

(1) Does the variant have a material effect upon the way the invention works? If yes, the variant is outside the claim. If no—
(2) Would this (*i.e.* that the variant had no material effect) have been obvious at the date of publication of the patent to a reader skilled in the art? If no, the variant is outside the claim. If yes—
(3) Would the reader skilled in the art nevertheless have understood from the language of the claim that the patentee intended that strict compliance with the primary meaning was an essential requirement of the invention? If yes, the variant is outside the claim.

These three questions have been approved and applied in: *Southco* v. *Dzus* ([1990] RPC 587 and SRIS C/86/91 (CA)); *A.C. Edwards* v. *Acme* ([1990] RPC 621 and SRIS C/80/91 (CA)); *Black & Decker* v. *Flymo* (SRIS C/7/91, *noted* IPD 14075); and *Vax* v. *Hoover* (SRIS C/8/91, *noted* IPD 14097; *otherwise reported*, [1991] FSR 307). They must, therefore, now be regarded as the standard test for infringement, at least before the Patents Court. The *Improver* case is further discussed in para. 125.16 *infra*. These three questions were also applied by the Patents County Court in *Daily* v. *Établissements Fernand Berchet* ([1991] RPC 587), where the infringing construction was held to be an obviously immaterial variant of the literally claimed embodiment and not excluded from protection by any wording used by the patent draftsman. The Comptroller also applied the third question in *Schmersal's Patent* (SRIS O/72/91) in proceedings under section 71 (for which see para. 71.06 *supra*), there being no evidence to enable him to consider the first two questions: he then held that there was nothing in the patent which pointed to any intention to include variants like that in issue and consequently found no infringement since otherwise the required reasonable certainty for third parties required by the Protocol would not exist.

The decision in *Harrison* v. *Project & Design (No. 2)* ([1987] RPC 151 (CA)), cited in the Main Work, can be regarded as a case where the doctrine of purposive construction was used to narrow, rather than broaden, the literal wording of the claim.

The extent of protection under subsections (1) and (3)

125.11 *—General*

Where patent claims have been construed in a previous action by the Court of Appeal, the Patents Court will regard that construction as binding upon it (*Filhol* v. *Fairfax*, [1990] RPC 293).

CPCaa. 29 and 30, referred to in the Main Work, have become CPCaa. 25 and 26 [1989], see para. 86.03 *supra*.

125.12 *—Conformity of interpretation with EPC and CPC*

Where a claim is in the recommended European form with a prior art part and a characterising part, a court (on an unsuccessful striking out action, for which see para. 61.23 *supra*) said that it is not unarguable that a court should more readily give a liberal construction to the applicant's description of the prior art than to the part of the claim in which he describes the point of his invention (*Mead Corp.* v. *McLaren Packaging*, SRIS C/51/90).

Limitation of literal wording 125.13

The EPO has held that, where a specification specifies a feature to be an overriding requirement of the invention, that feature should be read into the claim in the light of the Protocol to EPCa. 69 (*EPO Decision T* 416/87, "*Block copolymer/JSR*", OJEPO 10/1990, 415). Also, interpretation of a claim in accordance with examples in the specification has been applied in preference to its strictly literal interpretation (*EPO Decision T 361/88, "Hollow filaments/DU PONT*", [1991] EPOR 1); and, in *EPO Decision T* 416/87, "*Block copolymer/JSR*" ([1991] EPOR 25) a claim was interpreted as including a feature absent from the claim but indicated by the specification to be an overriding requirement of the invention.

Meaning of technical terms 125.15

In *A. C. Edwards* v. *Acme Signs* ([1990] RPC 621 and SRIS C/80/91 (CA)) an extended meaning was given to the word "spring", an attempt at limiting this meaning being dismissed as trying to import a feature that was not there; and, in *Bonzel* v. *Intervention (No. 3)* ([1991] RPC 553), the word "near" was construed according to the perception of the skilled man in the light of the problem which the invention set out to solve. In *Minnesota Mining* v. *Rennicks* (SRIS C/100/912) the word "adhesion" was construed in conformity with the specification, particularly because, if given the wider meaning contended for, no method was indicated or known whereby this parameter could be measured. Yet a further case in which a "squeeze" argument was run between non-infringement on a narrow claim construction and invalidity on a broader interpretation is *National Draeger* v. *Telegan* (SRIS C/102/91 (PCC)).

Applicability of former test to the present law 125.16

The substantive decision in *Improver Corp.* v. *Remington*, cited in the second paragraph of this commentary in the Main Work (SRIS C/61/89), has been reported ([1990] FSR 181). In this paragraph some words were omitted during its printing, and the first word of line 10 thereof should instead read:

> ". . . was found largely on the basis that the variant could not be made in".

Later decisions in the parallel case in Hong Kong (*Improver Corp.* v. *Raymond Industrial [Hong Kong]*, [1990] FSR 422) and [1991] FSR 233) eventually reached the same conclusion.

In *Anchor Building* v. *Redland Roof* ([1990] RPC 283) literal infringement was held to be unarguable and no evidence was submitted whether the absence of a claimed feature was an "obviously immaterial variant": the infringement action was therefore struck out, see para. 61.23 *supra*. Likewise, in *Willemijn Hondstermaatschappij* v. *Madge Networks* (SRIS C/55/90, *noted* IPD 13190; [1990] 2(8) IPBB 9), there was a finding of non-infringement because the alleged infringement fell outside the literal wording of the claim and it was a variant which had a material effect on the manner of operation and this would have been obvious to a skilled addressee. Had this decision been otherwise, the claims (of an existing patent) would have been found invalid (under s.32(1)(*i*) [1949]) for lack of fair basis, but this type of squeeze argument is not available as such under the 1977 Act, see para. 72.20 in the Main Work.

125.17 *The "squeeze argument"*

In *Bonzel* v. *Intervention (No. 3)* ([1991] RPC 553) a "squeeze argument" was run between non-infringement (if the claim had a narrow meaning, as was in fact held not to be the case), and invalidity for "added subject-matter" (if the claim had a broad meaning, because of lack of support for this in the description of the original application, which argument prevailed, see para. 72.26 *supra*).

125.18 *File wrapper estoppel*

In *Burton Mechanical Contractors* v. *Cowells* (SRIS C/41/90) it was pointed out that questions of estoppel arising from statements made by the patentee raise difficult questions of law and that, anyway, statements as to what a patentee intended his claim to mean can be no more than persuasive. In *Prestige Group* v. *Dart Industries [Australia]* ((1990) 19 IPR 275) it was pointed out that the doctrine of "file wrapper estoppel" could only apply to cases where there was not infringement on a literal construction of the claim, and there was no basis for applying the doctrine to narrow the ordinary reading of the claim. The existence of this doctrine was also doubted as a matter of Australian law, it being pointed out that the doctrine had its origins in the assessment of infringement under United States law on the basis of the doctrine of equivalents and that this latter doctrine was not applied in Australia [as it is also not now applied in the United Kingdom].

125.20 *Technical opinion by EPO on extent of protection*

It should be noted, however, that the EPO is only empowered to give a "technical opinion" and it takes the view that this precludes giving any opinion on the extent of protection under EPCa. 69 and its Protocol (EPO Guideline E-XII, 2.2).

125.21 *Priority dates of inventions (subs. (2))*

The decision in *Hallen* v. *Brabantia* (SRIS C/40/89), cited in the Main Work, has been reported ([1990] FSR 134). However, the claims here were not truly generic in the same way as is a claim to a generic chemical formula. Whether such a claim may be regarded as one for a plurality of separate "inventions" therefore remains to be decided. *EPO Decision T* 310/87, *Alpha-interferons/BIOGEN*" has been reported (OJEPO 8/1990, 335; [1990] 3 EPOR 190).

125A.01 **SECTION 125A**

Note. The prospective insertion of section 125A, noted in the Main Work, took effect from January 7, 1991 (S.I. 1990 No. 2168).

SECTION 125A—RELEVANT RULES

Rule 17 [1990]—*Micro-organisms* **125A.02**

This rule now reads:

17.—Schedule 2 shall have effect in relation to certain applications for patents, and patents, for inventions which require for their performance the use of micro-organisms.

Note. The detailed rules of new Schedule 2 are reprinted in paras. 125A.02A–125A–02E *infra*.

SCHEDULE 2—MICRO-ORGANISMS

Schedule 2: paragraph 1 [1990]—*Applications* **125A.02A**

1.—(1) The specification of an application for a patent, or of a patent, for an invention which requires for its performance the use of a micro-organism—

(a) which is not available to the public at the date of filing of the application; and
(b) which cannot be described in the specification in such a manner as to enable the invention to be performed by a person skilled in the art,

shall, in relation to the micro-organism itself, be treated for the purposes of the Act as disclosing the invention in such a manner only if one of the conditions set out in subparagraph (2) below is satisfied.

(2) The conditions referred to in subparagraph (1) above are—

(a) a condition that—
    (i) not later than the date of filing of the application, a culture of the micro-organism has been deposited in a depositary institution; and
    (ii) the name of the depositary institution, the date when the culture was deposited and the accession number of the deposit are given in the specification of the application; and
(b) a condition, in the case of a European patent (UK), an application for a European patent (UK) or an international application for a patent (UK) which is treated, by virtue of section 77, 81 or 89 as a patent under the Act, or, as the case may be, an application for a patent under the Act, that the corresponding provisions of the Implementing Regulations to the European Patent Convention or, as the case may require, the Patent Co-operation Treaty have been complied with,

and, where a new deposit is made under paragraph 4 below, a further condition that the applicant or proprietor makes a new deposit in accordance with that paragraph.

(3) Where the information specified in subparagraph (2)(a)(ii) above is not contained in an application for a patent as filed, it shall be added to the application—

(a) before the end of the period of sixteen months after the declared priority date or, where there is no declared priority date, the date of filing of the application;
(b) where, on a request made by the applicant, the comptroller publishes the application before the end of the period prescribed for the purposes of section 16(1), before the date of the request; or
(c) where the comptroller sends notification to the applicant that, in accordance with subsection (4) of section 118, he has received a request by any person for information and inspection of documents under subsection (1) of that section, before the end of one month after his sending to the applicant notification of his receipt of the request;

whichever is the earliest.

(4) The giving of the information specified in subparagraph (2)(a)(ii) above shall constitute the unreserved and irrevocable consent of the applicant to the depositary institution with which a culture (including a deposit which is to be treated as having always been available by virtue of paragraph 4(2) below) is from time to time deposited making the culture available on receipt of the comptroller's certificate authorising the release to the person who is named therein as a person to whom the culture may be made available and who makes a valid request therefor to the institution.

(5) The specification of an application for a patent described in paragraph (1) above shall mention any international agreement under which the micro-organism concerned is deposited.

(6) In relation to an application for a patent filed before this paragraph and paragraphs 2, 3 and 4 below come into force, rule 17 of the Patents Rules 1982 shall continue to have effect notwithstanding its revocation by rule 123(3) of these Rules.

Note. This paragraph 1 replaces former rule 17(1) and part of rule 17(2).

125A.02B Schedule 2: paragraph 2 [1990]—*Availability of cultures*

2.—(1) Save where paragraph 3 below has effect, a request that the comptroller certify a person as a person to whom a depositary institution may make available a sample of a micro-organism,—

(a) before publication of the application for a patent, to a person who has made a request under section 118(1) in the circumstances mentioned in paragraph 1(3)(c) above; and

(b) at any later time, to any person,

shall be made on Patents Form 8/77 (which shall be filed in duplicate) together, in the case of a micro-organism of which a culture is deposited under the Budapest Treaty with an international depositary authority, with the form provided for by the Regulations under that Treaty.

(2) The comptroller shall send copies of the forms lodged with him under subparagraph (1) above and of his certificate authorising the release of the sample—

(a) to the applicant for, or proprietor of, the patent;
(b) to the depositary institution; and
(c) to the person making the request.

(3) A request under subparagraph (1) above shall comprise, on the part of the person to whom the request relates, undertakings for the benefit of the applicant for, or proprietor of, the patent—

(a) not to make the culture, or any culture derived from it, available to any other person; and
(b) not to use the culture, or any culture derived from it, otherwise than for experimental purposes relating to the subject matter of the invention;

and—

(i) subject to (iii) below, both undertakings shall have effect during any period before the application for a patent has been withdrawn, has been taken to be withdrawn, has been treated as having been withdrawn, has been refused or is treated as having been refused (including any further period allowed under rule 100 or rule 110(1) or (4) but excluding, where an application is reinstated under either of those rules, the period before it is reinstated);
(ii) if a patent is granted on the application, the undertaking set out in subparagraph (a) above shall also have effect during any period for which the patent is in force and during the period of six months referred to in section 25(4); and
(iii) the undertaking set out in paragraph (b) shall not have effect after the date of publication in the Journal of a notice that the patent has been granted,

and, in this subparagraph, references to a culture derived from a deposited culture of a micro-organism are references to a culture so derived which exhibits those characteristics of the deposited culture essential for the performance of the invention.

(4) For the purpose of enabling any act specified in section 55 to be done in relation to the culture for the services of the Crown, the undertakings specified in subparagraph (3) above—

(a) shall not be required from any government department or person authorised in writing by a government department for the purposes of this paragraph; and
(b) shall not have effect in relation to any such person who has already given them.

(5) An undertaking given pursuant to subparagraph (3) above may be varied by way of derogation by agreement between the applicant or proprietor and the person by whom it is given.

(6) Where, in respect of a patent to which the undertaking set out in subparagraph 3(a) has effect,—

(a) an entry is made in the register under section 46 to the effect that licences are to be available as of right; or
(b) a compulsory licence is granted under section 48,

that undertaking shall not have effect to the extent necessary for effect to be given to any such licence.

Note. This paragraph 2 replaces former rule 17(2).

125A.02C **Schedule 2: paragraph 3 [1990]**—*Availability of cultures to experts*

3.—(1) Where, before the preparations for publication under section 16 of an application for a patent have been completed, the applicant gives notice to the comptroller on Patents Form 8A/77 of his intention that a sample of the micro-organism should be made available only to an expert, the provisions of this paragraph shall have effect.

(2) The comptroller—

(a) shall publish with the application notice that the provisions of this paragraph have effect; and
(b) notwithstanding paragraph 2 above, shall not, until the patent is granted or the application has been withdrawn, has been taken to be withdrawn, has been treated as having been withdrawn, has been refused or is treated as having been refused, issue any certificate authorising release of a sample otherwise than under this paragraph.

(3) Any person wishing to have a sample of the micro-organism made available ("the requester")—

(a) shall apply to the comptroller on Patents Form 8B/77 (which shall be filed in duplicate together, in the case of a micro-organism of which a culture is deposited under the Budapest Treaty with an international depositary authority, with the form provided for by the Regulations under that Treaty) nominating the person ("the expert") to whom he wishes the sample to be made available; and

(b) shall at the same time file undertakings by the expert as set out in subparagraph (3) of paragraph 2 above in accordance with the provisions of that paragraph.

(4) The comptroller shall send a copy of Patents Form 8B/77 filed under subparagraph (3) above to the applicant for the patent and shall specify the period within which the applicant may object, in accordance with subparagraph (5) below, to a sample of the micro-organism being made available to the expert.

(5) Unless, within the period specified by the comptroller under subparagraph (4) above (or within such longer period as the comptroller may, on application made to him within that period, allow), the applicant for the patent sends notice in writing to the comptroller that he objects to a sample of the micro-organism being made available to the expert and gives his reasons for his objection, the comptroller shall send a copy of any form lodged with him under subparagraph (3)(a) above and his certificate authorising the release of the sample—

(a) to the applicant for the patent,
(b) to the depositary institution concerned,
(c) to the requester, and
(d) to the expert.

(6) Where, in accordance with subparagraph (5) above, the applicant for the patent sends notice to the comptroller of his objection to the issue of a certificate in favour of the expert, the comptroller—

(a) shall decide, having regard to the knowledge, experience and technical qualifications of the expert and to any other factors he considers relevant, whether to issue his certificate in favour of the expert; and
(b) if he decides to authorise the release of the sample to the expert, shall send to the persons referred to in subparagraph (5) above a copy of any form lodged with him under subparagraph (3)(a) above and a certificate authorising the release of the sample to the expert.

(7) Before making a decision in accordance with subparagraph (6) above, the comptroller shall afford the applicant and the requester the opportunity of being heard.

(8) If the comptroller decides under subparagraph (6) above not to issue his certificate in favour of the expert, the requester may, by notice

in writing to the comptroller and the applicant, nominate another person as the expert for the purposes of this paragraph; and the comptroller shall give such directions as he shall think fit with regard to the subsequent procedure.

(9) Nothing in this paragraph shall affect the rights under section 55 of any government department or any person authorised in writing by a government department.

125A.02D Schedule 2: paragraph 4 [1990]—*New deposits*

4.—(1) Where the depositary institution with which a deposit or a new deposit of a culture has been made under this Schedule—

(a) notifies the applicant or proprietor that it—
  (i) cannot satisfy a request made in accordance with paragraph 2(1) or 3(3) above, or
  (ii) is not able lawfully, to satisfy such a request,
for the culture to be made available;
(b) ceases temporarily or permanently to carry out the functions of a depositary institution; or
(c) ceases for any reason to conduct its activities as a depositary institution in an objective and impartial manner,

subject to subparagraph (3) below, the applicant or proprietor may, unless the culture has been transferred to another depositary institution which is able to make it available, make a new deposit of a culture of that micro-organism.

(2) For the purposes of paragraph 1 above and of this paragraph, the deposit shall be treated as always having been available if, within three months of the receipt of such notification or of the depositary institution ceasing to perform the functions of a depositary institution or to conduct its activities as such an institution in an objective and impartial manner, the applicant or proprietor—

(a) in a case where the deposit has not already been transferred, makes the new deposit;
(b) furnishes to the depositary institution with which the new deposit is made a declaration that the culture so deposited is of the same micro-organism as was the culture originally deposited; and
(c) requests amendment of the specification under section 19 or section 27, as the case may be, so as to indicate the accession number of the transferred or new deposit and, where applicable, the name of the depositary institution with which the deposit has been made.

(3) The new deposit referred to in subparagraph (1) above—

(a) shall, save as provided in subparagraph (b) below, be made with the same depositary institution as was the original deposit; or
(b) in the cases referred to in subparagraphs (1)(a)(ii), (b) and (c) above, shall be made with another depositary institution which is able to satisfy the request.

Note. This paragraph 4 replaces former rule 17(4).

Schedule 2: paragraph 5 [1990]—*Interpretation of Schedule* **125A.02E**

5.—(1) In this Schedule—

"the Budapest Treaty" means the Treaty on the International Recognition of the Deposit of Micro-organisms for the purposes of Patent Procedure done at Budapest in 1977; and
"international depositary authority" means a depositary institution which has acquired the status of international depositary authority as provided in Article 7 of the Budapest Treaty.

(2) For the purposes of this Schedule a "depositary institution" is an institution which, at all relevant times,—

(a) carries out the functions of receiving, accepting and storing micro-organisms and the furnishing of samples thereof; and
(b) conducts its affairs in so far as they relate to the carrying out of those functions in an objective and impartial manner.

Note. This paragraph defines terms contained in paragraphs 1–4 of Schedule 2.

COMMENTARY ON SECTION 125A

General **125A.05**

The new form of former rule 17 is now provided by Schedule 2 to the 1990 Rules (reprinted in paras. 125A.02A–125A.02E *supra*). Paragraph 1(6) thereof provides a transitional provision whereby the provisions of former rule 17 continue to apply in the case of applications filed before January 7, 1991. Notes on the operation of rule 17 and the making of a deposit of micro-organisms, etc. are given periodically in the O.J., *e.g.* O.J. September 25, 1991.

The new rules more closely follow the practice under the EPC (for which see EPCrr. 28 and 28A and *EPH* (2nd ed.), Chapter 18) and therefore now apply the so-called "expert solution", for which see para. 125A.02D *supra* and 125A.12 *infra*.

Other cases in which a written description of recombinant DNA was sufficient, without reliance on a deposit, are two so far unreported decisions: *EPO Decisions T* 361/87, "*Micro-organisms/NABISCO* and *EPO Decision T* 181/87, "*Hepatitis B virus/UNIVERSITY OF CALIFORNIA*".

Types of claims **125A.06**

Claims to plants which do not specifically claim varieties have also been allowed, both in the United Kingdom and by the EPO, see para. 125A.07 *infra*.

125A.07 *Particular forms of claim for microbiological products*

The EPO has allowed claims to deposited mushroom fungi, as well as to the resultant whole mushrooms (*NRDC's Application No.* 84305097.5).

EPO Decision T 301/87, "*Alpha-interferons/BIOGEN*," cited in the Main Work, has been reported (OJEPO 8/1990, 335; [1990] 3 EPOR 190) and has been the subject of comment, particularly as to the breadth of claims allowed ((1988–89) 18 CIPA 396 and [1990] 2(2) IPB 24).

In relation to claims to recombinant DNA products, EPO examiners have been objecting to claims to recombinant DNA coding for a protein known *per se* on the ground that these merely define a problem and not the technical means of solving it, allegedly required by the first sentence of EPCa. 84 and by EPCr. 29(1). However, in *EPO Decision T* 181/87, "*Hepatitis B virus/UNIVERSITY OF CALIFORNIA*" (*unreported*), claims to a transfer vector containing DNA coding for hepatitis B surface antigen, but free of DNA coding for the core antigen, did not merely define a problem.

The EPO has granted a patent claiming a transgenic plant (*EPO Decision T* 320/87, "*Hybrid plants/LUBRIZOL*" (OJEPO 3/1990, 71; [1990] 3 EPOR 173); and has declared that animals are, in principle, patentable provided that they do not fall within the exceptions of EPCa. 53 (*EPO Decision T* 19/90, "*Onco-mouse/HARVARD*", OJEPO 12/1990, 488; [1990] EPOR 501). The Comptroller has also granted patents with product-by-process claims to transgenic plants in a scope greater than a "variety", see patents Nos. 2,183,660 and 2,200,367, but applications with claims related to animals have yet to be substantively examined.

125A.08 *Prior art issues applicble to biotechnology*

Claims to novel antibodies were held to lack inventive step in *Hybritech's Application* (SRIS O/76/89, *noted* IPD 12040) because such were merely substances similar to other substances already known and made for a similar purpose, see Main Work at para. 3.19.

125A.09 *Insufficiency issues in relation to biotechnology*

Para. 125A.07 *supra*, indicates that a patent description for a biotechnological invention need not be insufficient merely because no culture deposit has been made. The EPO also holds the view that a broad claim is not invalid for insufficiency merely because the invention has only been demonstrated by way of limited example (*EPO Decision T* 19/90, "*Onco-mouse/HARVARD*", OJEPO 12/1990, 488; [1990] 7 EPOR 501).

125A.11 *Deposit of micro-organism*

The new provisions for required micro-organism deposit are now contained in Schedule 2, paragraph 1, see para. 125A.02A *supra*. The former conditions for deposit continue to apply but, in addition (for applications filed after January 7, 1991), the depositary institution must (by virtue of the new definition of such an institution now contained in paragraph 5(2)) be one which: (a) carries out the function of receiving, accepting and storing micro-organisms, and the furnishing of samples thereof; and (b) conducts its affairs (relating to those functions) "in an objective and impartial manner". Unlike the EPO, the Patent Office does not issue an approved list of depositary institutions which meet these requirements and applicants therefore have the onus of choosing an institution for their deposit which meets these criteria and, in any subsequent challenge to validity of defending themselves against an attack that the criteria were not in fact met. If at any time these criteria cease to apply, a new deposit must be made within a period of three months (see paragraph 4(2), discussed in para. 125A.13 *infra*), which period is inextensible (r. 110(2)).

The required information must not only identify: (a) the culture collection, (b) the date of deposit; and (c) the accession number, but (d) must now also refer to "any international agreement under which the deposit is made" (*i.e.* refer to the Budapest Treaty if the deposit has been made thereunder). The information under (a), (b) and (c) can now be provided before the earliest of: (a) 16 months after the declared priority date, or if none the date of filing (a period which is extensible by one month under rule 110(3), see para. 123.10 *supra*); (b) the date of requesting early publication under section 16; and (c) one month after notification by the Comptroller that a request has been received for inspection of documents under section 118(4) (Sched. 2, para. 1(3)), but no date is specified for requirement (d), see Schedule 2, paragraph 1(5) [1990]. Indication that a deposit has been made under the Budapest Treaty can therefore probably be included in the specification by amendment at any time before grant in view of the distinction between subparagraphs (3) and (5) and because its addition to the specification would not involve adding matter extending beyond that disclosed in the application as filed contrary to section 76(2). In the case of a divisional or replacement application under sections 8(3), 12(6), 15(5) or 37(4), the requirements of (a), (b) and (c) must be met by the date of filing thereof, or by the date ascertained under Schedule 1, paragraph 1(3) [1990] if later (r. 26(1)(b)) (see para. 15.05 *supra*). The deemed "unreserved and irrevocable consent" to the depositary institution making the culture available following a proper request to the Comptroller is now contained in paragraph 1(4).

The EPO has refused correction of an application wherein the accession number of the culture deposit had not been provided within the 16 months' period required by EPCr. 28A ("*Deposit Number/ROCKEFELLER*", OJEPO 4/1990, 156; [1990] 4 EPOR 303), see para. 17.07 *supra*.

Obtaining a sample of a deposited micro-organism **125A.12**

The conditions for seeking a sample of the deposited micro-organism from the depositary institution are now contained in Schedule 2, paragraph 2 to the 1990 Rules (reprinted at para. 125A.02B *supra*). However, these conditions *do not apply* where PF 8A/77 (reprinted at para. 141.08A *infra*) has been filed before the date when preparations for publication of the application under section 16 are complete: the provisions of Schedule 2, paragraph 3 to the 1990 Rules then apply restricting sampling to a nominated expert, see para. 125A.12A *infra*.

When Schedule 2, paragraph 2 to the 1990 Rules applies, then a request for a sample of the deposited micro-organism to be furnished carries with it the undertakings set out in paragraph 2(3) to be effective so long as the application remains pending. These undertakings are now expressed to be for the benefit of the applicant/proprietor. This ought to avoid the rule of English contract law which makes a breach of contract actionable only by a party to that contract.

These undertakings are twofold: namely, while the application remains pending, (a) not to make the deposited culture available to any other; and (b) not to use the culture "otherwise than for experimental purposes relating to the subject matter of the invention". Each undertaking applies not only to the deposited culture, but also to any culture "derived from it", provided that the derived culture "exhibits those characteristics of the deposited culture essential for the performance of the invention". The phrase "application remains pending" used above includes any period of extension allowed under rule 100 or rule 110(1) or (4), but excludes any period during which the application had lapsed up to its reinstatement under either of these rules; and expires upon the date when grant of the patent is advertised in the O.J. (para. 2(3)(i) and (iii)). After grant, these undertakings are not needed because making the culture available to others would (if carried out in the United Kingdom) be an act of infringement, and experimental use (by s.60(5)(*b*)) is a non-infringing act, but the undertaking (under (a) above), not to make the undertaking available to others, is reinstated during the six months' period under section 25(4) during which a fee can be paid late at the option of the proprietor (para. 2(3)(ii)), but is not in force during any period allowed for restoration of a lapsed patent under section 28. The proprietor and the requester can agree to vary those undertakings (para. 2(5)).

The relaxation of the deemed undertakings in the case of Crown use of a deposited culture is now set out in paragraph 2(4), and paragraph 2(6) newly provides that the undertakings are not to apply: (a) where the patent has been made subject to "licences of right" under section 46(1); or (b) where a compulsory licence is granted under section 48, though in either case only to the extent for effect to be given to any such licence.

125A.12A *—For examination by nominated expert (Sched. 2, para. 3 [1990])*

Under the new provision of Schedule 2, paragraph 3 to the 1990 Rules (reprinted at para. 125A.02C *supra*), the applicant can, before preparations for publication of the application under section 16 are complete, make a request (on new PF 8A/77, reprinted at para. 141.08A *infra*) that a sample of the deposited micro-organism may be made available only to a nominated "expert" (para. 3(1)). The provisions of Schedule 2, paragraph 2 to the 1990 Rules (for which see para. 125A.12 *supra*) then cease to have effect until such time as the patent is granted or the application is withdrawn or refused or taken to be treated as withdrawn or refused (para. 3(2)(b)). The fact that PF 8A/77 has been filed has to be published with the application (para. 3(2)(a)).

Thereupon, during the period when this paragraph 3 applies, a sample of the deposited micro-organism may only be available to a "requester" consequent upon his filing PF 8B/77 (reprinted at para. 141.08B *infra*). PF 8B/77 must be filed in duplicate and be accompanied by the name of the nominated "expert" and by undertakings signed thereby in the form of those set out in Schedule 2, paragraph 2(3) of the 1990 Rules (for which see para. 125A.12 in the Main Work and *supra*). The Comptroller then sends a copy of the filed PF 8B/77 to the applicant for the patent, specifying the period within which the applicant may object to a sample of the micro-organism being made available to the nominated expert (para. 3(4)), but paragraph 3 does not affect the rights of Crown user under section 55 (para. 3(9)).

The applicant then has the period so specified within which he can send to the Comptroller a written objection to a sample of the micro-organism being sent to the nominated expert and giving his reasons for that objection. In the absence of such objection, the Comptroller must then send a copy of PF 8B/77, together with a certificate authorising release of the sample to: (a) the applicant; (b) the depositary institution concerned; (c) the requester; and (d) the expert (para. 3(5)). If, however, the applicant lodges a written objection (within the period specified under para. 3(4), which period may be extended, under para. 3(5), upon request made within that period), the Comptroller is required to adjudicate upon the suitability of the expert, having regard to his knowledge, experience and technical qualifications (para. 3(6)), with both the applicant and the requester having the opportunity to be heard before the Comptroller makes his decision on the objection (para. 3(7)). If the objection is rejected, the notification procedure of paragraph 3(5) is then followed; and, if the objection is sustained, the requester may nominate another expert, whereupon the Comptroller will give such directions as he thinks fit as to the subsequent procedure (para. 3(8)).

Renewal of deposited micro-organism **125A.13**

The provisions (formerly contained in r. 17(3)) for renewing a culture deposit are now to be found in Schedule 4, paragraph 4 to the 1990 Rules (reprinted in para. 125A.02D *supra*). They now apply where the depositary institution: (a) notifies the applicant that it (i) cannot, or (ii) cannot lawfully, satisfy a valid request to make a sample of the micro-organism available (a condition which it is believed relates only to matters within the control of the depositary institution, and therefore does not cover restrictions placed on the export or import of the micro-organism); (b) ceases (temporarily or permanently) to carry out the functions of a depositary institution; or (c) ceases (for any reason) to conduct its affairs as a depositary institution (para. 4(1)), which requires that institution to conduct its affairs in an objective and impartial manner (para. 5(2)). Thereupon, the applicant or proprietor has a period of three months to make a new deposit without loss of his rights (para. 4(2)). This period is inextensible (r. 110(2)).

It should be noted that provisions (b) and (c) above operate automatically, even apparently if the applicant/proprietor should be unaware that the "depositary institution" is failing to meet the requirements for such an institution as required by its definition in paragraph 5(2) of Schedule 2 [1990], for which see paras. 125A.02A and 125A.11 *supra*. Although, clearly, an applicant/proprietor is unlikely to be able to monitor the performance of a depositary institution, it would be prudent to make a periodic check of a chosen institute which is not recognised as an international depositary authority under the Budapest Treaty.

Where a new deposit has to be made under paragraph 4(2) of Schedule 2 [1990], in the case where a deposit has ceased to be viable, the new deposit must be made with the same depositary institution (para. 4(3)(a)), but otherwise can be made with another institution which can meet the requirements of paragraph 5(2) for a "depositary institution" (para. 4(3)(b)). The other requirements remain as stated in the Main Work.

Comparison with EPC and PCT requirements **125A.14**

The new provisions of the rules of Schedule 2 [1990] more closely approximate to, but are not exactly identical with, the EPC and PCT requirements (of EPCrr. 28 and 28A and of PCTr. 13*bis*) for inventions which make use of micro-organisms not readily available to the public. However, these provisions (now introduced by the new rule 17) do adopt, generally, the so-called "expert solution" applicable under the EPC and PCT, see para. 125A.12A *supra*. However, besides the advantage to the applicant mentioned in the Main Work of proceeding before the EPO because grant (and therefore the availability of the deposited culture to non-experts) may then be delayed, there is the further advantage that (under new rule 17) third parties have a potentially wider choice of expert than under EPCr. 28 which could be to the applicant's disadvantage, see also para. 125A.12A.

PRACTICE UNDER SECTION 125A

Procedure for deposit of micro-organisms

125A.17 *—Time limits for deposit of micro-organism in culture collection*

The references in the Main Work to rule 17 are now to be read as references to Schedule 2, paragraph 1 to the 1990 Rules, for which see paras. 125A.02A and 125A.11 *supra*.

Another warning of the need to alter conditions of deposit of a micro-organism to meet European requirements before the filing of a European application was given in *EPO Decision T* 39/88, "*Micro-organisms/CPC*" ([1990] 1 EPOR 41; *abridged* OJEPO 12/1989, 499).

125A.18 *—Factors influencing choice of culture collection*

The first United Kingdom IDA listed in the Main Work is more correctly called the "National Collections of Industrial and Marine Bacteria" (NCIMB): its address is now 23 St. Machar Drive, Aberdeen AB2 1RY (tel. 0224 273332) and it has extended its range of acceptable materials for deposit to include yeasts and most types of plant seeds. A seventh United Kingdom-domiciled IDA is now the National Collection of Food Bacteria at Shinfield, Reading (tel. 0734 883103), which accepts bacteria, possibly recombinant plasmids (either naked or within a host) and bacteriophages.

125A.19 *—Inadequate deposit*

The EPO has challenged the status of a deposit made by the applicant's subsidiary, but eventually held that this did satisfy EPCr. 28, though only because the parent company had effective control over the deposit (*EPO Decision T* 118/87, "*Amylolytic enzymes/CPC*", OJEPO 9/1991, 474; [1990] 4 EPOR 298, *noted* OJEPO 8/1990). In this Decision the Appeal Board interpreted EPCr. 28 as requiring that the depositor of a micro-organism must "in principle" be one and the same: Schedule 2 [1990] is possibly open to the same interpretation. Note the warnings given in paras. 125A.11 and 125A.12A *supra* concerning the onus on an applicant/proprietor for checking that a depositary institution meets, and continues to meet, the requirements of paragraph 5(2) of Schedule 2 [1990], namely that it remains able to receive, accept, store and furnish micro-organism samples and conduct its affairs in an objective and impartial manner.

125A.21 *Obtaining sample of deposited micro-organism*

Unless PF 8A/77 has been filed, and the application is still pending as indicated in para. 125A.12 *supra*, PF 8/77 has to be completed and filed as stated in the Main Work. Schedule 2, paragraph 2(2) and 3(3) [1990] (reprinted in para. 125A.02B and 125A.02B *supra*) now stipulate that, where the deposit has been made with an "international depositary authority" under "the Budapest Treaty" (each as defined in Sched. 2, para. 5, reprinted in para. 125A.02E *supra*), PF 8/77 must also be accompanied by the form required by the Regulations under that Treaty. This should be Form BP/12, as indicated in the Main Work.

125A.22 *Sequence listing*

The Patent Office recommends patent applicants to provide a "Sequence Listing" in standard form of amino acid sequences of four or longer, and nucleotide sequences of 10 or longer (O.J. May 16, 1990). The standard form is identical with that published by the EPO (OJEPO, Supplement to 12/1989), copies of which can be obtained from the Patent Office on request: this "standard form" is expected to become the subject of a new EPO rule during 1991. The United States and Japanese Patent Offices have adopted the same standard, mainly with a view to compiling a computer-searchable database. The Sequence Listing should begin on a separate page of the description immediately preceding the claims. It should be in an optical character readable typeface.

This Sequence Listing recommendation is to apply to all sequences (as defined above) of an unusual kind and throughout the specification. Wherever such a sequence is set forth, or is desired to be set forth, it must be referenced by a "Sequence Listing Number," *e.g.* "ID No. 1". This designation can be in lieu of, or in addition to, showing the sequence in context, but no sequence of the kind to which the recommendation applies is to appear unreferenced. Sequence listing does not apply to sequences which are not to be explicitly set forth, *e.g.* because these are described in words or by a literature reference.

The lay-out of the recommended standard form is too long to reproduce here, but is based on the three-letter amino code and single-stranded nucleotide sequences which, if non-coding, are to be in blocks of 10. Where nucleotide codons and amino acids are shown together, the amino acids go beneath the nucleotides. Amino acids are to be numbered every five beneath the code, nucleotides at the ends of lines. Maximum length lines are 16 amino acids or codons and 60 non-coding nucleotides.

To minimise the possibility of error, re-word-processing of long sequences is to be avoided. Where a specification is being prepared from the inventor's materials, the inventor should be asked to supply a floppy disk containing the sequences in as near as possible the correct lay-out, and the floppy disk sequence converted directly to a paper one. If filing in the United States is contemplated, a disk will ultimately be required anyway, because the United States Patent Office now insists upon one, see (1990–91) 20 CIPA 106.

SECTION 126 **126.01**

Note. CPCaa. 39 and 45 have been renumbered as CPCa. 38 and 44, see para. 86.03 *supra*.

SECTION 127—RELEVANT RULES

Rule 123 [1990]—*Transitional provisions and revocations* **127.02A**

This final rule of the 1990 Rules reads:

123.—(1) The reference to Schedule 2 to the Patents Rules 1968 in paragraph (a) of the proviso to rule 124 of the Patents Rules 1978 shall be construed as a reference to that Schedule with the substitution for forms 7, 9, 14 to 21, 23, 32 to 36, 38, 39, 43, 44, 46, 53 to 55, 63 to 65 and 69 of the correspondingly numbered forms in Schedule 5.

(2) In rule 124 of the Patents Rules 1978—

(a) for the words "the Patents Rules 1982" in each place where they occur there shall be substituted the words "the Patents Rules 1990";

(b) for paragraph (d) of the proviso to paragraph (1), there shall be substituted—

"(d) subject to sub-rule (3) below, rules 30, 39(1) and (3) to (6), 41 to 50, 52, 61 to 66, 68 to 74, 76, 88(1), 90, 92 to 95, 97 to 101, 103 to 108 and 114 to 116 of the Patents Rules 1990 shall apply.", and

(c) for the words "in rule 39(1)" in paragraph (4) there shall be substituted the words "in rule 39(1) of the Patents Rules 1990".

(3) The rules described in column 1 of Schedule 6 are hereby revoked to the extent specified in column 3 thereof.

(4) Where,—

(a) immediately before these Rules come into force, any time or period prescribed by the Rules hereby revoked has effect in relation to any act or proceeding and has not expired; and
(b) the corresponding time or period prescribed by these Rules would have expired or would expire earlier,

the time or period prescribed by those Rules and not by these Rules shall apply to that act or proceeding.

127.02B Schedule 6 [1990]—*Revocations*

Schedule 6 to the 1990 Rules revoked: the Patents Rules 1982 (S.I. 1982 No. 717), though subject to: the proviso to rule 39(2) [1990] (for which see para. 25.02 *supra*), rule 62(7) [1990] (for which see para. 46.03 *supra*), and Schedule 2, paragraph 1(6) [1990] (for which see para. 125A.02A *supra*); the Patents (Amendment) Rules 1983 (S.I. 1983 No. 180); the Patents (Amendment) Rules 1985 (S.I. 1985 No. 785); the Patents (Amendment) (No. 2) Rules 1985 (S.I. 1985 No. 1166); the Patents (Amendment) Rules 1987 (S.I. 1987 No. 288), except for rules 4 and 5 (for which see respectively paras. 77.02 and 78.02 in the Main Work); the Patents (Amendment) Rules 1988 (S.I. 1988 No. 2089); the Patents (Amendment) Rules 1989 (S.I. 1989 No. 116); and the Patents (Amendment) Rules 1990 (S.I. 1990 No. 1455).

127.03 Schedule 1 to Patents Rules 1990—*General Forms*

Note. The Patent Forms for use under the 1990 Rules are now set out in Schedule 1 to these Rules. Amendments to these Forms are indicated in paras. 141.01–141.58 *infra*.

127.04 Rule 124 [1978]—*Revocation of existing Rules*

Note. Rule 124 [1978] continues to have effect to apply, in the circumstances indicated in the Main Work, the revoked 1968 Rules to "existing patents", but all references therein to "the Patents Rules 1982" have been changed to "the Patents Rules 1990", see para. 127.02A *supra*. However, new rule 123(1) substitutes new forms for some of those still thought to be effective, for which see Schedule 5 to the 1990 Rules and para. A109 *infra*. The power to use replica forms does not seem to extend to these new Schedule 5 forms, see rule 4 [1990], reprinted in para. 123.06 *supra*.

Continuing effect of 1968 Rules and Forms thereunder **127.10**

Rule 124 [1978] continues to have effect with substitution therein of references to the 1990, rather than to the 1982, Rules, see para. 127.04 *supra*. However, several of the forms under the 1968 Rules have been revised, as set out in rule 123(1) [1990] (reprinted in para. 123.02A *supra*) and Schedule 4 to the 1990 rules. The revisions to these forms are indicated in paras. AA119–A138 *infra*.

SECTION 130 **130.01**

In subsection (1) after the definition of "employer" there has been added:

" 'enactment' includes an Act of Tynwald".

Notes. 1. The repeal of the definition of "patent agent" in subsection (1) took effect from August 13, 1990 (S.I. 1990 No. 1400). 2. The prospective amendment of the definition of "search fee" and the amendment of subsection (7), noted in the Main Work, each took effect from January 7, 1991 (S.I. 1990 No. 2168). 3. The definition of "enactment" was added by the Patents Act 1977 (Isle of Man) (Variation) Order 1990 (S.I. 1990 No. 2295).

Miscellaneous further definitions (subss. (2)–(5)) **130.07**

Subsection (3) causes the wording of claims as filed to constitute part of the original specification, but not as an independent disclosure (*Asahi's Application*, [1991] RPC 485 (HL)). The claims must therefore be read in context with the specification as a whole and their subject matter content is not to be confused with their breadth (*A. C. Edwards* v. *Acme Signs*, [1991] RPC 621 and SRIS C/80/91 (CA)).

COMMENTARY ON SECTION 131

General **131.02**

There is no judge specially assigned to hear patent matters in the High Court in Northern Ireland. Patent litigation there is infrequent but, when there have been cases, the pleading practice appears to have followed more that used in the Republic of Ireland than that under RSC Ord. 104.

COMMENTARY ON SECTION 132

Extension of the Act outside the United Kingdom **132.04**

Where a United Kingdom patent is registered abroad, for example in a (former) colony, this is under local law and the provisions of the United Kingdom

Act may not necessarily apply in the country of registration, see *Blackburn* v. *Boon Engineering [Brunei]* [1991] FSR 380).

132.05 *—Isle of Man (subs. (2))*

The Patents Act 1977 (Isle of Man) Order 1978 (S.I. 1978 No. 621) has been amended (by S.I. 1990 No. 2295, effective from January 7, 1991) by addition of a further article reading:

> "**4.** The Patents Act 1977 shall, in its application to the Isle of Man, be construed—
> (a) as if references to the Crown included the Crown in right of the Government of the Isle of Man;
> (b) as if references to a Government department included references to a Department of the Government of the Isle of Man, and in relation to such a Department as if references to the Treasury were references to the Treasury of the Isle of Man, and for the purposes of any arbitration in pursuance thereof and of the application thereto of the Arbitration Act 1976 (an Act of Tynwald), as if it were an Act of Tynwald".

S.I. 1990 No. 2295 also added a definition of "enactment" to section 130(1), see para. 130.01 *supra*.

The Copyright, Designs and Patents Act 1988 (Isle of Man) Order 1990 (S.I. 1990 No. 1505) extended to the Isle of Man the provisions of the 1988 Act relating to patent agents, *i.e.* sections 274–281, 285 and 286 [1988], including the repeals or partial repeals of sections 84, 85, 104, 105, 114, 115, 123(2)(*k*) and 130(1) [1977] effected by Schedule 8 [1988], but with some amendment of sections 278, 280, 284 and 285 [1988] in relation to their application to the Isle of Man. The remainder of the 1988 Act was given effect to in the Isle of Man by the Copyright, Designs and Patents Act 1988 (Isle of Man) (No. 2) Order 1990 (S.I. 1990 No. 2293) and, under this, any reference to an Act of Parliament or to a provision of such an Act in paragraphs 1 to 11, 17 to 23, 25, 26, 28 and 30 of Schedule 5 [1988] "shall be construed, unless a contrary intention appears, as a reference to that Act or provision as if it has effect in the Isle of Man". For the extent to which the ECJ considers itself competent to decide matters of the law of the Isle of Man, see the employment law case of *DHSS (Isle of Man)* v. *Barr* (ECJ Case C–355/89) ([1991] 3 CMLR 325).

137.01

SCHEDULE 5

The amendments to sections 10 and 10A of each of the Fair Trading Act 1973 (c. 41) and the Restrictive Trade Practices Act 1976 (c. 34), as noted in the Main Work in relation to former paragraphs 7 and 8 of Schedule 5, were brought into effect on August 13, 1990 (S.I. 1990 No. 1400).

139.01

THE PATENTS RULES 1990

S.I. 1990 No. 2384

ARRANGEMENT OF RULES

Note. From January 7, 1991 these Rules have totally replaced the Patents Rules

1982 around which the Main Work was prepared. However, the rule numbers generally remain unchanged, but the following amendments to the Arrangement of Rules set out in this para. of the Main Work should be noted in order that this Arrangement should now apply to the 1990 Rules.

The 1990 Rules are stated to be made in exercise of powers conferred by sections 5(2), 8(3), 12(6), 13(1) and (3), 14(1) and (6), 15(2), (3) and (5), 16(1), 17(1), (2) and (8), 18(1) and (4), 19(1), 20(1), 21(1), 24(2), 25(3) and (5), 28(1), (1A) and (2A), 32(2), (6) and (7), 40(1) and (2), 47(3) and (6), 52(1), 77(6), 78(4), 80(3), 81(2) and (2)(c), 89, 89A, 92(3) and (4), 97(1)(d), 118(1) and (3)(b), 120(1), 123(1) to (3A), (6) and (7), 124, 125A(1), (2) and (3), 127(6) and 130(2) and Schedule 1, paragraph 4A(5) and Schedule 4, paragraph 14, each of the 1977 Act.

Rule [1990]	*Title*	*Reprinted as para.*
Preliminary		
3.	Construction	123.05
25.	Periods prescribed under section 15(5)(a) and (b) and 17(1) for filing claims, abstract and request for preliminary examination and search	15.04
Examination and search		
28.	Preliminary examination and search under section 17	17.02
29.	Procedure where earlier application made	17.02A
32.	Searches under section 17(6) and (8)	17.04
Grant, amendment and continuation of patent		
38.	Certificates of grant	24.02
39.	Renewal of patent	25.02
Registration		
45.	Alteration of name or address	32.05
52.	Certificates and copies supplied by comptroller	32.10
Entitlement to patent		
54.	Reference of question to the comptroller under section 37(1)	37.02

Note. Rule 55 has been combined with rule 54 and rules 56 to 67 have been renumbered respectively as rules 55 to 66; and, in the title to new rule 62, "for" has been changed to "to settle".

Licences of right		
67.	Declaration under paragraph 4A of Schedule 1 to the Act	47.06
Compulsory licences		
70.	Procedure on receipt of application under section 48 or 51	48.03

139.02 *Notes on Patents Rules 1982*

1. Schedule 6 of the Patents Rules 1990 revoked the Patents Rules 1982 (S.I. 1982 No. 717), but subject to paragraph 1(5) of Schedule 2 to the 1990 Rules (for which see para. 17.03A *supra*), as well as the Amendment Rules thereto noted in the Main Work *re* this para., except as to rules 4 and 5 of the Patents (Amendment) Rules 1987 (S.I. 1987 No. 288), for which see paras. 77.02 and 78.02 in the Main Work.
2. The Patents Rules 1990 took effect from January 7, 1991, but without effect on time periods then running under the former Rules (r. 123(4) [1990], reprinted in para. 127.02 *supra*).

FEES 140.01

Note. The current fees are set out in the Patents (Fees) Rules 1991 (S.I. 1991 No. 1627), effective from August 12, 1991. As indicated in the Main Work, these Rules are *not* reproduced because they can be expected to change about mid-1992.

FORMS

SCHEDULE 1 TO PATENTS RULES 1990 140.02

Notes

1. The Forms designated under the Patents Rules for use in dealings with the Patent Office under the Act are now set out in Schedule 1 to the Patents Rules 1990, with some of the forms still applicable under the 1949 Act being designated in Schedule 5 thereto, see para. A109 *infra*.
2. The Forms designated under the 1982 Rules (as amended) were reprinted in the Main Work in paras. 141.01–141.58. The Form numbers remain unchanged and the newly designated forms are only reprinted *infra* where their format has substantially changed. Otherwise notes under the individual para. numbers indicate minor changes in more general terms and, where there is no such note, only the general changes noted below have been made.
3. All the forms have undergone some general changes. In particular, many forms are now printed on coloured paper in order to facilitate their internal transmission in the Patent Office. The colour coding is:—

Yellow — for pre-grant matters;
Blue — for assignments and other register entries;
Pink — for renewals;
Green — for translations of European patents and applications (UK);
Gold — for post-grant *inter partes* proceedings; and
White — for forms that can be used in either pre- or post-grant proceedings (*e.g.* PF 50/77),

see (1990–91) 20 CIPA 420. However, the use of these coloured forms is not obligatory and replicas can be used. For the possibility of computerised production of completed forms, see para. 123.19 *supra*.

Other general changes are noted below, rather than individually in each case, *viz*.—

(a) A note states (unless inapplicable) that:
"A prescribed fee is payable with this form. For details, please contact the Patent Office";
(b) A further note states (if applicable):
"This form should be filed in duplicate";
(c) Spaces are provided for giving the reference of the person filing the form, as well as for insertion of the "ADP No." of the appointed agent if this is known; and
(d) The former note drawing attention to rules 90 and 106 no longer appears.

4. For the use of replica or modified forms to those now prescribed (for which see paras. 141.01–141.57 *infra*), see para. 123.19 *supra*.
5. For the address of the Patent Office, see para. 123.16 *supra*, not para. 123.02 as stated in the Main Work.

FORMS OF SCHEDULE 1

141.01 Patents Form 1/77

Note. This form has been completely revised and is now an inconvenient four-page document, as reproduced below. If the applicant has not appointed an agent to act for him, he is now requested to give a name and address, in the United Kingdom, to which all correspondence will be sent: the applicant is also asked to specify a daytime telephone number if such be available.

For official use

Your reference

Notes
Please type, or write in dark ink using CAPITAL letters. A prescribed fee is payable for a request for grant of a patent. For details, please contact the Patent Office.

The Patent Office

Request for grant of a Patent

Form 1/77 **Patents Act 1977**

Rule 16 of the Patents Rules 1990 is the main rule governing the completion and filing of this form.

1 Title of invention

1 Please give the title of the invention

2 Do not give trading styles, for example, 'Trading as XYZ company', nationality or former names, for example, 'formerly (known as) ABC Ltd' as these are not required.

2 Applicant's details

☐ **First or only applicant**

2a If you are applying as a corporate body please give:

Corporate name

Country *(and State of incorporation, if appropriate)*

Warning
After an application for a Patent has been filed, the Comptroller of the Patent Office will consider whether publication or communication of the invention should be prohibited or restricted under Section 22 of the Patents Act 1977 and will inform the applicant if such prohibition or restriction is necessary. Applicants resident in the United Kingdom are also reminded that under Section 23, applications may not be filed abroad without written permission unless an application has been filed not less than 6 weeks previously in the United Kingdom for a patent for the same invention and either no direction prohibiting publication or communication has been given, or any such direction revoked.

2b If you are applying as an individual or one of a partnership please give in full:

Surname

Forenames

2c **In all cases,** please give the following details:

Address

UK Postcode *(if applicable)*

Country

ADP number *(if known)*

FORM 1/77 CONT. 1

2d, 2e and 2f: if there are further applicants please provide details on a separate sheet of paper.

☐ **Second applicant *(if any)***

2d If you are applying as a corporate body please give:

Corporate name

Country *(and State of incorporation, if appropriate)*

2e If you are applying as an individual or one of a partnership please give in full:

Surname

Forenames

2f In all cases, please give the following details:

Address

UK postcode *(if applicable)*

Country

ADP number (Ifknown)

***3** An address for service in the United Kindom must be supplied*

3 Address for service details

3a Have you appointed an agent to deal with your application?

Please mark correct box

Yes ☐ No ☐ ➧ ***go to 3b***

please give details below

Agent's name

Agent's address

Postcode

Agent's ADP number

3b: *If you have appointed an agent, all correspondence concerning your application will be sent to the agnet's United Kingdom address.*

3b If you have not appointed an agent please give a name and address in the United Kingdom to which all correspondence will be sent:

Name

Address

Postcode

Daytime telephone number *(if available)*

ADP number *(If known)*

FORM 1/77 CONT. 2

4 Reference number

4 Agent's or applicant's reference number *(if applicable)*

5 Claiming an earlier application date

5 Are you claiming that this application be treated as having been filed on the date of filing of an earlier application?

Please mark correct box

Yes ☐ No ☐ ➧ ***go to 6***

➧ ***please give details below***

☐ number of earlier application or patent number

☐ filing date *(day month year)*

☐ and the Section of the Patents Act 1977 under which you are claiming:

Please mark correct box

15(4) (Divisional) ☐ 8(3) ☐ 12(6) ☐ 37(4) ☐

6 Declaration of priority

6 *If you are declaring priority from a PCT Application please enter 'PCT' as the country and enter the country code (for example, GB) as part of the application number.*

6 If you are declaring priority from previous application(s), please give:

Please give the date in all number format, for example, 31/05/90 for 31 May 1990.

Country of filing	Priority application number *(if known)*	Filing date *(day, month, year)*

FORM 1/77 CONT. 3

7 The answer must be 'No' if:
- *any applicant is not an inventor*
- *there is an inventor who is not an applicant,* ***or***
- *any applicant is a corporate body.*

7 Inventorship

7 *Are you (the applicant or applicants) the sole inventor or the joint inventors?*
Please mark correct box

Yes ☐ No ☐ ➧ ***Statement of Inventorship on Patents Form 7/77 will need to be filed (see Rule 15).***

8 Please supply duplicates of claim(s), abstract, description and drawing(s).

8 Checklist

8a Please fill in the number of sheets for each of the following types of document contained in this application.

Continuation sheets for this Patents Form 1/77 ☐

Claim(s) ☐ Description ☐

Abstract ☐ Drawing(s) ☐

8b Which of the following documents also accompanies the application?

Please mark correct box(es)

Priority documents *(please state how many)* ☐

Translation(s) of Priority documents *(please state how many)* ☐

Patents Form 7/77—Statement of Inventorship and Right to Grant *(please state how many)* ☐

Patents Form 9/77—Preliminary Examination/Search ☐

Patents Form 10/77—Request for Substantive Examination ☐

9 You or your appointed agent (see Rule 90 of the Patents Rules 1990) must sign this request.

9 Request

I/We request the grant of a patent on the basis of this application.

Please sign here ➧ Signed Date *(day month year)*

A completed fee sheet should preferably accompany the fee.

Please return the completed form, attachments and duplicates where requested, together with the prescribed fee to:

☐ ***The Comptroller***
The Patent Office

141.03 Patents Form 3/77

Note. Note 2 now also refers to section 37(1)(c).

141.05 Patents Form 5/77

Note. This form is now applicable under rules 13 and 58. A box for indicating the name and United Kingdom address for service, with postcode and ADP No. is provided.

141.06 Patents Form 6/77

Note. A box is provided for entry of the name and United Kingdom address for service, including the postcode and ADP No. for this address.

Patents Form 7/77

141.07

For official use

Your reference

Notes
Please type, or write in dark ink using CAPITAL letters.

No fee is required with this form.

Rule 15 of the Patents rules 1990 is the main rule govening the completion and filing of this form.

If you do not have enough space please use a separate sheet of paper.

When an application does not declare priority at all, or declares priority from an earlier UK application, sufficient additional copies of this form must be supplied to enable the Comptroller to send one to each inventor who is not an applicant.

The Patent Office

Statement of inventorship and of right to grant of a Patent Form 7/77

Patents Act 1977

1 Application details

1a please give the patent application number *(if known)*:

1b Please give the full name(s) of the applicant(s):

2 Title of invention

2 Please give the title of the invention:

3 Derivation of right

3 Please state how the applicant(s) derive(s) the right to be granted a patent:

4 Declaration

4 I believe the person(s) named overleaf (and on any supplementary copies of this form) to be the inventor(s) of the invention for which the patent application has been made. I consent to the disclosure of the details contained in this form to each inventor named.

please sign here Signed Date *(day month year)*

Please turn over

(FORM 7/77 CONTINUED)

Please put the name(s) and address(es) of the inventors in the boxes below:

Please underline the surnames or family names.

ADP number *(if known)*:

ADP number *(if known)*:

ADP number *(if known)*:

Please give the names of any further inventors on the back of another form 7/77 and attach it to this form.

Reminder

Have you signed the declaration overleaf?

Patents Form 8/77 **141.08**

For official use

Your reference

Notes
Please type, or write in dark ink using CAPITAL letters.

A prescribed fee is payable with this form. For details, please contact the Patent Office.

Paragraph 2 of Schedule 2 to the Patents Rules 1990 governs the completion and filing of this form.

It should be filed in duplicate.

If the micro–organism of which a sample is required is deposited with an International Depositary Authority under the Budapest Treaty, the form provided for by the regulations under that Treaty should be filed with this form for certification by the Comptroller.

The Patent Office

Request for certificate authorising release of sample of micro–organism

Form 8/77 **Patents Act 1977**

1 Application or Patent details

1a Please give the patent application or patent number:

1b Please give the full name(s) of the applicant(s) / Proprietor(s):

2 Details of deposit of micro–organism

2a Please give the name of the depositary institution in which the micro–organism is deposited

2b Please give the accession number of the deposit:

3 Details of person(s) making this request

3a Please give your name and address:

Name

Address

Postcode

Please turn over

(FORM 8/77 CONTINUED)

3b: *The address to which the Comptroller's certificate is to be sent must be in the United kingdom.*

3b Please give the name and address to which your copy of the Comptroller's certificate should be sent if different from that at 3a:

Name

Address

Postcode

4 *If you are seeking release of a sample before publication of the application, by virtue of Section 118(4), a statutory declaration should also be furnished in accordance with Rule 96 of the Patents Rules 1990.*

These undertakings are subject to the provisions of paragraphs 2(3) to 2(6) of Schedule 2 to the Patents Rules 1990.

4 Declaration and undertaking

I/We declare:

- ☐ that the invention disclosed in the specification of the application or patent identified at 1 requires for its performance the use of the micro–organism identified at 2;
- ☐ that, where the application has not yet been published, I am/we are entitled to receive information and inspect documents by virtue of Section 118(4) or (5)

I/We undertake for the benefit of the applicant(s)/proprietor(s), if a sample of the micro–organism is made available as requested:

- ☐ not to make the culture, or any culture derived from it, available to any other person; ***and***
- ☐ not to use the culture, or any culture derived from it, otherwise than for experimental purposes relating to the subject matter of the invention.

I/We accordingly request that the Comptroller's certificate authorising the release of a sample of the micro–organism may be sent me/us.

Please sign here ➧ Signed Date *(day month year)*

Patents Form 8A/77

141.08A

For official use

Your reference

Notes
Please type, or write in dark ink using CAPITAL letters.

A prescribed fee is payable with this form. For details, please contact the Patent Office.

Paragraph 3 of Schedule 2 to the Patents Rules 1990 governs the completion and filing of this form.

In order to be effective, this form must be filed before the completion of preparations for the publication of your application under Section 16(1) of the Patents Act 1977.

The Patent Office

Notice of intention to restrict availability of samples of micro–organisms to experts

Form 8A/77 **Patents Act 1977**

1 Application details

1a please give the patent application number:

1b Please give the full name(s) and address(es) of the applicant(s):

Name

Address

Postcode

ADP number
(if known):

2 Details of deposit of micro-organism

2a Please give the name of the depositary institution in which the micro–organism is deposited:

2b Please give the accession number of the deposit:

3 Declaration

3 This election is effective only until grant of a patent on the application

I am/we are the applicant(s) identified at 1b and hereby give notice of my/our intention that samples of the culture identified at 2 shall be available only to experts in accordance with paragraph 3 of Schedule 2 to the Patents Rules 1990.

please sign here Signed Date *(day month year)*

141.08B Patents Form 8B/77

For official use

Your reference

Notes
Please type, or write in dark ink using CAPITAL letters.

A prescribed fee is payable with this form. For details, please contact the Patent Office.

Paragraph 3 of Schedule 2 to the Patents Rules 1990 governs the completion and filing of this form.

It should be filed in duplicate.

If the micro-organism of which a sample is required is deposited with an International Depositary Authority under the Budapest Treaty, the form provided for by the regulations under that Treaty should be filed with this form for certification by the Comptroller.

The Patent Office

Request for certificate authorising release of sample of micro-organism to expert

Form 8B/77 **Patents Act 1977**

1 Application details

1a Please give the patent application number:

1b please give the full name(s) of the applicant(s):

2 Details of deposit of micro-organism

2a Please give the name of the depositary institution in which the micro-organism is deposited

2b Please give the accession number of the deposit:

3 Details of person(s) making this request

3a Please give your name and address:

Name

Address

Postcode

Please turn over ➧

(FORM 8B/77 CONTINUED)

***3b:** The address to which the Comptroller's certificate is to be sent must be in the United Kingdom.*

3b Please give the name and address to which your copy of the Comptroller's certificate should be sent if different from that at 3a:

Name

Address

Postcode

***4** Paragraph 3 of Schedule 2 to the Patents Rules 1990 allows the applicant to restrict availability of the culture to 'experts' until the patent is granted, by filing form 8A/77.*

4 Nomination of expert

Please give the name and address of your nominated expert:

Name

Address

Postcode

***5** If you are seeking release of a sample before publication of the application, by virtue of Section 118(4), a statutory declaration should also be furnished in accordance with Rule 96 of the Patents Rules 1990.*

5 Declaration

I/We declare:

☐ that the invention disclosed in the specification of the application identified at 1 requires for its performance the use of the micro–organism identified at 2;

☐ that, where the application has not yet been published, I am/ we are entitled to receive information and inspect documents by virtue of Section 118(4) or (5).

I/We accordingly request that the Comptroller's certificate authorising the release of a sample of the micro–organism may be sent to me/us and to the person nominated at 4.

Person making the request please sign here ➧

Signed Date *(day month year)*

***6** These undertakings are subject to the provisions of paragraphs 2(3) to 2(6) of Schedule 2 to the Patents Rules 1990.*

6 Undertaking by expert

I am the person nominated at 4 and undertake for the benefit of the applicant(s), if a sample of the micro–organism is made available to me as requested:

☐ not to make the culture, or any culture derived from it, available to any other person; ***and***

☐ not to use the culture, or any culture derived from it, otherwise than for experimental purposes relating to the subject matter of the invention.

Expert please sign here ➧

Signed Date *(day month year)*

141.09 Patents Form 9/77

For official use

Your reference

Notes
Please type, or write in dark ink using CAPITAL letters.

A prescribed fee is payable for a preliminary examination and search, for a further search and a supplementary search. For details, please contact the Patent Office.

Rules 25, 28, and 32 of the Patents Rules 1990 are the main rules governing the completion and filing of this form.

The Patent Office

Preliminary Examination/ Search

Form 9/77 **Patents Act 1977**

1a Please give the patent application number *(if known)*:

1b Please give the full name(s) of the applicant(s):

*please mark **one** box only*

2 Are you:

a) requesting a preliminary examination and search under Section 17(1)? ☐

b) requesting a search of a further invention under Section 17(6)? ☐

c) paying for a supplementary search under Section 17(8)? ☐

You should complete this part only if you have marked question 2, box (b).

__3:__ If box 2b has been marked and no invention is specified here, the further search will be made in relation to the second invention specified in the Search Report previously made under Section 17(5).

3 Please identify the invention to be searched by reference to the claims:

Please sign here ➧

Signed

Date *(day month year)*

Patents Form 10/77 **141.10**

For official use

Your reference

Notes
Please type, or write in dark ink using CAPITAL letters.

A prescribed fee is payable with this form. For details, please contact the Patent Office.

Rule 33 of the Patents Rules 1990 is the main rule governing the completion and filing of this form.

The Patent Office

Request for substantive examination

Form 10/77

Patents Act 1977

1 Application details

1a Please give the patent application number *(if known)*:

1b Please give full name(s) of the applicant(s):

2 Request

I/We request a substantive examination under Section 18 of the Act.

Please sign here ➧ Signed

Date *(day month year)*

141.11 Patents Form 11/77

For official use

Your reference

Notes
Please type, or write in dark ink using CAPITAL letters.

A prescribed fee is payable with this form. For details, please contact the Patent Office.

Rules 35 and 36 of the Patents Rules 1990 are the main rules governing the completion and filing of this form.

If you wish to amend only the name of an applicant, please use form 20/77 instead.

The Patent Office

Request to amend application before grant

Form 11/77 **Patents Act 1977**

1 Application details

1a Please give the patent application number:

1b Please give the full name(s) of the applicant(s):

2 reasons for amandment

2 This request should be accompanied by a document clearly identifying the desired amendment. (The Comptroller may request you to file a copy of the unamended application on which the amendment is shown in red ink if the accompanying document is not itself in this form.)

2 Please give your reasons for making this amendment:

Please sign here

Signed Date *(day month year)*

Patents Form 12/77

Payment of renewal fee (and additional fee for late renewal)

Patents Act 1977

Form 12/77

For official use

Notes
Please type, or write in dark ink using CAPITAL letters. For details of the prescribed fees payable with this form, please contact the Patent Office.

Rules 39 and 41 of the Patent Rules 1990 are the main rules governing the completion and filing of this form.

1 Please give the patent number:

2 Please give the full name(s) of the proprietor(s):

3a When is the renewal fee due? ________ *(day month year)*

3b For which year are you paying ________ th

3c What renewal fee are you paying £

3b: please give the year in terms of the life of the patent, for example 6th.

4: Please complete this only if renewal is overdue. *If your renewal payment is overdue an additional fee will be payable under Section 25(4) of the Patents Act 1977.*

4a What additional fee payment are you making: £________

4b For how many months extension? *months*

5 Please give the name and address of the person paying fee:

Name

Address

Postcode

6: see Rule 39(5) of the Patents Rules 1990.

6 If next year's renewal fee is not paid by the due date a renewal reminder will be sent to the address for service on the register. If the proprietor wishes it to be sent to a different address in the United Kingdom, he should give that different address and add his signature.

Address

Postcode

Signature of proprietor

Date *(day month year)*

If you complete the certificate below, the Patent Office will stamp and return it to the address given in the box below.

Certificate of payment of renewal fee *(and additional fee if applicable)*

The Patent Office

Patent number ________ has been renewed until ________ *(day month year)*

Your reference

Patent Office date stamp

141.14 Patents Form 14/77

For official use

Your reference

Notes
Please type, or write in dark ink using CAPITAL letters.

A prescribed fee is payable with this form. For details, please contact the Patent Office.

Rule 40 of the Patents Rules 1990 is the main rule governing the completion and filing of this form.

If you do not have enough space please use a separate sheet of paper.

The Patent Office

Application to amend a specification after grant of a Patent

Form 14/77 **Patents Act 1977**

1a Please give the patent number;

1b Please give the full name(s) of the proprietor(s):

__2:__ This application should be accompanied by document(s) clearly showing the amendment sought, in accordance with Rule 40(6) of the Patents Rules 1990. (The Comptroller may request you to file a copy of the unamended specification on which the amendment is shown in red ink if the accompanying document is not itself in this form.)

2 Please give your reason for making the amendment:

Please mark correct box

3a Do you want the address for service to be altered?

Yes ☐ No ☐ ➧ ***go to declaration below***

__3:__ If an agent has been newly authorised form 51/77 should be completed instead of 3b.

3b Please give the full name and address in the United Kingdom to which all correspondence will be sent:

Name

Address

Postcode

ADP number *(if known)*:

I declare that no proceedings are pending before the court or the Comptroller in which the validity of the patent may be in issue.

Please sign here ➧ Signed Date *(day month year)*

Patents Form 16/77

For official use

Your reference

Notes
Please type, or write in dark ink using CAPITAL letters.

A prescribed fee is payable with this form. For details, please contact the Patent Office.

Rule 41 of the Patents Rules 1990 is the main rule governing the completion and filing of this form.

If you do not have enough space please use a separate sheet of paper.

The Patent Office

Application for restoration of a Patent

Form 16/77 **Patents Act 1977**

1a Please give the patent number;

1b Please give the full name(s) of the proprietor(s):

2 Please give your reasons for applying for this restoration

__2:__ Supporting evidence must be provided.

3 If you are not the proprietor(s) as at 1b above, please give your name and address:

Name

Address

Postcode

4 ***(See note 4)*** Please give name and address for service in the United Kingdom to which all correspondence will be sent:

__4:__ If you are the proprietor(s) of the patent:
- *do **not** complete this part unless you wish the register to be altered;*
- *use form 51/77 instead of completing this part if an agent has been newly authorised.*

Name

Address

Postcode

ADP number *(if known)*:

Please sign here ➧

Signed

Date *(day month year)*

141.18 Patents Form 18/77

Notes. 1. A note now states that "No fee is required with this form". 2. A box is provided for entry of the name and United Kingdom address for service, including the postcode and ADP No. for this address.

Patents Form 20/77 **141.20**

For official use	
Your reference	

Notes
This form is for use where a name which had previously been given to the Patent Office has since been changed.

Please type, or write in dark ink using CAPITAL letters.

One prescribed fee is charged for each application or patent affected. For details, please contact the Patent Office.

Rule 45 of the Patents Rules 1990 is the main rule governing the completion and filing of this form.

*If there is more than one patent application/patent number, please enter 'see attached list' and give the details requested in **1** (and **2** if more tha one owner) on a separate sheet of paper.*

***4:** Evidence of the alteration must be provided.*

please mark correct box

***5:** If you are the patent applicant(s) or the proprietor(s) of the patent:*

*• use form 51/77 instead of completing **5b** if an agent has been newly authorised.*

Please sign here

The Patent Office

Request for alteration of name

Form 20/77

Patents Act 1977

1a Please give the patent application or patent number:

2 Please give the full name(s) and address(es) of the existing applicant(s)/proprietor(s):

Name

Address

Postcode

ADP number *(if known)*:

3 Please give name to be altered:

ADP number *(if known)*:

4 Please give new name:

ADP number *(if known)*:

5a Do you want the address for service to be altered?

Yes ☐ No ☐ ***please sign below***

5b Please give the full name and address in the United Kingdom to which all correspondence will be sent:

Name

Address

Postcode

ADP number *(if known)*:

Signed

Date *(day month year)*

141.21 Patents Form 21/77

For official use

Your reference

Notes
Please type, or write in dark ink using CAPITAL letters.

A prescribed fee is payable with this form. For details, please contact the Patent Office.

Rule 46 of the Patents Rules 1990 is the main rule governing the completion and filing of this form.

The Patent Office

Application to register or to give notice of a transaction, instrument or event affecting the rights in a Patent or application for a Patent

Form 21/77 **Patents Act 1977**

1 Application or Patent details

1 If there is more than one patent application/patent number, please enter 'see attached list', and give the details requested on a separate sheet of paper.

1a Please give the patent application or patent number:

1b Please give the full name(s) and address(es) of the applicant(s)/ proprietors:

Name

Address

ADP number
(if known):

2 Details of transaction, instrument or event

2 See Section 33(3) which specifies the relevant transactions, instruments and events (which include assignments, licences and mortgages).

Registration will not be effected until a certified copy or extract establishing the transaction, instrument or event has been furnished, unless the Comptroller otherwise directs.

2 Please give details of the transaction, instrument or event together with its date and the names of all the parties involved including for corporate bodies the country and, if appropriate, state of incorporation:

Please turn over

(FORM 21/77 CONTINUED)

3 Details of person(s) making this application

3 If you are not the applicant(s)/proprietor(s) as at 1b overleaf, please give your name and address:

Name

Address

Postcode

4 Address for service

4a Please give the name and address for service in the United Kingdom to which all correspondence relating to this form will be sent:

Name

Address

Postcode

ADP number
(if known)

4b: *If you are the patent applicant(s) or the proprietor(s) of the patent, please use form 51/77 instead of completing this part if an agent has been newly authorised.*

4b If you are the patent applicant(s) or proprietor(s) is this a new address for service which you wish to be entered on the register?

Please mark correct box

Yes ☐ No ☐

Please sign here ➧ Signed Date *(day month year)*

141.22 Patents Form 22/77

PATENTS ACT 1977
PATENTS FORM 22/77
(Rule 47)

The Patent Office

Your reference

REQUEST FOR THE CORRECTION OF AN ERROR IN THE REGISTER OR IN ANY CONNECTED DOCUMENT

NOTES:

1 The person making the request should clearly identify in the space provided, the document containing the error to be corrected and should also supply a document clearly identifying the desired corrections unless it is not convenient to do so, in which case the correction sought may be stated in the space provided. The comptroller may request the filing of a copy of the defective document on which the corrections are shown in red ink.

2 Where any applicant/proprietor added or changed by the correction is a corporate body, the country and, if appropriate, state of incorporation of that body must be given.

3 A prescribed fee is payable with this form. For details contact the Patent Office.

I/We ....

....

....

request:-

(a) That the entry made in the register in relation to Patent Application/Patent No. ....

and/or

(b) that the undermentioned document filed in connection with such registration; be corrected

(i) as shown on the annexed copy of ...., or

(ii) as follows ....

....

....

....

....

Signature ....

If you are the patent applicant(s) or the proprietor(s) of the patent:

- do not complete this part unless you wish the register to be altered;
- use form 51/77 instead of completing this part if an agent has been newly authorised.

(See note opposite)
Please give name and address for service in the United Kingdom to which all correspondence will be sent.

Name

Address

Postcode ADP No.

For official use

Your reference

Notes
Please type, or write in dark ink using CAPITAL letters.

This form may be used to make more than one request. The requests need not all relate to the same patent or patent application. The fee payable is the total of the prescribed fees for each item. If the fee paid is insufficient, the requests will be actioned in the order they have been made on the form as far as the fee allows. For details, please contact the Patent Office.

Rules 48, 49, 52, and 93 and Schedule 4, paragraph 6 of the Patents Rules 1990 are the main rules governing the completion and filing of this form.

1* and *2 *Where a request in **1** or **2** is in relation to an unpublished patent application and relies on Section 118(4), the requirements of Rule 96 must be complied with.*

The Patent Office

Request for miscellaneous information

Form 23/77

Patents Act 1977

1 Inspection of register or documents

1 If you want to inspect the register and/or the original documents filed at or kept in the Patent Office in relation to any patent application, please give full details:

2 Supply of copies or extracts

2 If you want copies of, or extracts from, the register or documents relating to any patent or patent application, please give full details:

Please turn over

(FORM 23/77 CONTINUED)

3 If a request is made under 1 or 2, the information under 3 will be provided at no extra charge if requested in respect of the same patent.

3 Information about renewal

3 Please give the number of any patent for which you want to know whether, and when, a renewal fee has been paid:

4 Details of the person making the request(s)

4 Please give your name and address:

Name

Address

Postcode

Please sign here ➧ Signed Date *(day month year)*

Patents Form 25/77 141.25

Notes. 1. A note now states that "No fee is required with this form". 2. A box is provided for entry of the name and United Kingdom address for service, including the postcode and ADP No. for this address.

Patents Form 26/77 141.26

Note. This form is now applicable under rule 59.

Patents Form 27/77 141.27

Note. This form is now entitled "Application under section 41(8)" and is stated to be now applicable under rule 60. Also, a box is now provided for entry of the name and United Kingdom address for service, including the postcode and ADP No. for this address.

Patents Form 28/77 141.28

Note. This form is now applicable under rule 61.

Patents Form 29/77 141.29

Note. This form is now applicable under rule 62 and a box is provided for entry of the name and United Kingdom address for service, including the postcode and ADP No. for this address.

Patents Form 30/77 141.30

Note. This form is now applicable under rule 63 and a box is provided for entry of the name and United Kingdom address for service, including the postcode and ADP No. for this address.

Patents Form 31/77 141.31

Note. This form is now applicable under rule 64.

Patents Form 32/77 141.32

Note. This form is now applicable under rule 65.

141.34 Patents Form 34/77

PATENTS ACT 1977
PATENTS FORM 34/77
(Rule 69)

The
Patent
Office

Your reference

APPLICATION BY CROWN IN CASE OF MONOPOLY OR MERGER

NOTES:

1 The title of the appropriate Minister or Ministers should be entered in the first space below.

2 A prescribed fee is payable with this form, For details, please contact the Patent Office.

, following

a report of the Monopolies and Mergers Commission entitled

(which has been laid before Parliament) hereby makes/make application to the comptroller that he will take action under section 51 in respect of Patent No. and declares/declare that he/they have complied with the requirements of subsection (2) of that section in relation to this application.

Signature ....

Name and official capacity of person signing ....

Address for service in the ....

United Kingdom to which all ....

communications should be sent ....

ADP No

Patents Form 35/77

141.35

Note. A box is provided for entry of the name and United Kingdom address for service, including the postcode and ADP No. for this address.

141.36 **Patents Form 36/77**

PATENTS ACT 1977

PATENTS FORM 36/77

(Rule 72)

The Patent Office

Your reference

REFERENCE TO THE COMPTROLLER OF A DISPUTE AS TO INFRINGEMENT

NOTES:

1 The parties to the reference should enter their names and addresses in the appropriate spaces and the status of the first party should be indicated.

2 The parties should submit a joint statement, setting out fully the matters on which they are in agreement and those upon which they are in dispute.

3 A prescribed fee is payable with this form. For details, please contact the Patent Office.

We, ...

....

the proprietor of Patent No. ....

or the exclusive licensee under Patent No. ....

and ....

the persons alleged by the proprietor or exclusive licensee to have infringed the patent, refer to the comptroller the question whether such infringement has in fact taken place. We submit herewith a joint statement giving full particulars of the matters which are in dispute and those on which we are in agreement.

Signature of proprietor or exclusive licensee ....

If an agent has been newly authorised form 51/77 should be completed instead of b.

a Do you want the address for service to be altered?

Yes ☐ No ☐

b If yes, please give the full name and address in the United Kingdom to which all correspondence will be sent

Name

Address

Postcode ADP No (if known)

Signature of other party to the reference ....

Name of Agent (if any) ....

Address for service in the United Kingdom to which all communications should be sent ....

....

....

ADP No

Patents Form 39/77 **141.39**

Note. A box is provided for entry of the name and United Kingdom address for service, including the postcode and ADP No. for this address.

Patents Form 40/77 **141.40**

Note. A box is provided for entry of the name and United Kingdom address for service, including the postcode and ADP No. for this address.

141.43 Patents Form 43/77

For official use

Your reference

Notes
Please type, or write in dark ink using CAPITAL letters.

A prescribed fee is payable with this form. For details, please contact the Patent Office.

Rule 85 of the Patents Rules 1990 is the main rule governing the completion and filing of this form.

The Patent Office

Request for publication of translation

Form 43/77 **Patents Act 1977**

1 Application details

1a Please give the United Kingdom patent application number:

1b Please give the full name(s) of the applicant(s):

2 Translation details

2 Are you requesting publication of the translation of:

Please mark correct box

□ the application filed at the Patent Office under Section 89A(3)? □

□ the amendment filed at the Patent Office under Section 89A(5)? □

Please sign here Signed Date *(day month year)*

Patents Form 44/77 141.44

PATENTS ACT 1977

PATENTS FORM 44/77

(Rule 85)

The
Patent
Office

Your reference

APPLICATION TO THE COMPTROLLER FOR AN INTERNATIONAL APPLICATION TO BE TREATED AS AN APPLICATION UNDER THE ACT

NOTES:

1 The three irrelevant items (1)a, (1)b, (1)c or (2) below should be deleted.

2 This form should be accompanied by a statement of the facts being relied on.

3 A prescribed fee is payable with this form. For details, please contact the Patent Office.

In the case of international application No. ...., I/We ....

....

(1) request that the comptroller should treat the application as not withdrawn under the Act notwithstanding that it, or the designation of the United Kingdom in it, is deemed to be withdrawn under the Patent Co-operation Treaty -

a Because of an error or omission in an institution having functions under that Treaty; or

b because, owing to circumstances outside my/our control, a copy of the application was not received by the International Bureau before the end of the time limited for that purpose under that Treaty; or

c because, in the same or comparable circumstances in relation to an application under the Act (other than an international application) -

(i) the comptroller could have directed that an irregularity be rectified under rule 100 or an extension be granted under rule 110, and

(ii) he determines that the application would not have been treated as withdrawn under the Act,

as the case may require

(2) apply to the comptroller for -

a determination (the application having been refused a filing date under that Treaty) that the refusal was caused by an error or omission in an institution having functions under that Treaty; and

b direction that the application shall be treated as an application under the Act having such date of filing as he may direct.

Signature ....

Name of Agent (if any) ....

Address for service in the United Kingdom to which all communications should be sent ....

....

ADP No ....

141.45 Patents Form 45/77

Note. In the text on form 45/77 "section (1)" has been corrected to "section 1, subsection (1)".

141.46 Patents Form 46/77

Note. This form has been deleted.

Patents Form 47/77 141.47

For official use

Your reference

Notes
Please type, or write in dark ink using CAPITAL letters.

A prescribed fee is payable with this form. For details, please contact the Patent Office.

Rule 91 of the Patents Rules 1990 is the main rule governing the completion and filing of this form.

The Patent Office

Request for correction of error or mistake
Form 47/77

Patents Act 1977

1 Patent or application details

1a please give the patent application or patent number:

1b Please give the full name(s) of the proprietor(s) or applicant(s):

2 Error or mistake

2 This request should be accompanied by a document clearly identifying the desired correction. (The Comptroller may require you to file a copy of the defective document on which the correction is shown and may request that it be shown in red ink.) Where any applicant/proprietor added or changed by the correction is a corporate body, the country and, if appropriate, state of incorporation of that body must be given.

2 Please identify the document containing the error or mistake to be corrected:

3 Address for service

3a Do you want the address for service to be altered?

Please mark correct box

Yes ☐ No ☐ ➧ ***please sign below***

3b: If an agent has been newly authorised, form 51/77 should be completed instead of 3b.

3b Please give the full name and address in the United Kingdom to which all correspondence will be sent:

Name

Address

Postcode

ADP number *(if known)*:

Please sign here ➧ Signed Date *(day month year)*

141.48 Patents Form 48/77

Note. The title of form 48/77 has been changed to "Opposition to request for correction of error or mistake".

Patents Form 49/77 **141.49**

For official use

Your reference

Notes
Please type, or write in dark ink using CAPITAL letters.

A prescribed fee is payable with this form. For details, please contact the Patent Office.

Rule 92 of the Patents Rules 1990 is the main rule governing the completion and filing of this form.

Please use a separate form for each item of information.

The Patent Office

Request for information relating to a Patent or Application

Form 49/77 **Patents Act 1977**

1 Patent or application details

1a please give the patent application or patent number:

1b Please give the full name(s) of the proprietor(s) or applicant(s):

2 Information requested

2 The requests which may be made are specified in Rule 92(1) and (2).

2 What information do you require?

3 Details of person making request

3 Please give your name and address*(to which the information will be sent):*

Name

Address

Postcode

Please sign here ➧ Signed Date *(day month year)*

141.50 Patents Form 50/77

For official use

Your reference

Notes
Please type, or write in dark ink using CAPITAL letters.

A prescribed fee is payable with this form. For details, please contact the Patent Office.

The Patent Office

Request for extension of time or period under Rule 110(3)

Form 50/77 **Patents Act 1977**

1 Application or patent details

1a Please give the patent application or patent number *(if known)*:

1b Please give the full name(s) of the applicant(s) or proprietor(s):

2 Extension details

2 This form may not be used to extend more than one time or period unless the times or periods expire on the same day.

2 Which of the following Rules prescribe(s) the time(s) or period(s) to be extended?

Please mark correct box(es)

6(2) ☐	33(2) ☐	82(2) ☐
6(6) ☐	33(3) ☐	82(3) ☐
15(1) ☐	33(5) ☐	83(3) ☐
23 ☐	34 ☐	85(1) ☐
25(2) ☐	41(4) ☐	85(7) ☐
25(3) ☐	81(2) ☐	110(6) ☐
26 ☐	81(3) ☐	Schedule 2 Paragraph 1(3) ☐
		Schedule 4 paragraph 2 ☐

3 Signature

Please sign here ➧

Signed

Date *(day month year)*

Patents Form 51/77

141.51

For official use	
Your reference	

Notes
Please type, or write in dark ink using CAPITAL letters.

No fee is required with this form.

Rule 90 of the Patents Rules 1990 is the main rule governing the completion and filing of this form.

This form is for use only where, after a person has become a party to proceedings before the Comptroller, he appoints an agent for the first time or appoints one agent in substitution for another.

The form is to be completed by the newly appointed agent and filed in duplicate. Where the new agent has been appointed in substitution for another, the duplicate form is sent to the former agent.

1: *If more than one application or patent is affected, please enter 'see attached list' and give the details requested on a separate sheet of paper.*

The Patent Office

Appointment or change of agent

Form 51/77

Patents Act 1977

1 Please give the patent application or patent number to which the proceedings relate *(see note 1 below)*:

2 Have you been authorised to act in all matters relating to the above application/patent?
Please mark correct box Yes ☐ No ☐

Please give details of the extent of your appointment:

3 Please give full name(s) and address(es) of person(s) who have authorised you as agent:

Name

Address

Postcode

4 Please give your name and address:

Name

Address

Postcode

ADP number
(if known):

5 I declare that I/We have been appointed by the person(s) named at 3 above to act as agent as detailed in 2 above.

Please sign here ➧ Signed Date *(day month year)*

141.52 Patents Form 52/77

For official use

Your reference

Notes
Please type, or write in dark ink using CAPITAL letters.

A prescribed fee is payable with this form. For details, please contact the Patent Office.

This form should be accompanied by a statutory declaration or affidavit verifying the grounds for the request, unless the Comptroller otherwise directs.

The Patent Office

Request for extension of time or period under Rule 110(4)

Form 52/77 **Patents Act 1977**

1 Application or patent details

1a Please give the patent application or patent number:

1b Please give the full name(s) of the applicant(s) or proprietor(s):

2 Extension details

2 This form may not be used to extend more than one time or period unless the times or periods are to be extended to a common date.

2a Which of the following Rules prescribe(s) the time(s) or period(s) to be extended?

Please mark correct box(es)

6(2) ☐	33(2) ☐	82(2) ☐
6(6) ☐	33(3) ☐	82(3) ☐
15(1) ☐	33(5) ☐	83(3) ☐
23 ☐	34 ☐	85(1) ☐
25(2) ☐	41(4) ☐	85(7) ☐
25(3) ☐	81(2) ☐	110(6) ☐
26 ☐	81(3) ☐	Schedule 2 Paragraph 1(3) ☐
		Schedule 4 paragraph 2 ☐

2b Please enter the date on which the extension would expire if allowed:

Date

(day month year)

Remember to attach your declaration or affidavit

3 Signature

Please sign here ➧

Signed

Date *(day month year)*

For official use

Your reference

Notes
Please type, or write in dark ink using CAPITAL letters.

For details of the prescribed fee payable with this form, please contact the Patent Office.

The Patent Office

Additional fee for extension of time or period under Rule 110(6)

Form 53/77 **Patents Act 1977**

1 Application or Patent details

1a Please give the patent application or patent number:

1b Please give the full name(s) of the applicant(s) or proprietor(s):

2 Signature

Please sign here ➧ Signed Date *(day month year)*

141.54 Patents Form 54/77

For official use

Your reference

Notes
Please type, or write in dark ink using CAPITAL letters.

A prescribed fee is payable with this form. For details, please contact the Patent Office.

Paragraph 1 of Schedule 4 to the Patents Rules 1990 governs the completion and filing of this form.

This form must be filed in duplicate and must be accompanied by a translation into English, in duplicate, of:
- *the whole description*
- *those claims appropriate to the UK (in the language of the proceedings)*

including all drawings, whether or not these contain any textual matter but excluding the front page which contains bibliographic information. The translation must be verified to the satisfaction of the Comptroller as corresponding to the original text.

The Patent Office

Filing of translation of European Patent (UK) under Section 77(6)(a)

Form 54/77 **Patents Act 1977**

1 European Patent number

1 Please give the European Patent number:

2 Proprietor's details

2 Please give the full name(s) and address(es) of the proprietor(s) of the European Patent (UK):

Name

Address

Postcode

ADP number
(if known):

3 European Patent Bulletin date

3 Please give date on which the mention of the grant of the European Patent (UK) was published in the European Patent Bulletin or, if it has not yet been published, the date on which it will be published:

Date

(day month year)

Please turn over ◊

(FORM 54/77 CONTINUED)

4 Agents details

4 Please give name of agent (*if any*):

5 An address for service in the United Kingdom must be supplied.

5 Address of service

5 Please give a name and address in the United Kingdom to which all correspondence will be sent:

Name

Address

Postcode

ADP number (*if known*)

Signature

Please sign here ⇒

Signed

Date *(day month year)*

Reminder

Have you attached:

- □ *one duplicate copy of this form?*
- □ *two copies of the translation including any drawings (verified to the satisfaction of the Comptroller)?*
- □ *any continuation sheets (if applicable)?*

141.55 Patents Form 55/77

For official use

Your reference

Notes
Please type, or write in dark ink using CAPITAL letters.

A prescribed fee is payable with this form. For details, please contact the Patent Office.

Paragraph 1 of Schedule 4 to the Patents Rules 1990 governs the completion and filing of this form.

This form must be filed in duplicate and must be accompanied by a translation into English, in duplicate, of:
- *the whole description*
- *those claims appropriate to the UK (in the language of the proceedings)*

including all drawings, whether or not these contain any textual matter but excluding the front page which contains bibliographic information. The translation must be verified to the satisfaction of the Comptroller as corresponding to the original text.

The Patent Office

Filing of translation of an amended European Patent (UK) under Section 77(6)(b)

Form 55/77 **Patents Act 1977**

1 European Patent number

1 Please give the European Patent number:

2 *Proprietor's details*

2 Please give the full name(s) and address(es) of the proprietor(s) of the European Patent (UK):

Name

Address

Postcode

ADP number
(if known):

3 Publication of amended European Patent

3 Please give the date on which the amended European Patent (UK) was published by the European Patent Office or, if it has not yet been published, the date on which it will be published:

Date

(day month year)

Please turn over ◊

(FORM 55/77 CONTINUED)

4 Agent's details

4 Please give name of agent *(if any)*:

5 Address for service

5a Do you want the address for service to be altered:

Please mark correct box

Yes ☐ No ☐ ➧ ***please sign below***

5b: *If an agent has been newly authorised, form 51/77 should be completed instead of 5b.*

5b Please give a full name and address in the United Kingdom to which all correspondence will be sent:

Name

Address

Postcode

ADP number *(if known)*

Signature

Please sign here

Signed

Date *(day month year)*

Reminder

Have you attached:

☐ *one duplicate copy of this form?*

☐ *two copies of the translation including any drawings (verified to the satisfaction of the Comptroller)?*

☐ *any continuation sheets (if appropriate)?*

141.56 Patents Form 56/77

For official use

Your reference

Notes
Please type, or write in dark ink using CAPITAL letters.

A prescribed fee is payable with this form. For details, please contact the Patent Office.

Paragraph 3 of Schedule 4 to the Patents Rules 1990 governs the completion and filing of this form.

This form must be filed in duplicate and must be accompanied by a translation into English, in duplicate, of the claims of the application for a European Patent (UK). The translation must be verified to the satisfaction of the Comptroller as corresponding to the original text.

1 *The International publication number should be given only when paragraph 3(1)(b) of Schedule 4 to the Patents Rules 1990 applies.*

The Patent Office

Request for publication of translation of claims of application for European Patent (UK) filed under Section 78(7)

Form 56/77 **Patents Act 1977**

1 European publication number

1 Please give the European publication number (or international publication number) (*see note 1 below*):

2 Applicant's details

2 Please give the full name(s) and address(es) of the applicant(s) for the European Patent (UK):

Name

Address

Postcode

3 Agent's details

3 Please give name of agent (*if any*):

Please turn over ◊

(FORM 56/77 CONTINUED)

4 An address for service in the United Kingdom must be supplied.

4 Address for service

4 Please give a name and address in the United Kingdom to which all correspondence will be sent:

Name

Address

Postcode

ADP number
(if known)

Signature

Please sign here ➧

Signed

Date *(day month year)*

Reminder

Have you attached:

☐ *one duplicate copy of this form?*

☐ *two copies of the translation (verified to the satisfaction of the Comptroller)?*

☐ *any continuation sheets (if applicable)?*

141.57 Patents Form 57/77

For official use

Your reference

Notes
Please type, or write in dark ink using CAPITAL letters.

A prescribed fee is payable with this form. For details, please contact the Patent Office.

Paragraph 4 of Schedule 4 to the Patents Rules 1990 governs the completion and filing of this form.

This form must be filed in duplicate and must be accompanied by a corrected version, in duplicate, of the whole of the incorrect translation. The translation must be verified to the satisfaction of the Comptroller as corresponding to the original text.

The Patent Office

Request for publication of corrected translation of European Patent (UK) or application for European Patent (UK) filed under Section 80(3)

Form 57/77 **Patents Act 1977**

1 European Patent or publication number

1 please give the European patent or publication number:

2 Proprietor's or applicant's details

2 Please give the full name(s) and address(es) of the proprietor(s) of, or applicant(s) for, the European Patent (UK):

Name

Address

Postcode

3 Agent's name

3 Please give name of agent *(if any)*:

Please turn over

(FORM 57/77 CONTINUED)

4 Address for service

Please mark correct box

4a Do you want the address for service to be altered:

Yes ☐ No ☐ ➧ ***please sign below***

4b: *If an agent has been newly authorised, form 51/77 should be completed instead of 4b.*

4b Please give a full name and address in the United Kingdom to which all correspondence will be sent:

Name

Address

Postcode

ADP number
(if known)

Signature

Please sign here ➧

Signed

Date *(day month year)*

Reminder

Have you attached:

☐ *One duplicate copy of this form?*

☐ *Two copies of the translation including any drawings (verified to the satisfaction of the Comptroller)?*

☐ *any continuation sheets (if appropriate)?*

141.58 Patents Form 58/77

Declaration that licences of right shall not extend to excepted uses	**Patents Act 1977** **Form 58/77**

For official use

Notes
Please type, or write in dark ink using CAPITAL letters. No fee is required with this form. However, there will be no reduction of renewal fees for the final years of the patent's life.

Rule 67 of the Patent Rules 1990 is the main rule governing the completion and filing of this form.

***2b:** If an agent has been newly authorised, form 51/77 should be completed instead of 2b.*

1a Please give the patent number:

1b Please give the full name(s) of the proprietor(s):

2a Do you want the address for service to be altered?

(Please mark correct box) Yes ☐ No ☐

2b Please give the full name and address in the United Kingdom to which all correspondence will be sent:

Name

Address

Postcode

ADP number
(if known):

In the case of the patent (which is for an invention which is a product) I/We declare:

☐ that I/We desire that licences to which persons are entitled by virtue of paragraph 4(2)(c) of Schedule 1 to the Patents Act 1977 shall not extend to a use of the product which is excepted by or under paragraph 4A of that Schedule ('excepted use'); ***and***

☐ that there is:

- no existing licence for any description of excepted use of the product which takes effect at or after the end of the sixteenth year of the patent, ***and***
- so far as I am/we are aware, no outstanding application under Section 46(3)(a) or (b) for settlement by the Comptroller of the terms of a licence for any description of excepted use effective at or after the end of that year.

Please complete the confirmation slip below. The Patent Office will stamp and return it to the address in the United Kingdom given in the box below.

Please sign here Signed Date *(day month year)*

Confirmation of making an entry

The Patent Office

Patent number

This is to confirm that an entry has been made in the register under Rule 67(2) (Licences of right not to extend to an excepted use.).

Your reference

Patent Office date stamp

Form NP1 (for optional use under Rule 85) **143.01**

For official use

Your reference

Notes
Please type, or write in dark ink using CAPITAL letters.

For details of prescribed fees, please contact the Patent Office, telephone 071-829 6905.

This form is for use when paying the prescribed fee for national processing.

The Patent Office

National Processing of an International Application for a Patent (UK)

Form NP1 **Patents Act 1977**

1 Details of International Application

1a Please give international application number

1b Please give international publication number *(if known):*

1c Please give the international filing date

1d Please give the earliest priority date declared

2 Applicant's details

☐ **First or only applicant**

2a If you are applying as a corporate body please give:

Corporate name

Country *(and State of incorporation, if appropriate)*

2b If you are applying as an individual or one of a partnership please give in full:

Surname

Forenames

2c **In all cases**, please give the following details:

Address

UK postcode *(if applicable)*

Country

ADP number *(if known)*

(FORM NP1 CONTINUED 1)

2d, 2e and 2f: If there are further applicants please provide details on a separate sheet of paper.

☐ **Second applicant (*if any*)**
2d If you are applying as a corporate body please give:

Corporate name

Country (*and State of incorporation, if appropriate*)

2e If you are applying as an individual or one of a partnership please give in full:

Surname

Forenames

2f **In all cases**, please give the following details:

Address

UK postcode (*if applicable*)

Country

ADP number (*if known*):

3 An address for service in the United Kingdom must be supplied

Please mark correct box

3 Address for service details

3a Have you appointed an agent to deal with your application?

Yes ☐ No ☐ ➧ ***go to 3b***

please give details below

Agent's name

Agent's address

Postcode

Agent's ADP number

3b: If you have appointed an agent, all correspondence concerning your application will be sent to the agent's United Kingdom address.

3b If you have not appointed an agent please give a name and address in the United Kingdom to which all correspondence will be sent:

Name

Address

Postcode

Daytime telephone number (*if available*)

ADP number (*if known*)

(FORM NP1 CONTINUED 2)

Please mark the appropriate box for each item filed with this form

4 Check list

The following items must be filed within the prescribed period for the national phase of the application to begin:

Rule 85(1)	☐ National Fee.
Rule 85(5)	☐ Translation of the international application if not in English.
Rule 85(2)	☐ Where applicable translation of information, if not in English, filed with the International Bureau, and relating to the deposit of a micro-organism (the prescribed period may be extended for this purpose only).
	☐ Copy of the international application (only if requesting early processing under Section 89A(3)(b) and none has yet been sent to the UK Patent Office by the International Bureau).

The following items should also be filed within their appropriate prescribed periods:

Rule 85(1)	☐ A copy of any amendment of the international application made in accordance with the Patent Co-operation Treaty (only if requesting early processing under Section 89A(3)(b) and none has yet been sent to the UK Patent Office by the International Bureau, otherwise such amendments will be disregarded).
Rule 85(1) and (5)	☐ Translation of any amendment made in accordance with the Patent Co-operation Treaty if not in English (otherwise such amendments will be disregarded).
Rule 85(7)(a)	☐ Request for preliminary examination and search (Patents Form 9/77) and prescribed fee.
Rules 15(4) and 85(7)(a)	☐ Where required information specifying the inventor and derivation of right to apply (Patents Form 7/77).
Rule 85(7)(b)	☐ Request for substantive examination (Patents Form 10/77) and prescribed fee.
Rules 6(6) and (7) and 85(3)(c) and (d)	☐ Translation of any priority application if not in English.
Rule 85(3)(b)	☐ Where applicable a certificate relating to the display of the invention at an international exhibition.
Rule 85(3)(e)	☐ Translations should be verified as required by the Rules.

Rule 85(6)	☐ Request for publication of translation (Patents Form 43/77).

Warning *Applicants are advised to consult the indicated provisions of the Patents Rules 1990 to determine the precise requirements.*
Care should be taken that the translation of the right document and not some other document is filed.

Please sign here ➧ Signed   Date *(day month year)*

FEES

144.01 *Illustrative fee schedule*

Upon the introduction of the Patents Rules 1990, new Fees Rules were introduced to take account of the changes made in the substantive Rules (Patents (Fees) (No. 2) Rules 1990, S.I. 1990 No. 2517). These new Fees Rules provided: for new PF 8A/77 and 8B/77, each then attracting the same fee as PF 8/77; for PF 9/77 to be used for the payment of a supplementary search fee in the same amount as on an original PF 9/77; and for the fees formerly payable on PF 13/77 (now deleted) to be paid as additional fees on filing PF 12/77. However, the latest rules on fees under the Act are the Patents (Fees) Rules 1991 (S.I. 1991 No. 1627) effective from August 12, 1991. These abolished the fees previously payable on many of the forms, namely on PF 2–8B/77, 15/77, 19/77, 20/77, 22/77, 23/77, 26–31/77, 33–39/77, 41/77, 45/77 and 48/77.

The Fees Rules also provide that forms attracting fees are to be accompanied by those fees, unless payment may be made within a prescribed period thereafter in which case the fee is to be paid within that period, see para. 123.05 *supra*.

APPENDIX A

PATENTS ACT 1949

COMMENTARY ON SECTION 4 [1949]

A004.6 *General rules of construction*

In *Roussel Uclaf* v. *ICI* ([1991] RPC 51) it was suggested that the purposive construction of claims according to the *Catnic* test may now result in claims of the type found bad for inutility in *Norton & Gregory* v. *Jacobs* ((1937) 54 RPC 58 and 271) being construed functionally.

COMMENTARY ON SECTION 5 [1949]

A005.3 *The test of "fair basis" for according a priority date*

The tests of fair basis under sections 5 and 32(1)(*i*) [1949] have now been equated, the question being a matter of construction upon which evidence (other than of technical matters and background) will be of little assistance (*Insituform* v. *Inliner*, SRIS C/77/91).

A013.1

SECTION 13 [1949]

Note. The amendment to section 13 [1949], noted in the Main Work, came into effect on January 7, 1991 (S.I. 1990 No. 2168).

COMMENTARY ON SECTION 31 [1949]

A031.10 *Limitation to an intermediate generalisation by disclaiming amendment*

Amendment of this nature was refused in *Corning Glass Works' Patent* (SRIS O/88/90, *noted* IPD 13215) because there was insufficient support for the proposed limitation.

Correction

—Correction of obvious mistake **A031.13**

For a mistake to be obvious, there must be an immediacy of appreciation and the position has to be viewed from the standpoint of the reader, not that of the draftsman. Thus, if the specification accurately reflects the mistaken intention of the draftsman, the consequence is that there is no mistake but the application has not been drafted with the requisite skill and care (*Sperry-Sum's Patent*, SRIS O/122/89, *noted* IPD 13043). Here the proposed amendment was not obvious in this sense, but otherwise discretion to permit it would have been exercised because of the complexity of the subject-matter.

Amendment by "Explanation" **A031.14**

An explanatory amendment can be made for the avoidance of doubt, even unreasonable doubt, and can make the ambiguous clear, but not the insufficient sufficient (*Roussel Uclaf* v. *ICI*, [1991] RPC 51), see also para. A004.06 *supra*..

COMMENTARY ON SECTION 32 [1949]

Lack of novelty (subs. (1)(e))

—Prior use **A032.11**

A single demonstration of the invention with a view to securing financial support, or to offer a licence, has not been regarded as a "use" at all (*Vax* v. *Hoover*, [1991] FSR 307), where it was indicated a use requires some "commercial dealing" in the invention.

Inutility (subs. (1)(g))

Scope of the objection of inutility **A032.16**

An allegation of inutility can perhaps be avoided by construing the claim functionally, see para. A004.06 *supra*. In any event, the plea will fail if a fair embodiment of the claim is not shown to be "useless" (*Minnesota Mining* v. *Rennicks*, SRIS C/100/91). Also, the continued authority of *Norton and Gregory* v. *Jacobs* ((1937) 54 RPC 58 and 271, cited in the Main Work) has been doubted (*Roussel-Uclaf* v. *ICI*, [1991] RPC 51), see para. A004.06 supra.

Best method not disclosed

General **A032.23**

The "best method" of performing the invention is to be evaluated according to the invention "as claimed", but there is no requirement to identify this "as the best method", and the best method of preparing a product invention need not be the same as the best method of "using" the invention (*Van der Lely* v. *Ruston's Engineering (No. 2)*, SRIS C/44/91, *noted* IPD 14119 (CA)).

A032.24 *—Date of knowledge of "best method"*

The relevant date for determination of inclusion of the best method has now been held to be that of filing the complete specification (*Van der Lely* v. *Ruston's Engineering (No. 2)*, SRIS C/44/91, *noted* IPD 14119 (CA)). The point is discussed in a case comment by J. Linneker ([1991] EIPR 423).

"Ambiguity" and lack of fair basis (subs. (1)(i))

A032.28 *—When ambiguity arises*

In *Sperry-Sum's Patent* (SRIS O/122/89, *noted* IPD 13043) the Comptroller held claims invalid for lack of clarity after an attempt to correct an allegedly obvious mistake had failed, see this Supplement *re* para. A031.13.

A032.29 *—Lack of fair basis*

As a general principle, claims must not extend beyond what the patentee has disclosed as his inventive concept (*Black & Decker* v. *Flymo*, SRIS C/7/91, *noted* IPD 14075). In *Van der Lely* v. *Ruston's Engineering (No. 2)*, SRIS C/44/91, *noted* IPD 14119 (CA)) it was stressed that the objection has to be evaluated according to the invention "as claimed". However, a lack of fair basis was found because a feature of a sub-claim was accepted as essential: thus claims broader than this claim were invalid on this ground. Other claims were invalidated for the same reason because an integer thereof was intended to perform an unusual function, but this was not described and the claims therefore covered the normal function of the integer and hence were not fairly based on the invention. A validating amendment was then allowed.

The test for "fair basis" is the same as that for according priority, see para. A005.3 *supra*; and an inventor who discloses a new product, and a new way in which this can be used, is entitled to a monpoly for both the new product and the new method of use (*Insituform* v. *Inliner*, SRIS C/77/91).

A032.35 *Secret prior use (subs. (1)(l))*

When an invention is demonstrated in order to offer a licence or to secure financial support, this was not regarded as a "trial" (*Vax* v. *Hoover*, [1991] FSR 307); however, it was also not considered a "use", see para. A032.11 *supra*.

Commentary on Section 33 [1949]

A033.13 *Locus standi*

A case where *locus standi* was not, at least initially, established is *Fenwick-Wilson's Patent* (SRIS O/126/91) where the "opponent", who had no professional assistance, made only general and unsupported allegations of interest.

Commentary on Section 52 [1949]

A052.3 *Effect of the section*

It has been confirmed that section 52 only provides protection as regards disclosure of matter itself disclosed in the earlier priority document, but not as regards disclosure of matter not contained in the priority document (*Vax* v. *Hoover*, [1991] FSR 307).

SECTION 103 [1949]

Application in Scotland A103

Although the Main Work describes this section as "spent", strictly speaking it continues to provide the framework for litigation in Scotland under "existing patents" so far as these remain governed by the 1949 Act. However, section 103(2), which provided for the form of an action for revocation of the patent, has been repealed (Act of Sederunt (Rules of the Court of Session Amendment No. 7) (Patents Rules) 1991, S.I. 1991 No. 1621), this now being governed by new Scottish rules of court, see para. 98.09 *supra*.

THE PATENTS RULES 1968

S.I. 1968 No. 1389 [As Amended]

General A109

Schedule 5 to the Patent Rules 1990 (S.I. 1990 No. 2384) substitutes revised versions of certain of the forms which may continue to be required under the 1968 Rules for those previously contained in the 1968 Rules (as amended). These are Patents Forms Nos. 7, 9, 14 to 21, 23, 32 to 36, 38, 39, 43, 44, 46, 53 to 55, 63 to 65 and 69. However, many of these forms can be regarded as spent and are only likely to be used in the case of patent applications filed under the 1949 Act which have remained subject to continued secrecy orders. Moreover, except as noted in paras. A122, A125 and A135 *infra*, the changes made by the 1990 Rules are not of significance.

Patents Form No. 13 A122

This form is no longer required, see para. 101.05 *supra*.

Patents Form No. 35 A125

The reference to submission of requested amendments in red ink has been retained despite the fact that this is not necessary for amendments made under the 1977 Act, see para. 27.14 *supra*.

Patents Form No. 64 A135

The reference to submission of requested corrections in red ink has been retained despite the fact that this is not necessary for corrections made under the 1977 Act, see para. 117.13 *supra*.

FEES

A139 For some information on the fees payable on forms to the 1968 Rules, see para. 144.01 in the Main Work and *supra*. The Patents (Fees) Rules 1991 (S.I. 1991 No. 1627) abolished the fees previously payable on Forms Nos. 1 Add., 7, 8, 14, 15, 17–20, 23, 33, 36, 39, 43, 44, 46, 53–55, 65 and 68.

APPENDIX B

(OTHER FORMER PATENT STATUTES STILL EFFECTIVE)

PATENTS AND DESIGNS ACT 1907

(7 Edw. 7, c. 29)

B04 COMMENTARY ON SECTION 62 [1907]

From October 1, 1991 all operations of the Patent Office came under a trading fund established under the Government Trading Act 1990 (c. 30) (Patent Office Trading Fund Order 1991 (S.I. 1991 No. 1796)).

APPENDIX C

THE TREATY OF ROME

C09 BOOKS

R. Whish, "Competition Law" (2nd. ed.) (Butterworths, 1989);
C. W. Bellamy and G. D. Child, "Common Market Law of Competition: First supplement to third edition" (Sweet & Maxwell, 1991).

C09A ARTICLES

S. Kon, "Exhaustion of rights", (1990) 2(1) IPB 2 and 2(2) IPB 2;
S. Anderman, "E.C. Competition Law: Article 85", (1990) 2(4), 2 and 2(5), 2.
S. Anderman, "E.C. Competition law: Article 86", (1990) 2(6) IPB 23.

COMMENTARY ON THE TREATY OF ROME

C10 *Interpretation of the Treaty by the European Court of Justice*

Allen & Hanburys v. *Generics (Case No. 434/85)* ([1988] 1 CMLR 701; [1988] FSR 312 (ECJ) was a case referred to the ECJ which resulted in a reversal of decisions of the English courts, see para. 46.21 in the Main Work. Somewhat similar points of law have since also been referred to the ECJ, see *Smith Kline & French's (Cimetidine) Patents*, [1990] RPC 203 (CA)).

C11 *Anti-trust provisions of the Treaty*

The articles by S. Anderman, listed in para. C09A *supra*, highlight the impact of the E.C.'s competition rules on intellectual property licensing arrangements.

Exemption under TRa. 85(3) of prohibited licence clauses C12

The E.C. Commission is prepared to grant an individual exemption for a joint research and development venture when the existing know-how of the participants, plus further research and development, is necessary to develop, manufacture and market a new product as well as the machinery and technology linked to it, provided that there are no restrictions of the marketing policies of the joint venture and the exclusivity is limited to a narrowly defined field (*Re. Odin Developments*, [1991] 4 CMLR 832). For other individual exemptions of a somewhat similar nature, see *Continental Gummi/Michelin Agreement* ([1989] 4 CMLR 920, *noted* [1990] FSR 159) and *Agreements of KSB, Lowara and Others* ([1990] 4 CMLR 248). The E.C. Commission has also indicated a willingness to adopt a favourable position in relation to a joint venture for the development of a standardised framework for data transmission between different brands of consumer electronics products (*Re. D2B Systems Co. Ltd,* [1991] 4 CMLR 905).

The "exhaustion of rights" doctrine C15

An article by L. Defalque ([1989] EIPR 435) highlights the present relaxation of this doctrine as shown by recent decisions of the ECJ, particularly in cases concerning copyrights and rights relating thereto. The principles of the doctrine itself, and its development, are explained in the articles by S. Kon listed in para. C09A *supra*.

Warner Bros. v. *Christiansen*, cited in the Main Work, is now reported ([1990] 3 CMLR 684).

The exception of Spain from the exhaustion of rights doctrine in relation to certain products is expected to cease from October 7, 1995, consequent upon a revision of the Spanish Patent Law effective from October 7, 1992.

Principle of "common origin" C15A

This principle may, perhaps, also be derived from that of freely given, rather than imposed, consent by the original rights-owner. Thus, in the reverse of the original *Hag* case (cited in the Main Work), the original German trade mark owner was held entitled to prohibit imports from the successor in title to the Belgian owner of the mark who had assumed its title as a result of war-time expropriation of German property, there having been no free consent to that transfer by the original owner despite the common ownership of the mark in the two countries, [1991] FSR 99 (ECJ), but on the grounds that: the essential function of a trade mark is to guarantee the origin of the marked goods; and the doctrine of common origin has no place where the division of assets has arisen through an act of expropriation. This judgment may well have signalled the demise of the doctrine of common origin, see the papers by: W. A. Rothnie ([1991] EIPR 24); S. Kon ((1991) 3(1) IPB 24); and G. F. Kunze ((1991) 22 IIC 319).

Abuse of a dominant position (TRa. 86) C17

The European Commission's decision in *Eurofix and Bauco* v. *Hilti A.G.*, cited in the Main Work, has been fully reported ([1989] 4 CMLR 677).

An Article by S. Anderman, listed in para. C09A *supra*, summarises the application of TRa. 86 to intellectual property rights. Whether an agreement falls within a Block Exemption Regulation does not appear to be relevant when considering a possible abuse of dominant position under TRa. 86, see D32 *infra*.

An English court has stated that it is not *per se* an abuse of a dominant position for a patentee to seek, in good faith, to enforce a legal right which he thinks he has, or to threaten to do so (*Pitney Bowes* v. *Francotyp-Postalia*, [1991] FSR 72), see also paras. 61.17 and C18 in the Main Work. However, where the owner of an intellectual property right has a dominant position in a particular market, an abuse under TRa. 86 can arise by a discriminatory refusal to grant licences which has the effect of preventing the production and marketing of a new product for which there is a potential consumer demand, see *BBC* v. *E.C. Commission (Case T*-70/89, ECFI) ([1991] 4 CMLR 669) in relation to the exercise of copyright protection where no compulsory licence provision existed of which a potential licensee could take advantage.

C18 *Mere exercise of rights*

If an intellectual property right is exercised in ways and circumstances to persue an aim manifestly contrary to the objectives of TRa. 86, the doctrine of freedom of competition will then prevail over that right, see the copyright case of *BBC* v. *E.C. Commission (Case T*-70/89, ECFI) ([1991] 4 CMLR 669) and para. C17 *supra*.

C19 *Imposition of fines by European Commission*

The European Commission's decision in *Eurofix and Bauco* v. *Hilti A.G.*, cited in the Main Work, has been fully reported ([1989] 4 CMLR 677, see also [1988] FSR 473).

The Commission has power to levy fines up to 10 per cent. of the turnover of an undertaking held to infringe TRaa. 85 or 86 and has indeed imposed very heavy fines, the heaviest so far being ECU 75m. against *Tetra Pak* for abuse of a dominant position under TRa. 86 (*E.C. Commission Press Release IP* (91) 715, July 24, 1991), but subject to appeal.

APPENDIX D

LICENSING OF INTELLECTUAL PROPERTY UNDER EEC LAW

The Know-How Exemption Regulation (Regulation No. 556/89)

D20 *—Permissible provisions for exclusivity and territorial restrictions (Art. 1)*

The ECJ has upheld the view of the Commission in *Tetra-Pak's Agreement*, cited in the Main Work, that the acquisition of an exclusive licence by a company already dominant in its field can be an abuse falling within TRa. 86 (*Tetra-Pak* v. *E.C. Commission* (*Case T*–51/89), [1991] 4 CMLR 334, *noted* [1991] FSR 654 (ECFI)). This case, which was the first to be decided by the European Court of First Instance (the ECFI), is discussed by J. Daltrop and J. Ferry ([1991] EIPR 31).

D22 *—The "white clauses" (Art. 2)*

For an EC Commission press release, see *Re Post Term Use Bans in Know-How Licence Agreements* ([1989] 4 CMLR 851, *noted* [1990] FSR 21).

—The "black clauses" (Art. 3) **D23**

Bayer and Süllhöfer's Agreement, cited in the Main Work, has been reported ([1990] FSR 300 (ECJ)); and *Ottung* v. *Klee (Case 320/87*, ECJ), also cited in the Main Work, has been reported ([1989] ECR 1172; [1991] FSR 657; [1990] 4 CMLR 915).

The Patent Licensing Exemption Regulation No. 2349/84 **D26**

Art. 9 of this Regulation provides power for the E.C. Commission to remove exemption even though a patent licence is in accord with the Block Exemption Regulation. This would have been done in *Elopak* v. *Tetra Pak* ([1990] 4 CMLR 47, *noted* [1990] FSR 263) had not the offending provision for exclusivity been abandoned before the decision holding that the acquisition by assignment of an exclusive licence by a company already occupying a dominant position brought that licence within TRa. 85(1), with exemption under TRa. 85(3) not being appropriate because of the economic strength of the licensee. The ECFI rejected an appeal (*Case T*51/89, July 10, 1990, *noted* (1990) 2(6) IPB 24).

Later Commission decisions **D30**

For a commentary on three of the cases on exclusivity of know-how licences within the EEC, see [1990] 1 IPB 20.

ECJ Decisions on contractual licensing **D32**

An exclusive licence is caught by TRa. 85(1) when the licensee is already in a dominant position in the relevant market, even if the requirements of a Block Exemption Regulation are apparently met (*Elopak* v. *Tetra Pak*, [1990] 4 CMLR 47, *noted* [1990] FSR 263 and *ECFI Case T*–51/89, July 10, 1990, *noted* (1990) 2(6) IPB 24).

APPENDIX E

RULES OF THE SUPREME COURT

ORDER 3

TIME

Month of August excluded from time for service, etc., of pleadings (Ord. 3, r. 3) **E003.3**

Note. Order 3, rule 3 has been revoked (S.I. 1990 No. 1689).

ORDER 6

WRITS OF SUMMONS: GENERAL PROVISIONS

E006.7 Issue of Writ (Ord. 6, r. 7)

Rule 7(3) has been prefaced with the words "Subject to rule 7A" (S.I. 1990 No. 2599).

ORDER 14A

DISPOSAL OF CASE ON POINT OF LAW

E014A.1 Determination of questions of law or construction

1.—(1) The Court may upon the application of a party or of its own motion determine any question of law or construction of any document arising in any cause or matter at any stage of the proceedings where it appears to the Court that—

(a) such question is suitable for determination without a full trial of the action, and
(b) such determination will finally determine (subject only to any possible appeal) the entire cause or matter or any claim or issue therein.

(2) Upon such determination the Court may dismiss the cause or matter or make such order or judgment as it thinks just.

(3) The Court shall not determine any question under this Order unless the parties have either—

(a) had an opportunity of being heard on the question, or
(b) consented to an order or judgment on such determination.

(4) The jurisdiction of the Court under this Order may be exercised by a master.

(5) Nothing in this Order shall limit the powers of the Court under order 18, rule 19 or any other provision of these rules.

Note. This new rule was inserted by S.I. 1990 No. 2599, effective from February 1, 1991.

E014A.2 Manner in which application under rule 1 may be made (O. 14A, r. 2)

2. An application under rule 1 may be made by summons or motion or (notwithstanding Order 32, rule 1) may be made orally in the course of any interlocutory application to the Court.

Note. This new rule was inserted by S.I. 1990 No. 2599, effective from February 1, 1991.

ORDER 18

PLEADINGS

Service of defence (Ord. 18, r. 2) **E018.2**

In rule 29(1) the words "the plaintiff" have been replaced by "every other party to the action who may be affected thereby" (S.I. 1990 No. 2599, effective from February 1, 1991, but without effect on pre-existing actions).

Service of pleadings or amended pleadings in month of August (Ord. 18, r. 5) **E018.5**

Note. Order 18, rule 5 has been revoked (S.I. 1990 No. 1689).

Particulars of pleading (Ord. 18, r. 12) **E018.12**

Rule 12(1) has been amended by replacing "words—" at the end of the preamble by "," and adding at the end of the rule:

> "; and
> (*c*) where a claim for damages is made against a party pleading, particulars of any facts on which the party relies in mitigation of, or otherwise in relation to, the amount of damages".

Admission and denials (Ord. 18, r. 13) **E018.13**

In rule 13(4), the words "and any allegation as to the amount of damages" have been omitted.

ORDER 26

INTERROGATORIES

Discovery by interrogatories (Ord. 26, r. 1) **E026.1**

This rule has been replaced (from June 4, 1990) by:—

1.—(1) A party to any cause or matter may in accordance with the following provisions of this Order serve upon any other party interrogatories relating to any matter in question between an applicant and that other party in the cause or matter which are necessary either—

(*a*) for disposing fairly of the cause or matter, or
(*b*) for saving costs.

(2) Without prejudice to the provisions of paragraph (1), a party may apply to the Court for an order giving him leave to serve on any other

party interrogatories relating to any matter in question between the applicant and that other party in the cause or matter.

(3) A proposed interrogatory which does not relate to such a matter as is mentioned in paragraph (1) may not be administered notwithstanding that it might be admissible in oral cross-examination of a witness.

(4) In this Order,

"interrogatories without order" means interrogatories served under paragraph (1);

"ordered interrogatories" means interrogatories served under paragraph (2) or interrogatories which are required to be answered pursuant to an order made on an application under rule 3(2) and, where such an order is made, the interrogatories shall not, unless the Court orders otherwise, be treated as interrogatories without order for the purposes of rule 3(1).

(5) Unless the context otherwise requires, the provisions of this order apply to both interrogatories without order and ordered interrogatories.

Note. Rules 2–6 of Order 26 have also been revised and, although not reprinted herein, these rules are summarised at para. 61.34 *supra*.

ORDER 34

SETTING DOWN FOR TRIAL ACTION BEGUN BY WRIT

E034.3 **Lodging documents when setting down (Ord. 34, r. 3)**

3.—(1) In order to set down for trial an action which is to be tried before a judge, the party setting it down must, subject to any order of the Court to the contrary, deliver to the proper officer, by post or otherwise, a request that the action be set down for trial at the place determined in accordance with automatic directions or by order of the Court and lodge two bundles consisting of one copy of each of the following documents—

(*a*) the writ,
(*b*) the pleadings (including any affidavits ordered to stand as pleadings),
(*c*) any request or order for particulars and the particulars given, and any interrogatories and answers thereto,
(*d*) all orders made in the action except only any order relating only to time,
(*e*) in proceedings to which article 7(1) of the High Court and County Courts Jurisdiction Order 1991 applies, a statement of the value of the action,
(*f*) a note agreed by the parties or, failing agreement, a note by each party giving (in the following order)—
    (i) an estimate of the length of the trial,

(ii) the list in which the action is to be included,

(*g*) the requisite legal aid documents, if any.

(2) Each of the said bundles must be bound up in the proper chronological order, save that voluntary particulars of any pleading and particulars to which Order 18, rule 12(7) applies shall be placed immediately after the pleading to which they relate; and the bundle which is to serve as the record must be stamped with the stamp denoting payment of the fee payable on setting down the action and have indorsed thereon the names, addresses and telephone numbers of the solicitors for the parties or, in the case of a party who has no solicitor, of the party himself.

(3) . . .

(4) . . .

(5) In this rule "the proper officer" means—

. . .

(*c*) in relation to an action in the Chancery Division which is to be tried at the Royal Courts of Justice, the cause clerk in the Chancery Division.

Notification of setting down (Ord. 34, r. 8) **E034.8**

8.—(1) A party to an action who sets it down for trial must, within 24 hours after doing so, notify the other partes to the action that he has done so.

(2) It shall be the duty of all parties to an action entered in any list to furnish without delay to the officer who keeps the list all available information as to the action being or being likely to be settled, or affecting the estimated length of the trial, and, if the action is settled or withdrawn, to notify that officer of the fact without delay and take such steps as may be necessary to withdraw the record.

The Court bundle (Ord. 34, r. 10) **E034.10**

10.—(1) At least 14 days before the date fixed for the trial or, in the case of an action entered in any running list, within 3 weeks of the defendant's receiving notice of such entry, the defendant shall identify to the plaintiff those documents central to his case which he wishes included in the bundle to be provided under paragraph (2).

(2) At least 2 clear days before the date fixed for the trial the plaintiff shall lodge two bundles consisting of one copy of each of the following documents—

(*a*) witness statements which have been exchanged, and experts' reports which have been disclosed, together with an indication of whether the contents of such documents are agreed,

(*b*) those documents which the defendant wishes to have included in the bundle and those central to the plaintiff's case, and

(*c*) where a direction has been given under Order 25, rule 3(2), a note agreed by the parties or, failing agreement, a note by each party giving (in the following order)—

(i) a summary of the issues involved,
(ii) a summary of any propositions of law to be advanced together with a list of the authorities to be cited, and
(iii) a chronology of relevant events.

(3) Nothing in this rule shall—

(*a*) prevent the Court from giving, whether before or after the documents have been lodged, such further or different directions as to the documents to be lodged as may, in the circumstances, be appropriate; or
(*b*) prevent the making of an order for the transfer of the action to a county court.

(4) Where an action is to be tried with the assistance of assessors, additional copies of the bundles to be lodged under paragraph (2) shall be provided for the use of the assessors.

(5) For the purpose of this rule, "plaintiff" includes a defendant where an action is proceeding on a counterclaim and "defendant" includes any other party who is entitled under any order of the Court or otherwise to be heard at the trial.

ORDER 59

APPEALS TO THE COURT OF APPEAL

E059.3 Notice of Appeal (Ord. 59, r. 3)

Rule 3(4) has been reworded to read:

"(4) Every notice of appeal must specify the list of appeals to which the appellant proposes that the appeal should be assigned."

E059.5 Setting down appeal (Ord. 59, r. 5)

In rule 5(1) the word "lodge" has been replaced by "set down his appeal by lodging". Rule 5(2) has been reworded to read:

"(2) Upon the said documents being so lodged the registrar shall cause the appeal to be entered in the records of the Court and assigned to the appropriate list of appeals."

In rule 5(3) the word "proper" has been replaced by "appropriate; and rule 5(4) has been reworded to read:

"(4) Within 4 days of receipt of notification from the office of the registrar that the appeal has been entered in the records of the Court, the appellant must give notice to that effect to all parties on whom the notice of appeal was served, specifying the Court of Appeal reference allocated to that appeal."

Practice Statement E059.9A

Transcripts

Where the judge hands down a written judgment without a recording being taken, copies of the judgment (as signed by the judge) may be used instead of originals (*Practice Statement (Court of Appeal: Note of judgment under appeal): The Times*, July 12, 1990).

Applications to Court of Appeal (Ord. 59, r. 14) E059.14

Rule 14(2) has been replaced by:

"(2) An application to the Court of Appeal for leave to appeal shall—

(*a*) include, where necessary, any application to extend the time for appealing, and

(*b*) be made *ex parte* in writing setting out the reasons why leave should be granted and, if the time for appealing has expired, the reasons why the application was not made within that time;

and the Court may grant or refuse the application or direct that the application be renewed in open court either *ex parte* or *inter partes*.

(2A) If an application under paragraph (2) is refused otherwise than after a hearing in open court, the applicant shall be entitled, within 7 days after he has been given notice of the refusal, to renew the application; and such renewed application shall be heard *ex parte* in open court.

(2B) If an application under paragraph (2) is granted otherwise than after a hearing *inter partes*, notice of the order shall be served upon the party or parties affected by the appeal and any such party shall be entitled, within 7 days after service of the notice, to apply to have the grant of leave reconsidered *inter partes* in open court."

ORDER 65

SERVICE OF DOCUMENTS

Ordinary service: how effected (Ord. 65, r. 5) E065.5

By S.I. 1990 No. 2599, in paragraph (1) sub-paragraph (c) has been substituted by:

"(*c*) through a document exchange in accordance with paragraph (2A), or

(*ca*) by FAX in accordance with paragraph (2B), or";

and the final definition of "document exchange" has been omitted.

Paragraph (2A) has been substituted by:

"(2A) Where—

(*a*) the proper address for service includes a numbered box at a document exchange, or (*b*) there is inscribed on the writing paper of the party on whom the document is served (where such party acts in person) or on the writing paper of his solicitor (where such party acts by a solicitor) a document exchange box number, and such a party or his solicitor (as the case may be) has not indicated in writing to the party serving the document that he is unwilling to accept service through a document exchange,

service of the document may be affected by leaving the document addressed to that numbered box at that document exchange or at a document exchange which transmits documents every business day to that document exchange; and any document which is left at a document exchange in accordance with this paragraph shall, unless the contrary is proved, be deemed to have been served on the second business day following the day on which it is left.

(2B) Service by FAX may be effected where—

(*a*) the party serving the document acts by a solicitor,

(*b*) the party on whom the document is served acts by a solicitor and service is effected by transmission to the business address of such solicitor,

(*c*) the solicitor acting for the party on whom the document is served has indicated in writing to the solicitor serving the document that he is willing to accept service by FAX at a specified FAX number and the document is transmitted to that number; and for this purpose the inscription of a FAX number on the writing paper of a solicitor shall be deemed to indicate that such a solicitor is willing to accept service by FAX at that number in accordance with this paragraph unless he states otherwise in writing, and

(*d*) as soon a practicable after service by FAX the solicitor acting for the party serving the document dispatches a copy of it to the solicitor acting for the other party by any of the methods prescribed for service by paragraph (1), and if he fails to do so the document shall be deemed never to have been served by FAX."

In paragraph (3) the final definition of "business day" has been omitted; and a further paragraph (4) added as follows:—

"(4) In this rule—

(*a*) "document exchange" means any document exchange for the time being approved by the Lord Chancellor;

(*b*) "business day" means any day other than a Saturday, a Sunday, Christmas Day, Good Friday or a bank holiday as defined in Order 3, rule 2(5)."

ORDER 107

The County Courts Act 1984

Transfer of proceedings to or from a county court (O. 107, r. 2) **E107.2**

2.—(1) . . .

(1A) Where an order is made transferring proceedings to a county court, the proper officer shall, on the production of the order and the filing of a copy of it, send by post to the proper officer of the county court to which the proceedings are transferred all pleadings, affidavits and other documents filed in the High Court relating to the proceedings together with a copy of the order for transfer.

(1B) . . .

APPENDIX F

THE REGISTER OF PATENT AGENTS RULES

S.I. 1990 No. 1457)

Citation and commencement

1. These Rules may be cited as the Register of Patent Agents Rules 1990 and shall come into force on 13th August 1990. **F01**

Interpretation

2. In these Rules, unless the context otherwise requires— **F02**

"the Comptroller" means the Comptroller-General of Patents, Designs and Trade Marks;
"the Institute" means the Chartered Institute of Patent Agents;
"patent agency work" means work done in the course of carrying on the business of acting as agent for others for the purpose of applying for or obtaining patents in the United Kingdom or elsewhere or of conducting proceedings before the Comptroller relating to applications for, or otherwise in connection with, patents;
"the register" means the register required to be kept under these Rules; and
"registered patent agent" means a person whose name is entered in the register;
"the Registrar" means the person appointed in accordance with rule 7 below to maintain the register;
"the revoked Rules" means the Rules revoked under rule 23 below;
"the United Kingdom" includes the Isle of Man.

The register

F03 **3.**—(1) The register kept by the Institute under the revoked Rules shall be the register to be kept under these Rules and the Institute shall continue to keep the same, and any person whose name is, at the date of the coming into force of these Rules, entered in the register shall be a registered patent agent for the purposes of these Rules.

(2) There shall be entered in the register the name of each person who is entitled to be registered pursuant to rule 10 below, together with his business address, the date of his registration, his qualifications for registration, and such other particulars as the Registrar may, at the request of that person, think fit to include.

Special record

F04 **4.**—(1) The special record kept under rule 4 of the revoked Rules for the transfer thereto of the names and other particulars of persons whose names have been erased from the register kept under those Rules shall be the special record to be kept for the purposes of these Rules, and any name transferred thereto and not restored to the register under the revoked Rules shall, unless restored to the register under these Rules, remain a name erased from the register for the purposes of these Rules.

(2) The Registrar shall continue to keep the special record and shall transfer thereto the name and particulars of any person whose name has been erased under rule 12 or 13 or pursuant to a direction under rule 14 below and he shall enter therein, against such name, the reason for the erasure.

Inspection of register and special record

F05 **5.** The register and the special record or, if they are kept otherwise than in documentary form, entries therein made available in documentary form, shall be open to public inspection at such times and in such manner as the Registrar may, subject to any general directions of the Comptroller under rule 21 below, direct.

Publication of list of registered patent agents

F06 **6.** Not later than 1st April in each year the Institute shall cause to be printed, published and placed on sale a copy of the entries in the register (with the names arranged alphabetically) as at the end of the preceding calendar year.

The Registrar

F07 **7.**—(1) There shall be a Registrar who shall be charged with the duty of maintaining the register and the special record in accordance with these

Rules and who shall, subject thereto and to any general directions of the Comptroller under rule 21 below, be under the directions of the Institute.

(2) The Registrar shall be appointed by the Institute for a period of one year and shall on ceasing to hold office be eligible for reappointment. He shall hold and vacate his office in accordance with such terms and conditions as the Institute may, after consultation with the Comptroller, determine.

Qualifying examinations

8.—(1) The Institute may, by regulations made by it after consultation with the Institute of Trade Mark Agents and with the approval of the Comptroller, make provision for such educational qualifications, training and qualifying examinations (which examinations shall be offered at least once in every year) as it considers appropriate for the registration of persons under these Rules and shall, subject to any such regulations and any general directions of the Comptroller under rule 21 below, have the entire management and control of such examinations. **F08**

(2) Any such regulations may make transitional provision for candidates who have, before the coming into force of the regulations, entered for any examinations held or to be held by the Institute pursuant to rule 8 of the revoked Rules—

(a) to complete or take the same or part or parts thereof or such other examinations in lieu thereof within such time and subject to such conditions as may be specified, or

(b) in the case of candidates who have passed or been exempted from any examinations provided for under the said rule 8, to be exempted from any examination provided in lieu thereof.

Qualifications for registration

9. A person who has passed the qualifying examinations of the Institute and who has completed— **F09**

(a) not less than two years' full-time practice in the field of intellectual property, including substantial experience in patent agency work, under the supervision of either a registered patent agent or of a barrister, solicitor or, in Scotland or the Isle of Man, an advocate, being a barrister, solicitor or advocate who is engaged in or has substantial experience of patent agency work in the United Kingdom, or

(b) not less than four years' full-time practice in the field of intellectual property, including substantial experience in patent agency work in the United Kingdom,

shall qualify for registration under these Rules.

Entitlement to registration

F10 **10.**—(1) Unless a direction under paragraph (3) below in relation to him is in force, a person who qualifies for registration under rule 9 above shall be entitled to have his name entered in the register on production to the Registrar of evidence that he qualifies for registration under that rule and on the payment of the fee prescribed by regulations under rule 20 below.

(2) The Registrar may, for the purpose of satisfying himself that a person has completed the requisite number of years of practice, require that person to submit to him a statutory declaration attesting to that fact and may require such further particulars of that practice as he may consider necessary.

(3) The Secretary of State may, upon being satisfied after due inquiry in accordance with rule 15 below that a person (who would otherwise be entitled to be registered) has been guilty of misconduct, direct that the name of that person shall not be registered, and upon such direction the Registrar shall not, except with the prior consent of the Secretary of State, register the name of that person.

Amendment of the register

F11 **11.** A registered patent agent shall give notice to the Registrar of any change in the particulars relating to him entered in the register and the Registrar shall, on payment of the fee (if any) prescribed by regulations made under rule 20 below, amend the register accordingly.

Erasure of registration for failure to pay fee

F12 **12.**—(1) If any registered patent agent fails to pay any annual practice fee that may be prescribed by regulations made under rule 20 below within one month from the day on which it becomes payable, the Registrar shall send to him at his business address (as shown in the register) a notice requiring him to pay the fee on or before a day specified in the notice, and if that person fails to pay the fee on or before that date the Registrar may erase his name from the register.

(2) The name of a person erased from the register under this rule may be restored to it by direction of the Institute on payment by him of the fee or fees due from him, together with such further sum not exceeding the amount prescribed for the annual practice fee as the Institute may in each particular case direct.

Correction of entries in register

F13 **13.**—(1) The Registrar may, upon being satisfied in accordance with paragraph (2) below that any entry in the register has been made in error or that any entry is incorrect, erase or correct the same.

(2) No erasure or correction of any entry in the Register shall be made under paragraph (1) above unless the Registrar has first served notice of the proposed erasure or correction on the person appearing to him to be affected, has afforded that person the opportunity to make written representations regarding the same and has taken into account any such representations.

Erasure of registration after due inquiry into misconduct

14. Where the Secretary of State is satisfied, after due inquiry in accordance with rule 15 below, that a person has been guilty of misconduct, that is to say, conduct discreditable to a registered patent agent, he may at his discretion, having regard to the circumstances of the misconduct, direct that the name of that person be erased from the register, and he may further direct that the name shall remain erased during such period as he may specify; and upon a direction under this rule the Registrar shall erase the name and particulars of that person from the register accordingly. **F14**

Inquiry by Secretary of State

15.—(1) Where it appears to the Secretary of State under rule 10(3) or rule 14 above that a person may have been guilty of misconduct he shall serve on that person (hereinafter referred to as the person affected) a notice— **F15**

(a) informing him of the grounds on which it so appears to the Secretary of State and the substance of any allegations of misconduct made against him, and
(b) inviting him to submit to the Secretary of State, within such period (being not less than 21 days) as may be specified in the notice, his representations in writing and requiring him to serve notice, if he wishes, of his intention to make oral representations.

(2) A copy of the notice served on the person affected under paragraph (1) above and a copy of any written representations submitted by him to the Secretary of State shall be served by the Secretary of State on the Institute.

(3) Where the person affected has served notice under paragraph (1)(b) above of his intentions to make oral representations, the Secretary of State shall give him not less than 21 days notice, or such shorter notice as the person affected may request or consent to accept, of the date, time and place at which his representations will be heard.

(4) If the Secretary of State considers that he should proceed with his inquiry but for a reason which differs or on grounds which differ from those set out in the notice served under paragraph (1) above he shall give a further notice under that paragraph.

THE REGISTER OF PATENT AGENTS RULES]

Hearing of representations

F16 **16.**—(1) At the hearing of oral representations held pursuant to rule 15(3) above the Secretary of State shall, at the request of the person affected, permit any other person (in addition to the person affected) to make representations on his behalf or to give evidence or to introduce documents for him.

(2) The Secretary of State shall not refuse to admit evidence solely on the grounds that it would not be admissible in a court of law.

(3) The hearing may be adjourned at the discretion of the Secretary of State and if adjourned he shall give the person affected reasonable notice of the date, time and place at which the hearing is to be resumed.

(4) The Secretary of State shall inform the Institute of the date, time and place appointed for any hearing and the Institute shall be entitled to be represented at the hearing and to make submissions touching on the matters in issue.

Decision

F17 **17.** The Secretary of State shall, in deciding whether to issue a direction, take into account any written or oral representations made in accordance with rules 15 and 16 above and shall—

(a) if he decides not to issue a direction, give notice of that decision to the person affected, the Institute and, where the decision relates to any allegations of misconduct made by any person against the person affected, to that person (if known), but nothing in this rule shall require the Secretary of State to state the reasons for that decision;

(b) if he decides to issue a direction, give notice of his decision, the terms thereof and his reasons for the decision to the person affected, the Institute and, where the decision relates to any allegations of misconduct made by any person against the person affected, to that person (if known).

Restoration of name to register

F18 **18.**—(1) On an application made to him by a person whose name has been erased from the register under rule 14 above, the Secretary of State may, if he thinks fit, direct that the name of that person shall be restored to the register, and he may further direct that such restoration shall be made either without fee or on payment of such fee as he may fix not exceeding the fee prescribed by regulations made under rule 20 below for the registration of a name.

(2) The Registrar shall, upon a direction for the restoration of the name of a person under this rule, restore the name and particulars of that

person to the register and shall, in the case of a person whose name has been erased for a specified period and in respect of whom no direction has been issued under this rule, restore his name and particulars upon the expiration of that period and upon payment of the fee prescribed by regulations made under rule 20 below for the registration of a name.

Appeal to Comptroller from decision of the Institute or Registrar

19.—(1) A person aggrieved by any decision of the Institute or the Registrar under these Rules may appeal to the Comptroller by serving on the Comptroller, within one month from the date of the decision, a notice of appeal, stating the grounds of appeal with a statement of his case in support thereof. A copy of the notice with a copy of the statement of case shall, at the same time, be served by that person (the appellant) on the Institute or the Registrar, as appropriate. **F19**

(2) The Comptroller shall, on receipt of the notice of appeal, give such directions as he thinks fit for the purpose of hearing the appeal and shall give the appellant and the institute or the Registrar, as the case may be, not less than 14 days notice, or such shorter notice as the appellant and the Institute or Registrar may consent to accept, of the date, time and place appointed for the hearing of the appeal.

(3) At the hearing the Comptroller shall, at the request of any party, permit any other person (in addition to that party) to appear on his behalf.

(4) The Comptroller shall give his decision on the appeal in writing with a statement of his reasons and shall serve a copy thereof on the appellant and the Institute or Registrar.

(5) The Comptroller's decision on the appeal shall be final and for the purposes of giving effect to it he may give such directions to the Institute or Registrar as he thinks fit.

Fees

20.—(1) The Institute may, by regulations made by it with the approval of the Comptroller, prescribe the fees to be paid by— **F20**

(a) every candidate for any examinations (or part or parts thereof) held in accordance with regulations made under rule 8 above,
(b) every person for the registration of his name,
(c) every registered patent agent as an annual practice fee,
(d) a registered patent agent requesting an amendment of the register under rule 11 above,

and any such regulations may provide for the remission or refund of any fees in such circumstances as may be prescribed thereunder.

(2) When prescribing any fees for the purposes of paragraph (1)(a) above the Institute shall, as far as practicable, secure that the income

therefrom does not exceed the expenditure properly incurred in administering any examinations, taking one year with another.

Directions by Comptroller

F21 **21.** The Comptroller may from time to time give general directions to the Institute as to any matters relating to the register and in respect of such matters as in his opinion will be conducive to the better regulation of any examinations held by the Institute.

Report of the Institute

F22 **22.** The Institute shall before 30th April in each year send to the Comptroller a report stating—

(a) the number of applications for registration which were made in the preceding year and the number of registrations effected in that year;
(b) the examinations which were held in that year and the results thereof;
(c) the amount of the fees received by the Institute in that year; and
(d) that rule 20(2) above has been complied with and showing, by reference to income and expenditure, its compliance with that rule;

and shall include in the report a statement on such other matters in relation to the provisions of these Rules (including any regulations made by the Institute pursuant thereto) as the Comptroller may from time to time require.

Revocation and transitional provisions

F23 **23.** The Register of Patent Agents Rules 1978 [S.I. 1978 No. 1093] and the Register of Patent Agents (Amendment) Rules 1982 [S.I. 1982 No. 1428] are hereby revoked.

APPENDIX G

EXAMINATION REGULATIONS FOR ENTRY TO THE REGISTER OF PATENT AGENTS

G00 The Examination Regulations reprinted below are those referred to in para. 102.30 of the Main Work and have now been made jointly by The Chartered Institute of Patent Agents and The Institute of Trade Mark Agents with the approval of the Comptroller under rules 8 of each of the Register of Patent Agents Rules 1990 (S.I. 1990 No. 1457) and the Register of Trade Mark Agents

Rules (S.I. 1990 No. 1458). However, not reprinted here are the specific rules only applicable for entry in the Register of Trade Mark Agents, nor the transitional provisions applicable to those who, prior to October 31, 1991, had passed certain examinations under the previous Examination Rules and/or for membership of the Institute of Trade Mark Agents. Copies of the full Rules may be obtained from either of these Institutes.

Regulations for the Examinations for the Registration of Patent Agents and Trade Mark Agents 1991

Made by the Chartered Institute of Patent Agents (C.I.P.A.) and the Institute of Trade Mark Agents (I.T.M.A.) with the approval of the Comptroller-General of Patents, Designs and Trade Marks under Rule 8 of the Register of Patent Agents Rules 1990 and Rule 8 of the Register of Trade Mark Agents Rules 1990.

1. Commencement **G01**

These Regulations shall come into force on 1st June, 1991 and supersede all regulations for examinations made by C.I.P.A. or I.T.M.A. prior to that date.

2. Interpretation **G02**

In these Regulations unless the context otherwise requires:

2.1 "The Board" means the Joint Examination Board which is a joint committee of C.I.P.A. and I.T.M.A.

2.2 "Trade Mark Foundation Paper" means the Paper described in Schedule 1 and designated T2.

2.3 "Trade Mark Advanced Papers" means the Papers described in Schedule 1 and designated T3 and T4.

2.4 "Patent Foundation Papers" means the Papers described in Schedule 1 and designated P1 and P5.

2.5 "Patent Advanced Papers" means the Papers described in Schedule 1 and designated P2, P3, P4 and P6.

2.6 "Common Foundation Papers" means the Papers described in Schedule 1 and designated T1, T5, Law and D&C.

2.7 "G.C.S.E." means the General Certificate of Secondary Education issued by any recognised United Kingdom Examination Board; and includes the General Certificate at Ordinary level.

2.8 "G.C.E." means the General Certificate of Education at Advanced Level or Scholarship Level issued by any recognised United Kingdom Examination Board.

2.9 "C.N.A.A." means The Council for National Academic Awards.

2.10 "Q.M.W. Certificate" means the Certificate in Intellectual Property Law awarded by Queen Mary & Westfield College in the University of London.

2.11 "References to a "paragraph" and to a "Schedule" are references to a paragraph in and a Schedule to these Regulations.

G03 3. The Qualifying Examinations

3.1 The Board will hold each year qualifying examinations consisting of Foundation papers and Advanced papers ("the examinations") for persons wishing to be entered on the Register of Patent Agents and on the Register of Trade Mark Agents.

Register of Patent Agents

3.2.1 The qualifying examinations mentioned in Rule 8 of the Register of Patent Agents Rules 1990 shall be deemed to have been passed by a candidate who:

3.2.2 **either** has passed the Patent Foundation Papers, the Common Foundation Papers and the Patent Advanced Papers listed in Schedule 1 (or those of them from which he or she has not obtained exemption from the Board under paragraph 5.3);

3.2.3 **or** has passed the Trade Mark Foundation Paper **and** the Common Foundation Papers **and** the Patent Advanced Papers listed in Schedule 1 (or those of them from which he or she has not obtained exemption from the Board under paragraph 5.3);

3.2.4 **or** has passed the paper or papers appropriate to his or her case as is or are required to be passed to fulfil the condition in paragraph 3.2.2 or in paragraph 3.2.3 having regard to the transitional provisions set out in paragraph 5 of Schedule II.

Register of Trade Mark Agents

. . .

G04 4. Eligibility

Trade Marks

4.1 Foundation Papers

A person shall be eligible to sit the Trade Mark Foundation Paper and the Common Foundation Papers if he or she has obtained

(a) (i) The G.C.S.E. with Grades A, B or C in at least five subjects of which one shall be English Language; **and**

(ii) The G.C.E. in at least two subjects at least one of which shall be one of the subjects designated in Schedule III; **or**

(b) A degree conferred by a University or Polytechnic in the United Kingdom, or by the C.N.A.A., or a licence awarded by the University College of Buckingham before that College was granted University status; **or**

(c) Passes at any other examinations which the Board may accept from time to time as equivalent to any of the above examinations. Schedule IV lists other examinations which the Board has already decided should be regarded as equivalent to the examinations designated in paragraphs 4.1(a) and 4.1(b).

4.2. Advanced Papers

. . .

Patents

4.3. Foundation Papers

A person shall be eligible to sit the Patent Foundation Papers and the Common Foundation Papers if he or she has obtained:

(a) (i) The G.C.S.E. with Grades A, B or C in at least five subjects of which one shall be English Language;
(ii) The G.C.E. in at least two subjects at least one of which shall be one of the subjects designated in Schedule III; **or**

(b) A degree conferred by a University or Polytechnic in the United Kingdom, or by the C.N.A.A., or a licence awarded by the University College of Buckingham before that College was granted University status; **or**

(c) Passes at any other examinations which the Board may accept from time to time as equivalent to any of the above examinations. Schedule IV lists other examinations which the Board has decided should be regarded as equivalent to the examinations designated in paragraphs 4.3(a) and 4.3(b).

4.4. Advanced Papers

4.4.1 A person shall be eligible to sit the Patent Advanced Papers if he or she has passed:
(a) the Patent Foundation Paper P1; **or**
(b) the Trade Mark Foundation Paper **and** the Common Foundation Papers.

4.4.2 A candidate who has previously obtained a pass in Advanced Patent Paper P3 (but not Paper P4) and wishes to enter for Paper P4 in a subsequent year's examination, may be required to attend also for, but will not be required to attempt, Paper P3 of that year.

General

4.5. Candidates of Mature Years

A candidate of mature years with relevant work experience may apply to the Board for it in its discretion to waive the requirement for educational qualifications set out in paragraphs 4.1 and 4.3.

G05 **5. Examination information**

5.1 The designation, subject matter and duration of each paper comprising the Trade Mark Foundation Paper; the Patent Foundation Papers; the Common Foundation Papers; the Trade Mark Advanced Papers and the Patent Advanced Papers are as set out in Schedule I.

5.2 In order to pass any of the papers contained in Schedule I a candidate must obtain not less than 50% of the marks available in each paper. A pass in any single paper is independent of performance in any other paper.

5.3 A candidate may be deemed to have passed any of the papers if the candidate has passed another examination, or part of another examination, which the Board has deemed equivalent to the paper or papers. Schedule II lists other examinations, including previous examinations of C.I.P.A. and I.T.M.A., which the Board has decided to regard as equivalent to the papers designated in that Schedule.

G06 **6. Application for Candidacy**

6.1 Each candidate for the examinations, or any part of them, shall, not later than a date set by the Board prior to the date of the examination the candidate wishes to sit, furnish the Board with the following:

(i) His or her full name and permanent address, and if such address is not within the United Kingdom, then an address for service of correspondence within the United Kingdom;

(ii) Details of his or her educational attainments as required in paragraphs 4.1 or 4.3;

(iii) Proof in a form satisfactory to the Board of his or her educational attainments or qualifications which the candidate wishes the Board to consider in his or her application;

(iv) If applicable, a copy of any previous ruling of the Board under paragraph 4; and

(v) The titles of the paper or papers (as specified in Schedule I) the candidate wishes to sit and the amount of fees (in £ sterling and net of all bank charges) as may be required by the Board.

6.2. Requests for a Ruling

6.2.1 A request for a ruling under paragraph 4 (equivalent basic educational requirements) must be received by the Board by the

1st January and the 1st August immediately preceding the relevant examination in any calendar year.

6.2.2 In the case of a request under paragraph 6.2.1 the Board will issue a ruling as to the acceptability or non-acceptability of the candidate after such enquiries as the Board may wish to make.

6.2.3 If, for any reason, it is not possible for the Board to issue a ruling under paragraph 6.2.2 prior to the examinations, the candidate may be permitted to sit the relevant paper or papers but no result will be issued until the applicant's candidacy is approved.

6.3 In the event that the Board rules that a candidate is not eligible to sit the examinations the fees previously paid will be returned.

7. Communications to the Board **G07**

All communications under or in relation to these regulations should be addressed to the Board at either of the following addresses.

The Chartered Institute of Patent Agents
Staple Inn Buildings,
London, WC1V 7PZ

The Institute of Trade Mark Agents,
4th Floor, Canterbury House,
2–6 Sydenham Road,
Croydon, CR0 9XE

8. Appeals **G06**

Any appeal in connection with a ruling of the Board under these regulations shall be to the Comptroller-General of Patents, Designs and Trade Marks, whose decision shall be final.

Schedule I **G09**

Examination Papers

Trade Mark Foundation Paper

Designation	*Title*	*Duration*
T2	Basic United Kingdom Trade Mark Practice	3 hrs

Patent Foundation Papers

Designation	*Title*	*Duration*
P1	Basic United Kingdom Patent Law and Procedure	3 hrs
P5	Basic Overseas Patent Law and Procedure	3 hrs

Common Foundation Papers

Designation	*Title*	*Duration*
T1	Basic United Kingdom Trade Mark Law	2 hrs
T5	Basic Overseas Trade Mark Law and Practice	2 hrs
D&C	United Kingdom Designs and Copyright Law	3 hrs
Law	Basic English Law	2 hrs

Trade Mark Advanced Papers

. . .

Patent Advanced Papers

Designation	*Title*	*Duration*
P2	Patent Agents' Practice	4 hrs
P3	Preparation of specifications for United Kingdom and Overseas Patents	4 hrs
P4	Amendment of specifications for United Kingdom patents in revocation proceedings	2 hrs
P6	Infringement and validity of United Kingdom patents	4 hrs

G10 **Schedule II**

1. Other examinations or qualifications which the Board has deemed equivalent to the paper or papers forming part of or comprising the Trade Mark Foundation Paper, the Patent Foundation Papers, the Common Foundation Papers and the Patent Advanced Papers:

Deemed Equivalent	*Board Papers*
G.C.E. Law	Law
Law Degree	Law
Law Degree with IP Option	Law; P1; T1; D&C
Law Society Final Examination	Law
Bar Final Examination	Law
Q.M.W. Certificate	All Foundation Papers
European Qualifying Examinations	P3 and P4

2. . . .
3. A Registered Trade Mark Agent who wishes to sit the Patent Advanced Papers is exempted from all Foundation Papers.
4. **Transitional Provisions (Trade Marks)**

   . . .

G11 **Schedule III**

List of approved subjects for the purpose of paragraph 4.1(a)(ii):

English
History
Geography
Economics
Commerce
British Constitution
Business Studies
A modern language

Law
A science subject

Latin
Greek

List of approved subjects for the purposes of paragraph 4.3(a)(ii):

A science or engineering subject; or a subject the science or engineering content of which satisfies the Board.

Schedule IV G12

Other examinations which the Board has decided should be regarded as equivalent to G.C.S.E., G.C.E., or degree.

G.C.S.E. and G.C.E.
Degree

Highers (Scotland)
Law Society Final Examination;
Bar Final Examination.

RULES OF PROFESSIONAL CONDUCT OF THE CHARTERED INSTITUTE OF PATENT AGENTS G13

General

1. A Member shall practise competently, conscientiously and objectively, putting clients' interests foremost and respecting clients' confidence while observing the law and the Member's duty to any Court or Tribunal.
2. A Member's conduct shall be such as to promote well-founded public confidence in the intellectual property system, in the Institute and in its Members.

Availability

3. When unwilling to provide services, or withdrawing them, a Member shall make reasonable effort in the circumstances to enable the person wishing to use those services to make other arrangements.

Conflicts of interest

4. Except with the approval of the clients concerned, a Member shall not act for a client on any particular matter if, having acted for another client on a conflicting matter, the Member's professional duty to either client may thereby be compromised.

5. A Member shall not act for a client if, without the knowledge and approval of that client, the Member has, or acquires, any significant interest that the Member knows, or could reasonably be

expected to know, may conflict with the Member's professional duty to that client.

Liability

6. A Member in practice as a principal shall be responsible for ensuring that funds would be available to a reasonably practicable extent to provide compensation if a client were to suffer loss as a result of the Member's professional negligence.

Promotion

7. Promotional activity is permitted if it is fair, not undignified, wholly accurate, and gives a true impression.

Relations with others

8. A Member is responsible under these Rules not only for the Member's own acts and omissions, but also for those sanctioned, expressly or otherwise, by that Member.

Use of the Institute's name etc.

9. The President, Vice-President or Honorary Secretary may make public communication in the name of the Institute and may in doing so use any emblem of the Institute. Any other Member may do these things only on the authority of the President, of the Vice-President, or of the Council.

Professional guidance

10. A Member has the right to seek individual guidance from a Council Committee, known as the Professional Guidance Committee (PGC) and having a membership entirely separate from the Professional Conduct Committee, on the propriety under these Rules of any act or course of conduct he intends to undertake or sanction.

Interpretation

11. In these Rules:

(1) "The Institute" means The Chartered Institute of Patent Agents.

(2) "Member" means a patent agent who is a Member of the Institute, whether or not the Member is registered as a patent agent

in the United Kingdom. The Rules apply only to the conduct of Members in the course of work concerned with patents, trade and service marks, designs or copyright, or any other field insofar as any reference is made to the fact of Membership in connection with work in that field.

(3) A "client" includes, except in Rule 6, the employer of a Member whose job is concerned with intellectual property interests of the employer.

(4) RULES 3 TO 9 ARE ALL SUBJECT TO THE GENERAL RULES 1 AND 2.

(5) The headings to these Rules, and Guidelines on their observance, are not part of the Rules.

GUIDELINES CONCERNING THE OBSERVANCE OF THE RULES OF PROFESSIONAL CONDUCT G14

General Rules (Rules 1 & 2)

A.1 Rule 1 is about a Member's general duty to the public at large, and to clients in particular.

A.2 Members are expected to keep their relevant knowledge and expertise up to date to the best of their ability.

A.3 When asked to advise or act in a matter outside their expertise, Members should be frank with their clients and, whenever it seems in the client's best interest, recommend taking advice from, or transferring the whole matter to, someone better qualified to deal with the particular matter.

A.4 Rules 1 and 2 imply avoidance of situations which are compromising or likely to raise doubts about a Member's integrity. Thus, for example

(i) Faced with unreasonable conduct, Members should nevertheless be reasonable in handling the situation (though without prejudice to the pursuit of any appropriate legal remedy).

(ii) Members have a duty not to charge unjustifiable fees.

(iii) A Member shall not impugn, explicitly or otherwise, the competence, integrity or professional reputation of another Member without clear justification. This implies a general duty not to make unfair comparisons with other Members.

A.5 Members should observe these Rules independently of the Rules of any other body to which they may belong.

A.6.1 A Member, acting as a representative of a client:
in the preparation of a case for presentation;
in the conduct of proceedings, or
appearing on behalf of a client
in any Court, is expected to ensure that any money held on behalf of the client, in respect of the proceedings, is held on trust for the

client in an account which is entirely separate from the Member's personal or professional business account.

A.6.2 Money which would have to be kept in the separate account includes that which is intended, or which may be required to be paid to a third party or to the Court, by way of settlement or as the Court might direct. Money in the separate clients' account should be held to the order of the client or the Court and any interest accruing in the account should inure to the client.

A.6.3 Money which the Member is not required to keep in such a separate clients' account includes:
any money received on account of expected charges for the Member's services;
costs to be incurred on the client's behalf and
money paid in settlement of a debt owed by the client to the Member.

Availability (Rule 3)

B.1 A Member put in an unreasonable position, particularly if expected to continue services without payment, should nevertheless ensure that a client has the opportunity to make other arrangements, giving notice reasonable in all the circumstances. This may entail contact direct rather than through an associate, if due assurance cannot otherwise be obtained.

Conflicts of Interest (Rules 4 and 5)

C.1 In Rule 4, a "conflicting matter" is not necessarily the same matter as the one in which the second client is interested. On the other hand, the word "particular" is important. In the end, whether a conflict of interest exists—or whether a personal interest (Rule 5) is "significant"—must remain questions for judgment having regard the facts of the particular case. In any event, Members are reminded that Rules 1 and 2 are over-riding. If a client cannot be told of a possible conflict of interest beyond the bare indication that it exists, or if the client's approval cannot be sought without some breach of confidence, then the Member obviously cannot act for that client.

C.2 Where a conflict of interest might arise were two clients both represented by the same Member, then if they are in fact represented by two different Members (or if there is a proposal to this effect), but a connection exists between those Members, if it is possible without breach of confidence the first Member to find out must tell the other, and both clients must be told.

C.3 When receiving an enquiry or instructions from a new client, Members should consider the possibility of conflict.

Liability (Rule 6)

D.1 Members should consider taking out an appropriate policy of professional indemnity insurance.

Promotion (Rule 7)

E.1 Members will no doubt have regard to the E.P.I. rules and those of any other body outside the Institute to which they may belong, and to the provisions of Rule 2.

Relations with Others (Rule 8)

F.1 As far as these Rules are concerned, Members may practise as Companies, limited or otherwise, and in mixed partnerships.

F.2 Members employed by, or in partnership or co-directorship with anyone not a Member, should very carefully consider their position under Rule 6, especially as regards their liability for the actions of other people. Implicit in Rule 8 is the Member's responsibility to take whatever reasonable steps are practicable to ensure that neither the organization of which the Member is part, nor anyone in it, does anything to compromise the Member's duty to observe these Rules.

Use of the Institute's Name etc. (Rule 9)

G.1 For avoidance of doubt, there is no restriction on use of the name of the Institute to indicate the fact of a person's membership.

Professional Guidance (Rule 10)

H.1 The right in Rule 10 only applies when the Member himself actually intends (subject to being satisfied that it is proper) to do or sanction the course of action concerned.

H.2. The PGC is empowered by Council to publish the substance of guidance given to Members, while preserving the anonymity of the person asking for guidance, when it considers that the guidance may be of value to other Members.

H.3 The PGC is also empowered to issue statements of practice in respect of any matter governed by these Rules, setting out the view of the Committee for the general guidance of Members.

H.4 Neither individual nor general guidance will be binding on the Professional Conduct Committee or on Council in any formal professional conduct proceedings before them, but full account will be taken of the fact that such guidance was sought and given as well as of the content of that guidance.

H.5 In particular, activities compatible with guidance given by the PGC will ordinarily be considered by Council to be contrary to these Rules only in view of the manner in which they have been carried out, and not because of their inherent nature.

Interpretation (Rule 11)

I.1 Under Rule 11(2), the Rules apply to a Member working in some field, outside intellectual property as such, *e.g.* as a consultant in technology transfer, or as an executive director of an industrial company. Such people may well use their membership in connection with their work, for example by mentioning it on their business letterhead. To the extent set out in Rule 11(2), the Rules apply also to patent agents who are primarily members of other professions or of overseas professional bodies of practitioners within the field of intellectual property.

1.2 The conduct of Members working abroad will be judged with due regard to all the circumstances, including the prevailing standards of professional conduct in the country concerned.

APPENDIX H

COUNTY COURT RULES (ORDER 48A)

H00.1 *Note.* This new Appendix reprints new Order 48A of the County Court Rules ("CCR") introduced by S.I. 1990 No. 1495 and operative from September 3, 1990. This order sets out the basic rules of procedure for those county courts designated as "Patents County Courts" (for which see para. 96.17 *supra*). For information on the other applicable County Court Rules, the current version of "*The County Court Practice*" ("The Green Book") and its latest cumulative supplement should be consulted. That book reprints all the County Court Rules and contains extensive notes on practice thereunder. It should be consulted for the origin of these Rules and for their possible amendment as reference to the appropriate statutory instruments is only given here in relation to Order 48A.

In the County Court Rules, "the Act" means the County Courts Act 1984 (c. 28), as amended.

ORDER 48A

PATENTS AND DESIGNS

Application and interpretation

H48A.01 **1.**—(1) This Order applies to proceedings in respect of which patents county courts have jurisdiction under section 287(1) of the 1988 Act.

(2) In this Order:—

"The 1988 Act" means the Copyright, Designs and Patents Act 1988 [c. 48];

"patents county court" means a county court designated as a patents county court under section 287(1) of the 1988 Act;
"patents judge" means a person nominated under section 291(1) of the 1988 Act as the patents judge of a patents county court.

Patents judge

2.—(1) Subject to paragraph (2), proceedings to which this Order applies shall be dealt with by the patents judge. **H48A.02**

(2) When an interlocutory matter needs to be dealt with urgently and the patents judge is not available, the matter may be dealt with by another judge.

Commencement

3. Every summons, notice, pleading, affidavit or other document relating to proceedings to which this Order applies must be marked in the top left hand corner with the words "patents county court". **H48A.03**

Pleadings

4.—(1) Every summons issued in accordance with rule 3 shall be endorsed with or accompanied by a statement of case. **H48A.04**

(2) Where a claim is made by the plaintiff in respect of the infringement of a patent, the statement of case shall give full particulars of the infringement relied on, setting out:—

(a) which of the claims in the specification of the patent are alleged to be infringed; and
(b) in respect of each claim alleged to be infringed the grounds relied on in support of the allegations that such claim has been infringed; and all facts, matters and arguments relied on as establishing those grounds, including at least one example of each type of infringement alleged.

(3) Where, in any proceedings, the validity of a patent is put in issue, the statement of case shall give particulars of the objections to the validity of the patent which are relied on; and in particular shall explain the relevance of every citation to each claim, with identification of the significant parts of each citation, and shall give all facts, matters and arguments which are relied on for establishing the invalidity of the patent.

(4) Without prejudice to paragraph (3) above, RSC Order 104, rule 6(2) to (4) shall apply to particulars of objections given under paragraph (3) as they apply to particulars given under paragraph (1) of that rule.

(5) Every statement of case shall be signed:—

(a) by the plaintiff, if he sues in person; or

(b) by the plaintiff's solicitor in his own name or the name of his firm;

and shall state the plaintiff's address for service.

(6) Where a defendant wishes to serve a defence to any claim he shall serve it, together with any counterclaim including a statement of case under paragraph (2) or (3) above, upon the plaintiff within 42 days of service upon him of the summons.

(7) Where a party wishes to serve a reply or a defence to counterclaim, he shall do so within 28 days of the service of the previous pleading upon him.

(8) Pleadings will close seven days after the expiry of the time for service of a reply.

(9) No time limit mentioned in this rule may be extended more than once (and then by no more than 42 days) save by order of the court; and such order shall, in the first place, be applied for in writing, whereupon the judge shall either grant the application, refuse it or order a hearing.

(10) The parties to proceedings shall notify the court of any agreed extension of any time limit mentioned in this rule.

Service

H48A.05 **5.**—(1) In their application to proceedings to which this Order applies, rules 10 and 13 of Order 7 shall apply as if:—

(a) before the words "an officer" in paragraph (1)(b) of each rule there were inserted the words "the plaintiff or"; and
(b) in paragraph (4) of rule 10 (and in that paragraph as applied by rule 13) after the words "sent by post" there were inserted the words "by an officer of the court".

(2) Where a pleading is served which refers to any document, the party serving the pleading must also serve with it a copy of any such document together with an English translation of any foreign language text, certified as being accurate.

Interrogatories and notices to admit facts

H48A.06 **6.**—(1)(a) Interrogatories under Order 14, rule 11, and
(b) a notice to admit facts under Order 20, rule 2,

may not be served without the leave of the court unless (in the case of a notice to admit facts) it is served within 14 days of the close of pleadings; and accordingly those provisions of Order 14, rule 11 (and of the RSC which are applied by that rule) which relate only to interrogatories without order shall not apply to proceedings under this Order.

(2) An application for leave to serve interrogatories or a notice to admit facts may only be made on notice at the preliminary consideration under rule 8.

Scientific advisers, assessors and Patent Office reports

7.—(1) The court may at any time, on or without the application of any party:— **H48A.07**

(a) appoint scientific advisers or assessors to assist the court; or
(b) order the Patent Office to inquire into and report on any question of fact or opinion.

(2) RSC Order 104, rule 15 shall apply to the appointment of a scientific adviser under this rule.

(3) Where the court appoints an assessor under this rule without the application of a party, paragraphs (3) and (6) of Order 13, rule 11 shall apply, and paragraph (4) of that rule shall apply with the omission of the words from "the applicant shall" to "and thereupon" inclusive.

Preliminary consideration

8.—(1) Within fourteen days of the close of pleadings, all parties shall file and serve an application for directions, signed by the person settling it. **H48A.08**

(2) Each application for directions shall:

(a) summarise the outstanding issues in the proceedings;
(b) summarise the further steps necessary to prove the applicant's contentions in the proceedings and prepare his case for a hearing;
(c) give full particulars of any experiments the applicant intends to conduct, stating the facts which he intends to prove by them and the date by which he will submit a written report of the results; and
(d) set out all orders and directions the applicant will ask for at the preliminary consideration of the action.

(3) As soon as is practicable after receipt of each party's application for directions, the proper officer shall set a date for the preliminary consideration.

(4) On the preliminary consideration the judge may, with or without the application of any party and either after a consideration of the papers or having adjudicated upon a point of law strike out any point raised in the proceedings.

(5) On the preliminary consideration, the judge shall give such directions as are necessary to prepare the proceedings for hearing and in particular shall consider and (where appropriate) give directions in respect of each or any of the following matters, namely:—

(a) the witnesses who may be called;
(b) whether their evidence should be given orally or in writing or any combination of the two;

(c) the exchange of witness statements;
(d) the provision of Patent Office Reports;
(e) the use of assessors at the hearing;
(f) transfer to the High Court;
(g) reference to the Court of Justice of the European Communities;
(h) applications for discovery and inspection;
(i) applications for leave under rule 6 above; and
(j) written reports of the results of any experiments of which particulars have been given under rule 8(2)(c).

General modification of County Court Rules

H48A.09 **9.** In their application to proceedings to which this Order applies, county court rules shall be subject to the following modifications:—

(a) Order 3 rules 3(1) and (2)(c) shall have effect as if for the words "particulars of claim" there are substituted the words "statement of case";
(b) in Order 3, rule 3(2)(a), the words from "and in the case" to "return day" inclusive shall be omitted;
(c) Order 3, rule 3(3) shall not apply;
(d) Order 6, rule 7 shall not apply;
(e) Order 9 shall not apply, with the exception of Order 9 rule 19, which shall apply to every defence or counterclaim delivered under rule 4(6) above as it applies to those delivered under Order 9 rule 2.

Application of Rules of the Supreme Court

H48A.10 **10.**—(1) RSC Order 104, rule 3 shall apply to applications by a patentee or the proprietor of a patent intending to apply under section 30 of the Patents Act 1949 or section 75 of the Patents Act 1977 for leave to amend his specification, save that references therein to an application by motion shall be construed, for the purposes of an application to a patents county court, as an application on notice to the patents judge.

(2) RSC Order 104, rule 17 shall apply to actions to which this Order applies, with the omission of the words "by originating summons".

(3) RSC Order 104, rule 16(3), rule 20 and rule 23 shall apply to actions to which this Order applies.

SUPPLEMENTARY INDEX

(This Index is supplementary to that at page 1171 et seq. of the Main Work and refers to the para. numbers therein. Thus, both indexes should be consulted and then the indicated paras. studied both in the Main Work and as regards the additional commentary thereon in this Supplement.)
A marginal asterisk indicates that the index entry thus noted also appears in the Index in the Main Work, the present entry relating to further relevant paras. so far as this Supplement is concerned.